John Edgar McFadyen

The Psalms in Modern Speech and Rhythmical Form

Second Edition

John Edgar McFadyen

The Psalms in Modern Speech and Rhythmical Form
Second Edition

ISBN/EAN: 9783337020675

Printed in Europe, USA, Canada, Australia, Japan

Cover: Foto ©Lupo / pixelio.de

More available books at **www.hansebooks.com**

THE PSALMS
IN MODERN SPEECH
AND RHYTHMICAL FORM

BY

JOHN EDGAR McFADYEN, D.D.

PROFESSOR OF OLD TESTAMENT LANGUAGE, LITERATURE,
AND THEOLOGY, UNITED FREE CHURCH COLLEGE, GLASGOW;
AUTHOR OF "THE MESSAGES OF THE PSALMISTS," "STUDIES
IN THE PSALMS," "INTRODUCTION TO THE OLD TESTA-
MENT," "A CRY FOR JUSTICE," ETC.

SECOND EDITION

LONDON
JAMES CLARKE & CO., 13 & 14 FLEET STREET, E.C.

PREFACE

THIS translation aims at reproducing, in modern speech, something of the impression created by the rhythmical form of the Hebrew Psalter. From lovers of the Bible much of its beauty is not infrequently hidden, because it is so persistently presented to them in the garb of prose. Doubtless it is true that Hebrew poetry loses less through translation into prose than does the poetry of other languages; and this because one of its chief characteristics is the so-called " parallelism," in virtue of which the second line of a verse is usually an echo of, or contrast to, the first—a feature which no translation, however inadequate, can altogether obliterate. But between lines thus related there is also a certain correspondence of accent, and any translation which would do approximate justice to the original must seek to satisfy the ear as well as the mind.

In a translation which attempts to be faithful, this is not easy; for it frequently happens that one Hebrew word demands for its adequate, or at any rate for its literal, interpretation six or even more English words; and probably no translation which was narrowly faithful could invariably produce its effect within lines so short and with accents so few as those which characterize the Hebrew original. At the same time I have sought to reproduce, or at least to suggest, something of its music and cadence, and to convey an impression not only of its spirit, but also of its form.

The translation, while faithful, is free; indeed, perhaps the most faithful translation would be that

PREFACE

which, within certain recognized limits, would claim the greatest liberty. Owing to differences of idiom and outlook, a pedantically accurate translation may be obscure even to the point of being unintelligible. Superficial familiarity with Biblical language sometimes blinds us to its real remoteness from our common ways of speech, and may even lead us to assign to phrases meanings which do not correspond to facts. For example, *my soul* in Hebrew may mean nothing more than *I* or *me* : *His name* may be practically equal to *He* or *Him*. There are reasons for this, rooted in Hebrew psychology and in Hebrew conceptions generally ; but bearing the facts in mind, we may roundly say that a translation which may seem to be less precise may nevertheless convey a more clear and even a more accurate impression to the uninitiated reader than one that is strictly literal.

Similarly the Hebrews speak as naturally of *lifting up the horn* as we should of *increasing in strength or dignity* ; and, while the translator must not wantonly obliterate distinctive or pictorial touches, his first concern is to be intelligible. Again, the Hebrew word for *to know* is often as much emotional as intellectual, so that it may mean something like *to care for*, and *those who know Him* are almost = *His worshippers* or *friends*. Further, some of the most characteristic words of the Psalter have really no single English equivalent at all. The words commonly rendered by *saints, poor, afflicted,* etc., have a rich historic background and far more comprehensive implications than these English words suggest ; and any rigid uniformity in the translation of words so rich and suggestive would be rather a hindrance than a help to true interpretation.

PREFACE

The original *Jahweh* I have rendered almost throughout by *the Lord*. This may seem a lamentably reactionary step, calculated to injure the historical appreciation and the primarily national flavour of the Psalter. But I have retained the familiar, though strictly inaccurate, rendering of the Authorized Version, for the following reasons: (i.) We may be quite sure that so foreign-looking a word as *Jahweh* will never be domesticated in English religious speech. Scholars will very properly use it in critical and scientific discussions; but a volume which has, in part, devotional interests in view, may well retain a form sanctioned by immemorial usage. (ii.) Long before the Psalter was finally edited, Jahweh, the national God of Israel, was recognised to be, and was worshipped as, the only God and the Lord of all the earth. The retention of the more correct, but primarily local and national name *Jahweh*, really tends to obscure, for the average reader, the fact—which is suggested by *the Lord*—that He is the God of all (*cf.* Pss. VIII. 1, C., etc.); and, as the Psalter is no longer the book of the praises of Israel only, but the hymn-book of humanity, the term which carries the wider implications is really —*for modern worship or devotional reading* as contrasted with critical and historical study—the more appropriate. (iii.) Further, it is well known that the second and third books of the Psalter were deliberately edited in such a way as to replace, on an extensive scale, an original *Jahweh* by the regular word for *God*. In this connection a comparison of Ps. XIV. with Ps. LIII. is instructive: the latter, in the main, but repeats the former, with the significant and deliberate change just alluded to. Here we have proof enough that ancient Jewish worshippers themselves were willing

PREFACE

to displace the personal name of their God, with its local and national implications, in favour of a name that did better justice to the nation's later and wider thoughts of Him. For these reasons, then, I have adopted the venerable rendering familiarized to us by the Authorized Version, retaining *Jehovah*[1] almost exclusively for passages in which an original *Jahweh* stood side by side with the proper word for *Lord*, as in Ps. VIII. 1.

The translation here offered rests upon a strictly critical basis. Where it differs—as it will frequently be found to do—from the familiar English versions, the reader may be assured that there are good reasons for the modifications. They rest either on the evidence of some of the ancient versions, or on some more or less highly probable emendation. No attempt has been made to explain or defend the reasons for the readings adopted, or for the very few additions or omissions which will be noted; to have attempted this would have been to write a volume of another kind and of twice the length. Suffice it to say that the changes are not arbitrary, but are based on material familiar to scholars. The more important of them are very briefly referred to in the *Notes*, which are relegated to the end of the volume, in order not to distract attention from the substance of the psalms themselves.

The numbering of the verses is that of the English Bible. Refrains are printed in italics.

JOHN E. McFADYEN.

[1] This form, though relatively modern and indefensible, is now an inalienable part of our religious speech, from which we may feel sure it will never be dislodged by *Jahweh*. It is worth remembering that, for popular purposes, the form *Jehovah* has the high authority of no less great and conscientious a scholar than the late Professor W. Robertson Smith.

CONTENTS

BOOK I.

PSALM		PAGE
I.	THE TWO WAYS	1
II.	THE VICTORY AND UNIVERSAL DOMINION OF JEHOVAH'S ANOINTED KING	1
III.	A MORNING PRAYER FOR PROTECTION.	2
IV.	AN EVENING PRAYER	3
V.	A MORNING PRAYER FOR GUIDANCE	4
VI.	A CRY FOR HELP IN TIME OF MORTAL DISTRESS	6
VII.	A PRAYER TO THE GOD OF JUSTICE	6
VIII.	NATURE'S TESTIMONY TO GOD'S LOVE FOR MAN	8
IX.	A SONG OF PRAISE FOR THE DESTRUCTION OF THE ENEMY	9
X.	A PRAYER FOR HELP	11
XI.	THE COURAGE OF FAITH	12
XII.	A PRAYER FOR THE PRESERVATION OF THE FAITHFUL IN A FALSE WORLD	13
XIII.	A PRAYER FOR HELP IN TROUBLE	14
XIV.	THE FOLLY OF DENYING GOD	14
XV.	THE TRUE CITIZEN OF ZION	16
XVI.	THE JOY OF FELLOWSHIP WITH GOD	16
XVII.	A PRAYER FOR DELIVERANCE FROM INSOLENT FOES.	17
XVIII.	A KING'S SONG OF GRATITUDE FOR VICTORY	19
XIX. 1–6.	THE GLORY OF GOD IN THE HEAVENS.	23
XIX. 7–14.	IN PRAISE OF THE LAW	23
XX.	A PRAYER FOR THE KING ON THE EVE OF BATTLE	24
XXI.	A PRAYER FOR THE KING AFTER A VICTORY.	25
XXII.	THE SUFFERER'S TRIUMPH	27
XXIII.	THE GOOD SHEPHERD	29
XXIV. 1–6.	THE TRUE WORSHIPPER	30

CONTENTS

PSALM		PAGE
XXIV. 7-10.	JEHOVAH'S TRIUMPHAL ENTRY INTO THE SANCTUARY	31
XXV.	A PRAYER FOR FORGIVENESS AND PROTECTION	31
XXVI.	PRAYER OF A DEVOUT WORSHIPPER	33
XXVII. 1-6.	IF GOD BE FOR ME	34
XXVII. 7-14.	THE SERENITY OF FAITH	35
XXVIII.	AN ANSWERED PRAYER FOR HELP	36
XXIX.	JEHOVAH'S GLORY IN THE STORM	37
XXX.	A SONG OF THANKSGIVING FOR DELIVERANCE	38
XXXI.	A PRAYER FOR DELIVERANCE FROM SORE DISTRESS	39
XXXII.	THE JOY OF CONFESSION AND RECONCILIATION	42
XXXIII.	A NATIONAL HYMN OF THANKSGIVING	43
XXXIV.	THE LORD IS MINDFUL OF HIS OWN	45
XXXV.	A PRAYER FOR DELIVERANCE FROM MALICIOUS FOES	46
XXXVI.	THE TRIUMPHANT POWER OF THE DIVINE LOVE	49
XXXVII.	A VINDICATION OF THE MORAL ORDER	50
XXXVIII.	A CONFESSION OF SIN AND PRAYER FOR DELIVERANCE	54
XXXIX.	THE PATHOS OF LIFE	56
XL.	THANKSGIVING AND PETITION	57
XLI.	A PRAYER FOR HEALING AND VINDICATION	59

BOOK II.

XLII, XLIII.	YEARNING FOR GOD	63
XLIV.	A LAMENT IN DEFEAT	65
XLV.	SONG FOR THE MARRIAGE OF A KING	67
XLVI.	A SAFE STRONGHOLD OUR GOD IS STILL	69
XLVII.	JEHOVAH'S UNIVERSAL SOVEREIGNTY	70
XLVIII.	THE MARVELLOUS DELIVERANCE OF ZION	71
XLIX.	THE PROBLEM OF THE PROSPERITY OF THE WICKED	72
L.	TRUE WORSHIP	74
LI.	GOD BE MERCIFUL TO ME, THE SINNER	76
LII.	THE DOOM OF ARROGANCE	78

CONTENTS

PSALM		PAGE
LIII.	THE FOLLY OF DENYING GOD	79
LIV.	A PRAYER FOR DELIVERANCE FROM OPPRESSION	80
LV.	PRAYER FOR HELP AGAINST A TREACHEROUS FRIEND	81
LVI.	THE TEARS OF THE SAINTS	83
LVII.	A PRAYER FOR PROTECTION FROM PERSECUTION	84
LVIII.	A PRAYER FOR VENGEANCE UPON UNJUST JUDGES	85
LIX.	A PRAYER FOR VENGEANCE UPON INSOLENT FOES	86
LX.	A PRAYER AFTER DEFEAT IN BATTLE	88
LXI.	A PRAYER FOR THE KING	89
LXII.	QUIETNESS AND CONFIDENCE	90
LXIII.	ATHIRST FOR GOD	91
LXIV.	A PRAYER FOR DELIVERANCE FROM MALICIOUS FOES	92
LXV.	HYMN FOR A THANKSGIVING FESTIVAL	93
LXVI.	THANKSGIVING FOR NATIONAL DELIVERANCE	94
LXVII.	A HARVEST THANKSGIVING	96
LXVIII.	VICTORY	97
LXIX.	A PRAYER FOR DELIVERANCE AND VENGEANCE	100
LXX.	A CRY FOR HELP IN PERSECUTION	103
LXXI.	FORSAKE ME NOT, WHEN I AM OLD	104
LXXII.	A PRAYER FOR A JUST AND GLORIOUS REIGN	106

BOOK III.

LXXIII.	FELLOWSHIP WITH GOD HERE AND HEREAFTER	111
LXXIV.	LAMENT ON THE DEVASTATION OF THE TEMPLE	113
LXXV.	GOD THE ARBITER OF DESTINY	115
LXXVI.	A SONG OF VICTORY	116
LXXVII.	A PRAYER FOR PRESERVATION AS IN THE DAYS OF OLD	117

CONTENTS

PSALM		PAGE
LXXVIII.	THE WARNINGS OF HISTORY	119
LXXIX.	A NATIONAL PRAYER FROM THE DEPTHS OF A BITTER NEED	125
LXXX.	A PRAYER FOR THE PRESERVATION OF ISRAEL, JEHOVAH'S VINE	126
LXXXI.	FOR THE FEAST OF TABERNACLES: A WARNING AGAINST DISOBEDIENCE	128
LXXXII.	GOD THE UPHOLDER OF JUSTICE	129
LXXXIII.	A PRAYER FOR THE DESTRUCTION OF THE ENEMIES OF JUDAH	130
LXXXIV.	THE SONG OF THE PILGRIMS	131
LXXXV.	A PRAYER FOR NATIONAL RESTORATION	132
LXXXVI.	A PRAYER FOR THE DIVINE GUIDANCE AND FAVOUR	133
LXXXVII.	MOTHER ZION	135
LXXXVIII.	THE PRAYER OF DESPAIR	136
LXXXIX.	THE PROMISE TO DAVID AND THE PRESENT DISTRESS	137

BOOK IV.

XC.	HYMN OF ETERNITY	145
XCI.	IN THE SHELTER OF THE MOST HIGH	146
XCII.	THE WAYS OF GOD	148
XCIII.	JEHOVAH, KING OF ALL THE WORLD	149
XCIV.	A PRAYER FOR VENGEANCE UPON THE CRUEL: UNSWERVING CONFIDENCE IN THE MORAL ORDER	150
XCV.	FOR A FESTIVAL: A HYMN OF PRAISE AND A SOLEMN WARNING	151
XCVI.	THE WORLD-KING AND THE WORLD-JUDGMENT	152
XCVII.	THE WORLD-KING A KING OF JUSTICE	154
XCVIII.	THE HOMAGE OF NATURE AND MAN TO JEHOVAH, THE MIGHTY JUDGE OF THE WORLD	155
XCIX.	JEHOVAH'S JUST AND HOLY RULE	156

CONTENTS

PSALM		PAGE
C.	A CALL TO WORSHIP	157
CI.	A MODEL KING	157
CII.	A PRAYER FOR PITY AND FOR THE RESTORATION OF ZION	158
CIII.	BLESS THE LORD, O MY SOUL	161
CIV.	THE HYMN OF CREATION	162
CV.	THE INSPIRATION OF THE PAST	165
CVI.	THE NATION'S SIN AGAINST THE DIVINE LOVE	168

BOOK V.

CVII.	THE SONG OF THE REDEEMED	175
CVIII.	A PRAYER FOR VICTORY	178
CIX.	AN IMPRECATION	179
CX.	DIVINE PROMISE OF VICTORY AND DOMINION TO THE PRIEST-KING	181
CXI.	IN PRAISE OF THE DIVINE GOODNESS	182
CXII.	THE BLESSINGS OF GODLINESS	183
CXIII.	THE LORD LOVETH THE LOWLY	184
CXIV.	THE MARVEL OF THE EXODUS	185
CXV.	ISRAEL'S INCOMPARABLE GOD	185
CXVI.	SONG OF THANKSGIVING FOR DELIVERANCE	187
CXVII.	A CALL TO PRAISE	189
CXVIII.	THANKSGIVING FOR VICTORY	189
CXIX.	THE POWER AND COMFORT OF THE WORD OF GOD	191
CXX.	PRAYER FOR DELIVERANCE FROM SLANDER AND TREACHERY	203
CXXI.	THE OMNIPOTENT KEEPER	204
CXXII.	THE JOY AND THE PRAYER OF THE PILGRIMS	205
CXXIII.	A PRAYER FOR THE DIVINE PITY	206
CXXIV.	A MAGNIFICENT DELIVERANCE	206
CXXV.	A SURE DEFENCE	207
CXXVI.	SOWING IN TEARS	208
CXXVII. 1, 2.	THE NEED OF HEAVENLY HELP	209
CXXVII. 3-5.	THE BLESSING OF CHILDREN	209
CXXVIII.	THE BLESSINGS OF HOME	210

CONTENTS

PSALM		PAGE
CXXIX.	A Prayer for the Discomfiture of the Enemies of Zion	210
CXXX.	Out of the Depths	211
CXXXI.	As a Little Child	212
CXXXII.	The Ancient Promise to David and Zion	212
CXXXIII.	Brothers Together	214
CXXXIV.	An Evening Invocation	214
CXXXV.	The Divine Power as Revealed in Nature and History	215
CXXXVI.	The Divine Love as Revealed in Nature and History	216
CXXXVII.	By the Waters of Babylon	218
CXXXVIII.	The Constancy of the Divine Care	219
CXXXIX.	The Ever-Present God	220
CXL.	A Prayer for Preservation	222
CXLI.	A Prayer for Protection from Persecutors	224
CXLII.	A Prayer for Deliverance from Persecutors	225
CXLIII.	A Prayer for Deliverance and Guidance	226
CXLIV. 1–11.	The Warrior's Stay	227
CXLIV. 12–15.	The Prosperity of Jehovah's People	228
CXLV.	The Gracious Kingdom Everlasting	229
CXLVI.	The Great Protector	231
CXLVII.	The Divine Love and Power as Revealed in Nature	232
CXLVIII.	The Universal Chorus of Praise	233
CXLIX.	Song of Victory	235
CL.	Hallelujah!	236

Notes		237
The Psalms arranged Topically		246
Bibliography		248

BOOK I

PSALM I
The Two Ways

  HAPPY the man who goes on his way,
     Unheeding the counsels that wicked men offer,
Not halting in ways frequented by sinners,
    Nor taking his seat in a session of scoffers.
2 But the law of the Lord is his joy,
    He muses on it night and day.
3 For he is like to a tree
    Planted by runlets of water,
Yielding its fruit in due season,
    With leafage that fadeth never.
    In all that he does, he prospers.

4 Not so fare the wicked, not so;[1]
    But like chaff are they, driven by the wind.
5 So the wicked shall not rise up in the judgment,
    Nor sinners appear, when the righteous are gathered.
6 For the way of the righteous is dear to the Lord,
    But the way of the wicked shall end in ruin.

PSALM II
The Victory and Universal Dominion of Jehovah's Anointed King

  WHEREFORE this tumult of peoples,
     This idle noise of the nations,
2 With kings of the earth conspiring,
    And rulers consulting together,
    Against the Lord and against His anointed,[1]

PSALM III

3   To snap their bonds in sunder
     And fling their cords away ?

4   He whose throne is in heaven laughs,
     The Lord mocketh at them.
5   Then He speaks unto them in His wrath,
     And in His hot anger confounds them.
6   " This my king is installed by me,
     Upon Zion my holy mountain."

7   I will tell of Jehovah's decree.
    He said to me, " Thou art my son,
     Begotten this day by me.
8   Only ask, and I make thee the heir of the nations,
     And lord of the world to its utmost bounds.
9   Thou shalt break them with sceptre of iron,
     And dash them like potter's vessel."

10 Now therefore, ye kings, be wise :
     Be admonished, ye rulers of earth.
11 Serve ye Jehovah with fear,
     Kiss ye His feet with trembling,[2]
12 Lest, indignant, He hurl you to ruin ;
     For soon will His anger blaze.
     Happy all who take refuge in Him.

PSALM III

A Morning Prayer for Protection

How many, O Lord, are my foes !
    Those that rise up against me are many.
2 Many are those who declare of me,
     " There is no help for him in his God."

PSALM IV

3 But Thou, Lord, art Shield about me,
    My Pride, who dost lift up my head.
4 When loudly I call to the Lord,
    From His holy hill He gives answer.

5 I laid me down and slept :
    Now I wake, for the Lord doth sustain me.
6 I fear not the myriads of people
    Who beset me round and round.

7 Arise, Lord : save me, my God,
    Who dost smite all my foes on the cheek,
    And shatter the teeth of the wicked.
8 Salvation belongs to the Lord :
    Let Thy blessing descend on Thy people.

PSALM IV
An Evening Prayer

ANSWER my cry,
    Thou God of my cause.
Oft from straits Thou hast brought me
    To spacious places,
So now show me Thy favour
    And hear my prayer.

2 How long, ye proud men,
    Shall mine honour be stained
By the slanders ye love,
    And the lies that ye follow ?
3 See ! the Lord hath shown me
    His wonderful kindness :
The Lord doth hear,
    When I call unto Him.

PSALM V

4 Sin not in your anger :
　　But speak in your heart
　　On your bed, and be still.
5 Offer true sacrifice,
　　Trust in the Lord.

6 Many are longing
　　For fortune to smile.
　　Lift Thou upon us
　　The light of Thy face.[1]
7 Thou hast put in my heart, Lord,
　　A deeper joy
　　Than was theirs who had corn
　　And wine in abundance.

8 So in peace I will both
　　Lay me down and sleep ;
　　For 'tis Thou, Lord, that makest me
　　Dwell securely.

PSALM V

A Morning Prayer for Guidance

GIVE ear to my words, O Lord :
　　Give heed to my whisper.
2 Attend to my loud cry for help,
　　My King and my God.
3 When I pray to Thee, Lord, in the morning,
　　O hear Thou my voice.
　　I make ready for Thee in the morning,
　　And look for a sign.

PSALM V

4 For Thou art no God that takes pleasure in wickedness :
    No evil man can be guest of Thine.
5 No braggarts can stand in Thy presence,
    Thou hatest all workers of wrong.
6 Thou destroyest all speakers of lies,
    Men of blood and deceit Thou abhorrest.
7 But I, through Thy kindness abundant,
    May enter Thy house,
   And towards the shrine of Thy temple
    May reverently bow.

8 Lead me, O Lord, in Thy righteousness
    Because of mine enemies.
    Make Thy way level before me.
9 For their mouth is a stranger to truth,
    Their heart is a pit of destruction.
   Their throat is a wide open grave,
    Their tongue the smooth tongue of the hypocrite.

10 Hold them guilty, O God ;
    Let their schemes bring them down to the ground.
   For their numberless sins thrust them down—
    For playing the rebel against Thee.
11 But let all who take refuge in Thee
    Ring out their gladness for ever.
   Protect those that love Thy name,
    So that they may exult in Thee.
12 For Thou givest Thy blessing, O Lord, to the godly,
    And the crown of Thy favour dost set on his head.

PSALMS VI—VII

PSALM VI

A Cry for Help in Time of Mortal Distress

R EPROVE me not, Lord, in Thine anger,
And chasten me not in Thy wrath.
2 Lord, be gracious to me in my weakness.
Heal me, for racked is my body;
3 Utterly racked is my soul.
And Thou, Lord, why so long?

4 Turn, O Lord, and rescue me;
Save me, for Thy love's sake.
5 For in death none can call Thee to mind;
In the world below, who can praise Thee?

6 I am so weary of sighing.
All the night I make my bed swim,
And wet my couch with my tears.
7 Mine eye is wasted with grief;
Grown old, through all them that vex me.

8 Begone, all ye workers of wrong,
For the Lord hath heard my loud weeping,
9 The Lord hath heard mine entreaty,
The Lord accepteth my prayer.
10 My foes, in their turn, shall be all brought to shame—
Brought to shame and dismay in a moment.

PSALM VII

A Prayer to the God of Justice

O LORD my God, I take refuge in Thee.
Deliver and save me from all who pursue me;

PSALM VII

2 Lest, like lions, they tear me in pieces,
   And rend me, past hope of deliverance.

3 O Lord, my God, if my life hath been such—
   If my hands have been stained with injustice,
4 If friends I requited with evil,
   If I vexed even those that were wrongly my foes,
5 May the enemy chase till he find me,
   May he trample my life to the ground,
   And mine honour lay low in the dust!

6 Arise, O Lord, in Thine anger,
   Against my foes lift Thee in fury.
   Awake Thou for my help
   In the judgment that Thou hast ordained.
7 Gather the nations about Thee,
   And sit on Thy lofty throne,
8   As the Lord, the Judge of the peoples.
   Judge me, O Lord, in mine innocence
   And according to mine integrity.

9 Put an end to the wrong of the wicked,
   Establish the righteous.
   Thou searcher of heart and of reins,
   Thou God that art righteous.
10 God is my shield over me:
   He saveth the upright in heart.

11 God is a righteous judge,
   A God who is daily indignant.
12 He will whet his sword without fail,
   His bow is bent and ready,
13 His deadly weapons are ready,
   His arrows He maketh of flame.

PSALM VIII

14 Behold! he[1] travails with wickedness;
   He is big with mischief, he bringeth forth falsehood.
15 A pit he hath made and dug;
   But into the hole that he made shall he fall.
16 On his own head his mischief comes back;
   On his own crown his violence descends.
17 I will render thanks to the Lord for His justice,
   And praise the name of the Lord Most High.

PSALM VIII

Nature's Testimony to God's Love for Man

O JEHOVAH our Lord!
   How glorious in all the earth is Thy name!
Thou hast set [1] Thy majesty high in the heavens.

2 In the lisping of babes and of sucklings
   Thou hast founded a bulwark
   Because of Thine enemies,
To silence the foe and the rebel.

3 When I look at Thy heavens, the work of Thy fingers,
   The moon and the stars, which Thou hast set there,
4 What is mortal man, that Thou thinkest of him,
   And the son of man, that Thou visitest him?

5 Yet Thou madest him little less than divine,
   And didst crown him with glory and majesty,
6 Lord of the work of Thy hands Thou hast made him,
   And Thou hast put all things under his feet.

PSALM IX

7 Sheep and oxen, all of them ;
   Yea, and the wild beasts also :
8 Birds of the air, and fish of the sea,
   And whatso crosses the paths of the ocean.

9 O Jehovah our Lord !
   How glorious in all the earth is Thy name !

PSALM IX [1]

A Song of Praise for the Destruction of the Enemy

With all my heart I will praise the Lord,
   All Thy wonders I will rehearse.
2 I will rejoice and exult in Thee,
   Singing praise to Thy name, O Thou Most High ;
3 Because my foes were backward turned,
   Before Thy presence they stumbled and perished.

4 My right and my cause Thou hast maintained,
   Thou didst sit on the throne dealing judgment just,
5 Rebuking the heathen, destroying the wicked,
   And blotting their name out for ever and ever.
6 The foe is vanished in ruin eternal,
   His cities destroyed, his memory perished.

7 Behold ! the Lord is seated for ever
   On the throne that He hath established for judgment ;
8 And He doth rule the world with justice,
   He judgeth the nations with equity.

PSALM IX

9 Thus the Lord proves a sure retreat to the wretched,
     A sure retreat in times of distress.
10 Well may they trust Thee who know Thy name,
     For those that seek Thee Thou never forsakest.

11 Sing ye praise to the Lord, whose home is in Zion,
     Declare His doings among the nations.
12 As avenger of blood, He keeps them in mind,
     He doth not forget the cry of the wretched.

13 Graciously look on my misery, Lord,
     Thou who liftest me up from the gates of death;
14 To the end that I, in Thy help exulting,
     May tell forth Thy praise in the gates of Zion.

15 The heathen are sunk in the pit which they made,
     In the net that they hid hath their own foot been taken.
16 The Lord is revealed in the judgment He wrought,
     The wicked are snared in their own handiwork.

17 Let the wicked depart to the world below,
     All the nations that live forgetful of God.
18 For the needy shall not be forgotten for ever,
     Nor the hope of the helpless be lost for aye.

19 Arise, Lord; let not man be triumphant:
     Before Thy face let the nations be judged.
20 Ordain Thou terror for them, O Lord:
     Convince the nations how frail they are.

PSALM X

PSALM X

A Prayer for Help

WHY, O Lord, art Thou standing afar,
Hiding Thyself in times of distress?
2 Wicked men, in their pride, are pursuing the helpless:
O let them be caught in the schemes they have plotted.

3 For the wicked boasts of his wanton greed,
The robber renounces the Lord, and blasphemes Him.
4 In his wicked pride, he fears no retribution,
Fancying the while that there is no God.

5 Never a season that he doth not prosper;
Thy judgments are far above out of his sight:
As for his foes, he puffs at them all.

6 He says in his heart, " I shall never be shaken;
I shall live for all time untouched by misfortune."
7 His mouth is full of deceit and oppression:
Under his tongue lurk mischief and wrong.

8 Lying in secret in some village ambush,
And stealthily watching, he murders the innocent.
9 Like a lion he lurks in his secret lair—
Lurks with intent to catch the defenceless;
He catches and drags him away in his net.

10 Crushed, he sinketh down to the ground.
Under his claws the hapless fall.
11 He says in his heart that God has forgotten,
Has hidden His face, and will never see it.

PSALM XI

12 Arise, O Lord, and lift up Thine hand,
    Forget not Thou the cry of the wretched.
13 Why doth the wicked treat God with contempt,
    And say in his heart, "There is no retribution"?

14 For Thou hast indeed seen the trouble and sorrow;
    Thou markest it all, and wilt take it in hand.
    Thou wilt assuredly come to the help
    Of the hapless and orphan who leaves it to Thee.

15 Break Thou the arm of the godless and wicked:
    Search out his sin, till it no more be found.
16 The Lord is King for ever and ever:
    The heathen are perished out of His land.

17 Thou hast heard, O Lord, the desire of the humble,
    Lending attentive heart and ear.
18 Rights Thou hast won for the crushed and the orphan,
    That mortals of earth may strike terror no more.

PSALM XI

The Courage of Faith

IN the Lord I take refuge.
   How then can ye tell me
   To flee like a bird to the mountains?

The Challenge of Cowardice

2 "See! The wicked are bending the bow,
    Their arrow is set on the string,
    To shoot in the dark at the upright.
3 In this tearing down of foundations
    What good can the just man do?"

PSALM XII

The Answer of Faith

4 The Lord in His holy temple,
   The Lord in heaven is enthroned.
 His eyes behold the world,¹
   They narrowly scan all men.
5 The Lord scans righteous and wicked,
   And the lover of wrong He hates.
6 On the wicked He rains coals of fire and brimstone,
   And scorching wind is their portion allotted.²
7 For the Lord is just, and justice He loves ;
   So the upright shall see His face.

PSALM XII

A Prayer for the Preservation of the Faithful in a False World

HELP, O Lord, for the good are all gone,
   From the sons of men the faithful are vanished.
2 One to another, men speak empty lies,
   With flattering lips and false hearts they speak.

3 May the Lord cut off all the flattering lips,
   And the tongue that uttereth arrogant things—
4 Even those that declare, "Our tongue is our strength,
   Our allies our lips : who is lord over us ? "

5 " The poor are despoiled, and the needy are sighing ;
   So now I will rouse me "—the Lord declareth—
 " And set him in safety at whom they snort."

6 The words of the Lord are words that are pure,
   Silver smelted, seven times refined.

PSALMS XIII—XIV

7 (Most surely, then) Thou wilt keep us, O Lord,
  And guard us from this generation for ever,
8 In a world where wicked men strut about,
  And worthless men are exalted.

PSALM XIII

A Prayer for Help in Trouble

How long, Lord, wilt Thou forget me for ever?
  How long wilt Thou hide Thy face from me?
2 How long must I nurse grief in my soul,
  And in my heart a daily sorrow?
  How long are my foes to exult over me?

3 O look and answer me, Lord my God.
  Fill mine eyes with Thy light, that I sleep not in death.
4 Else would mine enemies claim to have triumphed;
  My foes would rejoice at mine overthrow.

5 As for me, I trust in Thy kindness:
  My heart shall rejoice in Thy help.
6 I will sing to the Lord for His bounty to me.

PSALM XIV[1]

The Folly of Denying God

Fools say in their heart,
  "There is no God."
Vile, hateful their life is;
  Not one doeth good.

PSALM XIV

2 From heaven the Lord looked
    Upon men, to see
  If any was wise,
    And cared for God.

3 But all have swerved,
    The taint is on all;
  Not one doeth good,
    No, not one.

4 But they learned their lesson,
    Those workers of evil,
  Who ate up my people,
    Eating, devouring,
    And feared not the Lord.

5 Sore afraid were they there; [2]
    For God was among
  The folk that was righteous,
    Confounding the purpose
  Against the helpless,
    Whose refuge the Lord was.

6 O that from Zion
    Came help for Israel!
  When the Lord brings His people
    A change of fortune,
  How glad shall be Jacob,
    And Israel how joyful!

PSALMS XV—XVI

PSALM XV
The True Citizen of Zion

Lord, who can be guest in Thy tent?
    Who may dwell on Thy holy mountain?

2 He whose walk is blameless,
    Whose conduct is right,
Whose words are true and sincere;
3   On whose tongue there sitteth no slander,
Who will not harm his friend,
    Nor load his neighbour with insult.
4 Reprobates he regards with contempt;
    But who feareth the Lord, he honoureth.
He keepeth his oath, though he suffer for it,
5   His money he putteth not out to usury,
He taketh no bribe against the innocent.

    He who doeth these things will abide unshaken.

PSALM XVI
The Joy of Fellowship with God

Keep me, O God, for in Thee I take refuge.
    I said to Jehovah, " My Lord art Thou:
My happiness resteth in Thee altogether.
3 As for the saints in the land,
    They, they alone, are the noble ones;
    All my delight is in them."

4 Manifold sorrows have they
    Who make choice of another god.
Their offerings of blood I will never pour out
    Nor take their name on my lips.

PSALM XVII

5 The Lord is my share and my portion,[1]
   My lot is in Thy strong hands.

6 In delightsome places my lines have fallen,
   My heritage pleaseth me well.
7 I will bless the Lord for His counsel,
   Which so stirs my heart in the night.
8 I have set the Lord ever before me:
   With Him at my hand, I can never be moved.

9 So my heart is glad, there is joy in my bosom;
   Yea, and in safety of body I dwell.
10 For Thou wilt not give me up to the grave[2]
   Nor let any who loves Thee behold the pit.
11 Thou wilt show me the path that leadeth to life,
   To that fulness of joy which is in Thy presence,
   And the pleasures dispensed by Thy hand evermore.

PSALM XVII

A Prayer for Deliverance from Insolent Foes

LISTEN, O Lord, to mine innocence;
   Attend to my piercing cry.
Give ear to my prayer
   Out of lips unfeigned.
2 Let my sentence come forth from Thy presence.
   Thine eyes behold the truth.

3 When Thou triest my heart in Thy night visitations,
   And provest me—then Thou canst find nothing evil.

PSALM XVII

4 I was still at Thy doing. 4 My mouth transgressed not;
 I gave earnest heed to the words of Thy lips.
5 My steps have held fast to the paths of Thy precepts[1]
 And in Thy tracks have my feet never stumbled.

6 So I call thee, O God, with assurance of answer;
 Incline Thine ear to me, hear what I say.
7 Show Thy marvellous love, Thou who savest from enemies
 Those that take refuge at Thy right hand.

8 Keep me as the apple of the eye,
 Hide me in the shelter of Thy wings
9 From wicked men who do me violence,
 From enemies of mine who raven round me.

10 They have closed their hearts to pity,
 The words of their mouths are haughty.
11 Now they dog us at every step,
 Keenly watching, to hurl us to the ground,
12 Like a lion, longing to tear,
 Like a young lion, lurking in secret.

13 Arise, Lord, face him and fell him.
 By Thy sword set me free from the wicked,
14 By Thy hand, O Lord, from the men—
 From the men who are but of this world.
 Fill their maw with Thy treasures (of wrath)
 And the rest let them leave to their children.[2]

15 Mine shall it be to behold Thy face,
 And to gaze on Thy form to my heart's desire.

PSALM XVIII

PSALM XVIII[1]

A King's Song of Gratitude for Victory

With my whole soul I love Thee, O Lord, my strength.
2 The Lord is my rock, my fortress, deliverer,
   My God, my rock, whereon I take refuge,
   My shield, my defender,[2] my saviour, my tower,
   My refuge, my saviour, who saves me from violence.[3]
3 Worthy of praise is the Lord whom I call on,
   For He is my Saviour from all my foes.

4 The waves of death broke about me,
   Fearful floods of perdition.
5 The nether world threw cords around me,
   Snares of death came to meet me.
6 In distress I cried to the Lord,
   And shouted for help to my God;
   He heard my voice out of His palace,
   And into His ears came my cry.

7 Then the earth shook and quaked,
   Mountains trembled to their foundations,
   And quaked because of His wrath.
8 Smoke went up at His nostrils,
   Devouring fire from His mouth,
   Coals were kindled therefrom.

9 Then He bowed the heavens and came down,
   Thick darkness was under His feet.
10 He rode on a cherub and flew,
   Darting on wings of wind,

PSALM XVIII

11 With His covert of darkness about Him,
   Even thick dark clouds of water.

12 At the radiance before Him there passed
   Hailstones and coals of fire.
13 The Lord thundered from heaven,
   The Most High uttered His voice.
14 He shot His arrows and scattered them,
   Flashed lightnings, and discomfited them.
15 The channels of the sea were revealed,
   The world was laid bare to its base,
   At Thy rebuke, O Lord,
   At the blast of the breath of Thy nostrils.

16 He stretched from on high, He seized me,
   Drew me up from the mighty waters,
17 And saved me from those that hated me—
   Fierce foes, too mighty for me.
18 In my day of distress they assailed me,
   But the Lord proved my stay.
19 To a spacious place He brought me,
   And, for love of me, He saved me.

20 The Lord recompenses mine innocence,
   He requites my cleanness of hands.
21 For I kept the ways of the Lord,
   Nor have wickedly strayed from my God.
22 His commandments were all before me,
   His statutes I put not away.
23 And I was blameless before Him,
   Guarding myself from sin.
24 So the Lord requited mine innocence,
   My cleanness of hands in His sight.

PSALM XVIII

25 With the loving Thou art loving,
    And with the blameless blameless.
26 With the pure Thou showest Thyself pure,
    And perverse with the froward.
27 For the lowly people Thou savest,
    But haughty eyes Thou abasest.
28 Yea, Thou art my lamp, O Lord,
    My God who enlightens my darkness.
29 For in Thee I can break through a wall,
    In my God I can leap o'er a rampart.
30 As for God, His way is perfect;
    The word of the Lord is tried.
    He is shield to all who take refuge in Him.

31 For who is God but Jehovah?
    And who is a rock save our God?
32 The God who girt me with strength,
    Who cleared and smoothed my way.
33 He made my feet like hinds' feet,
    And set me up on the heights.
34 He taught my hands how to fight,
    And mine arms how to bend a bronze bow.

35 The shield of Thy help Thou gavest me,
    And didst cover me with Thy buckler.[4]
36 In Thy strength I took giant strides,
    And mine ankles never tottered.
37 So I chased the foe till I caught them,
    And turned not, till I made an end of them.
38 I smashed them—they could not rise,
    They fell beneath my feet.

PSALM XVIII

39 Thou didst gird me with strength for war,
    Thou didst bow mine assailants beneath me.
40 Thou madest my foes turn their back to me,
    And those that did hate me I finished.
41 They cried for help, but none saved them ;
    To the Lord, but He answered them not.
42 I beat them like dust of the market-place,
    Stamped them like mud of the streets.

43 From the strife of the peoples Thou savedst me,
    Thou madest me head of the nations,
    Peoples I knew not did serve me.
44 On the instant they hear, they obey me,
    Aliens come to me cringing.
45 Aliens wither away,
    And come out of their fastnesses quaking.

46 Hail, Lord ; blest be my rock.
    Exalted be God, my Saviour—
47 The God who gave me revenge,
    And brought down nations beneath me,
48 Who saved me from angry foes,
    And set me above mine assailants,
    Safe from the violent man.

49 For this I will praise Thee among the nations,
    Making music, O Lord, to Thy name :
50 For great triumphs He grants to His king,
    And leal love He shows His anointed,
    Even David and his seed evermore.

PSALM XIX

PSALM XIX, 1—6

The Glory of God in the Heavens

EVERMORE are the heavens declaring God's glory,
  The firmament tells what His hands have done.
2 Day unto day is a well-spring of speech,
  Night unto night a revealer of knowledge.
3 Speech there is none, and words there are none;
  The voice of them cannot be heard.
4 Yet through all the earth their sound has gone out,
  And their words to the end of the world.

  In them hath He set a tent for the sun,
5   Who is like to a bridegroom leaving his chamber;
  He runneth his course like a hero with joy.
6   From one end of the heavens forth he goes,
  And round he runs to the end thereof,
  And nothing is hid from his glow.

PSALM XIX, 7—14

In Praise of the Law

THE Law[1] of Jehovah is perfect,
  Refreshing the soul.
The charge of Jehovah is trusty,
  Making simple ones wise.

8 The behests of Jehovah are right,
  Rejoicing the heart.
  The command of Jehovah is pure,
  Giving light to the eyes.

PSALM XX

9 The fear of Jehovah is clean,
   It abideth for ever.
 Jehovah's judgments are true
   And right altogether.

10 More precious are they than gold—
   Yea, than fine gold in plenty,
 And sweeter they are than honey,
   That drops from the comb.

11 Yea, by them is Thy servant warned;
   Who keeps them has rich reward.
12 Lapses—who can discern them?
   Absolve me from those that I know not.

13 Thy servant hold back from the reckless—
   From falling under their sway:
 Then blameless and clear shall I be
   From manifold transgression.

14 May the words of my mouth and the thoughts
   Of my heart be well-pleasing
 In Thy sight for ever, O Lord,
   My rock and redeemer.

PSALM XX

A Prayer for the King on the Eve of Battle

THE Lord answer thee in the day of distress,
   The name of the God of Jacob protect thee,
2 Sending thee help from the temple,
   And out of Zion supporting thee.

PSALM XXI

3 All thy meal-offerings may He remember,
    Thy burnt-offerings look on with favour.
4 May He grant thee thy heart's desire,
    And bring all thy designs to fruition.
5 We will shout then for joy at thy victory,
    And rejoice in the name of our God.
    May the Lord fulfil all thy petitions.

6 Now I am sure that the Lord
    Will give victory to His anointed.
    From His temple in heaven He will answer
    By His mighty triumphant right hand.
7 Some in chariots are strong, some in horses;
    But *our* strength is the Lord our God.
8 As for them, they shall bow down and fall,
    While *we* rise and stand erect.

9 Give victory, Lord, to the king,
    And answer this day, when we call.

PSALM XXI

A Prayer for the King after a Victory[1]

IN Thy might, O Lord, the king doth rejoice,
    And because of Thy help how exultant is he!
2 Thou hast granted to him the desire of his heart,
    The request of his lips Thou hast not withheld.

3 Thou didst go forth to meet him with blessing and weal,
    Thou didst set on his head a crown of fine gold.

PSALM XXI

4 He asked of Thee life, Thou gavest it him—
 Even length of days for ever and ever.

5 Great is his glory because of Thy help,
 Honour and majesty Thou layest upon him.
6 For Thou dost make him most blessed for ever,
 With the joy of Thy presence Thou makest him glad.

7 Yea, the king putteth ever his trust in the Lord;
 The Most High, in His love, will preserve him unshaken.
8 Thy hand shall reach unto all Thy foes,
 And those that hate Thee Thy right hand shall shatter.

9 Thou shalt make them like furnace of fire,
 What time Thou appearest, O Lord.[2]
10 Their fruit Thou shalt sweep from the earth,
 And their seed from the children of men.

11 When they threaten thy crown with disaster
 And hatch evil plots—they shall fail.
12 For thou makest them turn their back,
 And dost aim with thy bow at their faces.

13 Be exalted, O Lord, in Thy strength,
 To Thy might we will sing and make music.

PSALM XXII

PSALM XXII
The Sufferer's Triumph

My God, my God, why hast Thou left me,
 Gone afar from my cry, from the words of my roaring?
2 I cry in the day-time, but Thou dost not answer;
 Even in the night I am never still.

3 Yet Thou, O Lord, art the Holy One,
 Throned on the praises of Israel.
4 In Thee did our fathers trust,
 They trusted and Thou didst deliver them.
5 They cried unto Thee, and found safety,
 In Thee did they trust and were not put to shame.

6 But I am a worm, and no man;
 Insulted of men and despised of the people.
7 All they that see me mock me,
 With mouths wide open and wagging heads:
8 "He has rolled (his cause) on the Lord; let Him save him.
 Let Him rescue him, since He takes pleasure in him."

9 But 'twas Thine own self drew me out of the womb,
 Made me trustfully lie on my mother's breast.
10 On Thy care was I cast from my very birth,
 Thou art my God from my mother's womb.
11 Be not far from me, for trouble is nigh,
 And there is none to help.

PSALM XXII

12 I am circled by many bulls,
    Beset by the mighty of Bashan,
13 Who face me with gaping jaws,
    Like ravening roaring lions.
14 Poured out am I like water,
    And all my bones are loosened.
    My heart is become like wax,
    Melted within my bosom.

15 My palate is dry as a sherd,
    My tongue cleaves to my jaws;
    In the dust of death Thou dost lay me.
16 For dogs are round about me,
    A band of knaves encircles me,
    Gnawing my hands and my feet.
17 I can count my bones, every one.
    As for them, they feast their eyes on me.
18 They divide my garments among them,
    And over my raiment cast lots.

19 But Thou, O Lord, be not far,
    O Strength of mine, haste Thee to help me.
20 Deliver my life from the sword—
    My soul[1] from the power of the dogs.
21 Save me from the jaws of the lion,
    From the horns of the wild oxen help me.[2]

22 I will tell of Thy fame to my brethren,
    And in the assembly will praise Thee.
23 Praise the Lord, ye that fear Him.
    All Jacob's seed, give Him glory.
    All Israel's seed, stand in awe of Him.

PSALM XXIII

24 For He hath not despised nor abhorred
         The sorrow of him that was sorrowful.
     He hid not His face from him,
         But He listened to his cry for help.

25 Of Thee is my praise in the great congregation;
         My vows I will pay before those that fear Him.
26 The afflicted shall eat to their heart's desire,
         And those that seek after the Lord shall praise Him.
     Lift up your hearts for ever.
27 All shall call it to mind, to the ends of the earth,
         And turn to Jehovah;
     And all tribes of the nations shall bow down before Thee.
28 For the kingdom belongs to Jehovah:
     He is the Lord of the nations.
29 Yea, to Him shall bow down all who sleep in the earth,
     And before Him bend all who go down to the dust,
     And whoso kept not his soul alive.
30 The sons of His servants shall tell of the Lord
         To the next generation;
31 And men shall declare to a folk yet unborn
         Of the victory He wrought.

PSALM XXIII

The Good Shepherd

   THE Lord is my shepherd: no want have I.
2   He layeth me down in pastures green.

PSALM XXIV

    To waters of rest He gently leads me,
3   Refreshing my soul.
    He guideth me ever in paths that are straight
        For His own name's sake.

4   And when my way lies through a valley of gloom,
        I fear no evil, for Thou art with me.
    Thy rod and Thy staff—in them is my comfort.

5   Thou settest a table before me
        In face of my foes ;
    With oil Thou anointest my head,
        And my cup runneth over.
6   Surely goodness and love shall pursue me
        All the days of my life.
    In the house of the Lord I shall dwell
        Through the length of the days.

PSALM XXIV, 1—6

The True Worshipper

THE earth is the Lord's and its fulness,
    The world and the dwellers therein.
2   For *He* founded it on the seas,
        And He on the floods doth sustain it.

3   Who may ascend the hill of the Lord,
        Or who may stand in His holy place ?
4   The clean of hands, the pure of heart,
        Who sets not his soul upon sinful things,
        Nor swears with intent to deceive.

PSALMS XXIV—XXV

5 This is he who wins from the Lord a blessing:
   God is his champion and saviour.
6 Such must be those who resort to Him,
   And seek the face of the God of Jacob.

PSALM XXIV, 7—10

Jehovah's Triumphal Entry into the Sanctuary

LIFT high your heads, ye gates—
   Higher, ye ancient doors;
   Welcome the glorious King.
8 "Who is the glorious King?"
   "The Lord strong and heroic,[1]
   The Lord heroic in battle."

9 Lift high your heads, ye gates—
   Higher, ye ancient doors;
   Welcome the glorious King.
10 "Who is the glorious King?"
   "The Lord, the God of hosts,
   He is the glorious King."

PSALM XXV[1]

A Prayer for Forgiveness and Protection

To Thee, O Lord, I lift up my soul:
   All the day I wait for Thee.
2 In Thee I trust, put me not to shame;
   Let not my foes exult over me.
3 Yea, none shall be shamed that wait for Thee,
   But shame shall fall upon wanton apostates.
4 Make me, O Lord, to know Thy ways:
   Teach Thou me Thy paths.

PSALM XXV

5 In Thy faithfulness guide me and teach me,
    For Thou art my God and my Saviour.
6 Remember Thy pity, O Lord, and Thy kindness,
    For they have been ever of old.
7 The sins of my youth remember not;
    In Thy kindness remember Thou me,
    For Thy goodness' sake, O Lord.
8 Good is the Lord and upright,
    So He teaches sinners the way.
9 The humble He guides in the right,
    He teaches the humble His way.
10 All His ways are loving and loyal
    To those who observe His charges and covenant.
11 For Thy name's sake, O Lord,
    Forgive my many sins.
12 Who then is the man that feareth the Lord?
    He will teach him the way to choose.
13 He himself shall abide in prosperity,
    And his seed shall inherit the land.
14 The Lord holds communion with those that fear Him,
    And with His covenant He makes them acquainted.
15 Mine eyes are ever toward the Lord,
    For out of the net *He* brings my foot.
16 Turn unto me with Thy favour,
    For I am lonely and crushed.
17 In my heart are strain and storm;
    Bring me out of my distresses.
18 Look on my misery and trouble,
    And pardon all my sins,
19 Look on my foes—oh, so many!
    And their cruel hatred towards me.
20 Deliver me, keep me, and shame not
    One who takes refuge in Thee.

PSALM XXVI

21 May integrity and innocence preserve me,
   For I wait for Thee, O Lord.
22 Redeem Israel, O God,
   Out of all his distresses.

PSALM XXVI
Prayer of a Devout Worshipper

DEFEND me, O God, for my walk has been blameless;
   In the Lord have I trusted unswervingly:
2 Prove me, O Lord, and test me;
   Try my heart and my mind.
3 For Thy love is before mine eyes,
   And Thy faithfulness governs my way.

4 I never sat down with the worthless,
   Nor companied with dissemblers.
5 I hate the assembly of knaves,
   I would never sit down with the wicked;
6 But, with hands washed in innocence,
   I would march round Thine altar, O Lord,
7 Singing loud songs of thanks,
   And telling of all Thy wonders.
8 O Lord, I love Thy house,
   The place where Thy glory dwelleth.

9 Take me not off with sinners;
   Slay me not with men of blood,
10 Whose hands are stained with villainy,
   And whose right hand is filled with bribes.
11 As for me, my walk is blameless.
   O redeem me, be gracious to me.
12 My foot standeth on even ground,
   In the choirs I will bless the Lord.

PSALM XXVII

PSALM XXVII, 1—6

If God be for Me

THE Lord is my light and my saviour;
  Whom then shall I fear?
The Lord protecteth my life;
  Whom then shall I dread?

2 When the wicked drew nigh to assail me
    And eat up my flesh,
  It was those that distressed and opposed me
    Who stumbled and fell.

3 Though against me a host should encamp,
    Yet my heart would be fearless:
  Though battle should rise up against me,
    Still would I be trustful.

4 One thing have I asked of the Lord,
    And that do I long for—
  To dwell in the house of the Lord
    All the days of my life,
  To gaze on the grace of the Lord
    And inquire in His temple.

5 For He treasureth me in His bower
    In the day of misfortune.
  In His sheltering tent doth He hide me:
    He lifteth me up on a rock.

6 And now that my head He hath lifted
    Above mine encircling foes,

PSALM XXVII

I will march round[1] the altar and sacrifice,
    Shouting with joy, in His tent,
    Making music and song to the Lord.

PSALM XXVII, 7—14

The Serenity of Faith

Hear, O Lord, my loud cry,
    And graciously answer me.
8 My heart hath said unto Thee,
    " Thy face, O Lord, I seek."

9 Hide not Thy face from me,
    Reject not Thy servant in anger:
    For Thou hast been my help.
Abandon me not, nor forsake me,
    O God of my salvation:
10 For father and mother have left me;
    But the Lord will take me up.

11 Teach me Thy way, O Lord:
    Lead me in an even path,
    Because of mine enemies.
12 Give me not up, O Lord,
    Unto the rage of my foes;
    For against me have risen false witnesses,
    Breathing out cruelty.

13 Firm is the faith I cherish,
    That I, in the land of the living,
    Shall yet see the goodness of God.
14 Let thy heart be courageous and strong
    And wait on the Lord.

PSALM XXVIII

PSALM XXVIII
An Answered Prayer for Help

Unto Thee, O Lord, do I cry;
  My Rock, be not deaf unto me:
Lest, through holding Thy peace, I become
  Like them that go down to the pit.
2 Hear Thou my loud entreaty,
  As I cry for help unto Thee
Lifting my hands, O Lord,
  Towards Thy holy chancel.

3 Take me not off with the wicked,
  Nor with the workers of wrong,
Whose speech to their neighbours is friendly,
  While evil is in their heart.
4 Give them as they have done,
  As their wicked deeds deserve.
As their hands have wrought, so give Thou unto them:
  Requite unto them their deserts.
5 They are blind to all that the Lord does,
  To all that His hands have wrought;
And so He will tear them down,
  To build them up no more.

6 Blest be the Lord, who hath heard
  The voice of my supplication.
7 The Lord is my strength and my shield;
  My heart trusteth in Him.
I was helped: so my heart is exultant,
  And in my song I will praise Him.

PSALM XXIX

8 The Lord is the strength of His people,
    The fortress who saves His anointed.
9 O save Thy people,
    And bless Thine inheritance.
  Be Thou their shepherd
    And carry them for ever.

PSALM XXIX
Jehovah's Glory in the Storm

ASCRIBE to Jehovah, ye Beings celestial,[1]
    Ascribe to Jehovah glory and power
2 Ascribe to Jehovah the glory He manifests,
    Bow to Jehovah in holy array.

3 Jehovah's voice peals on the waters.
    The God of glory has thundered.
    He peals o'er the mighty waters.
4 Jehovah's voice soundeth with strength,
    Jehovah's voice soundeth with majesty.

5 Jehovah's voice breaketh the cedars,
    He breaketh the cedars of Lebanon,
6 Making Lebanon dance like a calf,
    Sirion[2] like a young wild ox.

7 Jehovah's voice cleaves flames of fire.
8 Jehovah's voice rendeth the desert,
    He rendeth the desert of Kadesh.

9 Jehovah's voice whirleth the oaks,
    And strippeth the forests bare;
    And all in His temple say " Glory."

PSALM XXX

10 Jehovah was King at the flood,
   Jehovah sits throned for ever.
11 Jehovah gives strength to His people,
   He blesses His people with peace.

PSALM XXX

A Song of Thanksgiving for Deliverance

I WILL extol Thee, O Lord,
   Because Thou hast lifted me up,
And not suffered my foes to rejoice over me.

2 I cried unto Thee for help,
   O Lord my God, and Thou healedst me.
3 Thou hast brought me up, Lord, from the world below,
   From my way to the pit back to life Thou hast called me.

4 Sing praise to the Lord, ye His saints;
   Give thanks to His holy name.
5 For His anger lasts only a moment,
   His favour endures for a life-time.
Weeping may lodge for the night,
   But the morning brings shouts of joy.

6 When all went well, I imagined
   That never should I be shaken.
7 For by Thy favour, O Lord,
   Thou hadst set me on mountains strong:
But Thou hiddest Thy face,
   And I was confounded.

PSALM XXXI

8   Then to Thee, O Jehovah, I cried,
      To the Lord I made supplication.
9   " What profit is there in my blood,
      If I go down to the pit ?
    Canst Thou be praised by dust ?
      Can it tell of Thy faithfulness ?
10 Hear, Lord, and show me Thy favour,
      Lord, be a helper to me."

11 Thou hast turned my mourning to dancing ;
      My sackcloth Thou hast unloosed,
      And given me a girdle of joy :
12 That unceasingly I should sing Thy praise,
      And give thanks to Thee, Lord my God, for ever.

PSALM XXXI

A Prayer for Deliverance from Sore Distress

   IN Thee, O Lord, I take refuge ;
      Let me never be put to shame.
    Rescue me in Thy faithfulness ;
2   Incline unto me Thine ear.
    Deliver Thou me speedily.
      Be to me a rock of defence,
    A fortified house, to save me.[1]
3   For my rock and my fortress art Thou ;
    For Thy name's sake lead me and guide me.
4   Draw me out of the net they have hid for me,
    For Thou Thyself art my refuge.
5   Into Thy hand I commend my spirit :
      Thou dost ransom me, Lord, Thou faithful God.

PSALM XXXI

6   Those that regard vain idols Thou hatest;
      But, as for me, I trust in the Lord.
7   I will rejoice and be glad in Thy love,
      Because Thou hast looked on my misery,
      And cared for my soul's distress.
8   Thou hast not given me into the enemy's hand,
      Thou hast set my feet in a spacious place.

9   Be gracious to me, Lord, for I am distressed;
      Mine eye is wasted away with sorrow.
10 For my life is consumed with grief,
      And my years with sighing.
    My strength is broken with misery,
      My bones waste away.
11 The scorn of all my foes,
      The butt of my neighbours am I,
      A terror to mine acquaintance.
    At the sight of me in the street
      Men run away from me.
12 I am clean forgotten like the dead,
      Am become like a ruined vessel.
13 Yea, I hear the whispers of many—
      Terror on every side—
    Scheming together against me,
      Plotting to take my life.

14 As for me, my trust is in Thee, Lord.
    " Thou art my God," I say;
15 My times are in Thy hand, save me
      From the hand of the foes that pursue me.
16 Make Thy face to shine on Thy servant,
      Save me in Thy love.

PSALM XXXI

17 Put me not, O Lord, to shame,
    For I have called upon Thee.
  Let the wicked be put to shame
    In the silent world below.
18 Strike the false lips dumb,
    That speak proudly against the righteous
    With haughtiness and contempt.

19 How manifold is the goodness
    Thou hast treasured for those that fear Thee,
  And wrought for those who take refuge in Thee,
    Before the children of men!
20 In Thy sheltering wings Thou dost hide them
    From plottings of men,
  Thou keepest them safe in a bower
    From the chiding of tongues.

21 Blest be the Lord
    For the wonderful love He has shown me
    In time of distress.
22 As for me, I had said in alarm,
    " I am driven clean out of Thy sight."
  But Thou heardest my loud supplication,
    When I cried for help unto Thee.

23 Love the Lord, all ye His saints;
    The Lord preserveth the faithful,
  And recompenseth abundantly
    The man that haughtily dealeth.
24 Let your hearts be courageous and strong,
    All ye who wait on the Lord.

PSALM XXXII

PSALM XXXII

The Joy of Confession and Reconciliation

Happy he whose transgression is pardoned,
  Whose sin is covered.
2 Happy the man, free from falseness of spirit,
  To whom the Lord reckons no debt of guilt.

3 When I held my peace, my bones wore away
  With mine endless groaning ;
4 For day and night did Thy hand
  Lie heavy upon me.
The sap of my life was dried up
  As with fierce summer-heat.

5 I began to acknowledge my sin,
  Not concealing my guilt ;
And the moment I vowed to confess
  To the Lord my transgression,
Then Thou Thyself didst pardon
  The guilt of my sin.

6 For this cause let every true saint
  Pray to Thee in the time of distress ;
Then, when the great waters rush,
  They shall not reach unto him.
7 For Thou wilt be his shelter,
  Preserving him in his straits,
  And compassing him with deliverance.

8 " With mine eye steadfastly upon thee,
  I will instruct and teach thee
  The way thou shouldst go.

PSALM XXXIII

9 Be ye not like the horse or the mule,
   That have no understanding,
   But need bridle and halter to curb them,
   Else they will not come nigh unto thee."

10 The godless have manifold sorrows,
   But he that trusts in the Lord
   Shall be compassed about by His kindness.
11 Be glad in the Lord, and rejoice, ye righteous;
   And ring out your joy, all ye upright in heart.

PSALM XXXIII
A National Hymn of Thanksgiving

SHOUT for joy in the Lord, ye righteous:
   Praise for the upright is seemly.
2 Give thanks to the Lord on the lyre,
   Play to Him on a ten-stringëd harp.
3 Sing unto Him a new song,
   Play skilfully and shout merrily.
4 For the Lord is straight in His promise;
   And all that He does is in faithfulness.
5 Justice and right He loveth;
   The earth is full of His kindness.

6 By His word the heavens were made,
   All their host by the breath of His mouth.
7 He gathers the sea in a bottle,
   The ocean He puts into store-houses.
8 Let the whole world reverence the Lord,
   Let all dwellers on earth be in awe.
9 For at *His* word it came into being,
   At *His* command it stood forth.

PSALM XXXIII

10 The Lord frustrates the designs of the heathen,
   What the nations have purposed, He bringeth to nought,
11 But the Lord's own design shall stand for ever,
   And what *His* heart hath purposed, through all generations.
12 Happy the nation whose God is Jehovah,
   The people He chose for Himself as His own.

13 The Lord looketh down from heaven,
   He sees all the children of men ;
14 From His dwelling-place He gazeth
   On all who inhabit the earth.
15 He fashions the hearts of them all,
   And gives heed to all that they do.

16 It is not by great armies that kings are victorious,
   It is not by great strength that a warrior saves himself ;
17 Vain is the war-horse to usher in victory,
   Nor brings he to safety for all his great might.

18 See ! the eye of the Lord is on them that fear Him,
   On them that hope in His kindness ;
19 To deliver their life from death,
   And to keep them alive in famine.

20 Our soul waits for the Lord :
   He is our help and our shield.
21 For in Him our heart is glad,
   We trust in His holy name.

22 Let Thy kindness, O Lord, be upon us,
   Even as we hope in Thee.

PSALM XXXIV

PSALM XXXIV[1]

The Lord is Mindful of His Own

1. I WILL bless the Lord at all times,
   In my mouth shall His praise be for ever.
2. In the Lord shall my soul make her boast,
   The humble shall hear and be glad.
3. O magnify the Lord with me
   And let us extol His name together.
4. I sought the Lord, and, in answer,
   He saved me from all my terrors.
5. Look to Him and ye shall be radiant,
   With faces unashamëd.
6. Here is a man who was crushed,
   But he cried and was heard by the Lord,
   And brought safe out of all his distresses.
7. Jehovah's angel encamps
   About those that fear Him, and rescues them.
8. O taste and see that the Lord is good,
   Happy the man who takes refuge in Him.
9. Fear the Lord, ye His saints,
   For they that fear Him lack nothing.
10. Apostates[2] are poor and hungry,
    But those who seek the Lord
    Shall not lack any good thing.

11. Come, children, listen to me.
    I will teach you the fear of the Lord.
12. What man is desirous of life,
    Loveth many and happy days?
13. Then guard thy tongue from evil,
    And thy lips from speaking deceit.

PSALM XXXV

14 Depart from evil, and do good;
  Seek thou peace, and pursue it.
15 The Lord sets His face against them that do evil,
  To root their memory out of the earth.*
16 The eyes of the Lord are towards the righteous,
  His ears are towards their cry for help.
17 When they cry, they are heard by the Lord,
  And He saves them from all their distresses.
18 The Lord is nigh to the broken-hearted,
  He helpeth those whose spirit is crushed.
19 Many misfortunes befall the righteous,
  But the Lord delivers him out of them all.
20 He keepeth all his bones,
  Not one of them is broken.
21 Misfortune shall slay the ungodly;
  Those who hate the righteous are doomed.
22 The Lord doth ransom the life of His servants,
  And none shall be doomed who takes refuge in Him.

PSALM XXXV

A Prayer for Deliverance from Malicious Foes

CONTEND, Lord, with those that contend with me,
  Do battle with those that do battle with me.
2 Grasp shield and buckler,
  And rise up as my help.
3 Draw spear and battle-axe,
  Confront those who pursue me.
  Assure me that Thou wilt help me.

PSALM XXXV

4 Dishonour and shame be on those
    'Who are seeking my life!
  Defeat and confusion on those
    Who are planning my hurt!
5 As chaff before wind may they be,
    With Jehovah's angel pursuing them.
6 Slippery and dark be their way,
    With His angel thrusting them on.
7 For they wantonly hid their net for me,
    And dug a pit to destroy me.

8 Upon them may ruin come unawares;
  May the net which they hid catch themselves,
    And into the pit may they fall.
9 Then my soul shall exult in the Lord,
    And be joyful because of His help;
10 And all my being[1] shall say,
    " Who, O Lord, is like Thee,
  That savest the helpless from those too strong for them,
    The poor and the helpless from those that despoil them?"

11 Violent witnesses rise,
    And ask of me things that I know not.
12 Evil for good they requite me,
    Leaving me inwardly comfortless.[2]

13 But when *they* were sick, *I* put on sackcloth,
    And chastened my soul with fasting.
  I prayed with head bent on my bosom,
14   As though 'twere my friend or my brother.

PSALM XXXV

    I went about bowed and in mourning,
        As one that lamenteth his mother.

15 When I stumbled, they gleefully gathered,
       They gathered against me like aliens,
       And tore without ceasing,
16 Impiously mocking and mocking,
       And gnashing on me with their teeth.

17 How long, Lord, wilt Thou look on?
       O recover my soul from their roaring,
       My precious life³ from the lions.
18 I will then give Thee thanks in the great congregation,
       And praise Thee before many people.
19 Suffer not those to rejoice over me
       Who are falsely my foes,
    Suffer not those who without cause abhor me
       To wink with the eye.

20 For it is not peace that they speak
       Of those that are quiet in the land;
    But treacherous charges they plot.
21   With wide open mouths they shout,
    "Hurrah! Hurrah!
    With our own eyes we saw it."

22 But Thou hast seen, too, O Jehovah,
       Keep not silence, O Lord,
       Be not Thou far from me.
23 Bestir Thee, awake, for my right—
       My God, my Lord, for my cause.

PSALM XXXVI

24 Thou art just, Lord : win for me justice,
   Let them not rejoice over me,
25 Inwardly saying, " Hurrah !
   The desire of our hearts at last !
   Now we have swallowed him up."
26 Shame and confusion together
   On those that rejoice at my hurt !
   Clothed with shame and dishonour
   Be those that are haughty to me !

27 Let such as delight in my cause
   Ring out their gladness,
     And say evermore,
   " Great is the Lord whose delight
   Is the well-being of His servant."
28 Then my tongue shall tell of Thy justice,
   And all the day long of Thy praise.

PSALM XXXVI

The Triumphant Power of the Divine Love

The Rise and Progress of Sin

SIN whispers within the bad man's heart,
   Who hath no dread of God before his eyes.
2 Yea, she flattereth him in his eyes
   That his sin will not be found out.[1]

3 First, his speech becomes wicked and false,
   He gives up acting wisely and well.
4 Then he plots deliberate wrong,
   Takes his stand on the wicked way,
   Without the least shrinking from evil.

PSALM XXXVII

The Abounding Love of God

5 Thy love, O Lord, touches the heavens,
   Thy faithfulness reaches the clouds.
6 Thy justice is like the great mountains,[2]
   Thy judgments are like the broad sea.
   Man and beast Thou savest, O Lord.
7 How precious Thy love, O God!
   'Neath Thy sheltering wings men take refuge.
8 They feast on the fat of Thy house,
   They drink of Thy brook of delights.
9 For with Thee is the fountain of life,
   In the light that is Thine we see light.

10 O continue Thy grace to the faithful,
   Thy love to the upright in heart.
11 Let no arrogant foot tread upon me,
   No wicked hand drive me to exile.

12 There [3] the workers of wrong lie prostrate,
   Thrust down—to rise up no more.

PSALM XXXVII[1]

A Vindication of the Moral Order

BE not kindled to wrath at the wicked,
   Nor envious of those that work wrong;
2 For, like grass, they shall speedily wither,
   And fade like the green of young grass.

3 Trust in the Lord, and do good;
   Remain in the land, and deal faithfully:
4 Then the Lord shall be Thy delight,
   He will grant Thee thy heart's petitions.

PSALM XXXVII

5 Commit Thy way unto the Lord;
     Trust in Him, and *He* will act,
6 Making clear as the light thy right,
     And thy just cause clear as the noon-day.

7 In silence and patience wait on the Lord.
     Be not kindled to anger at those who prosper.
     At those who execute evil devices.

8 Desist from anger, abandon wrath :
     Be not kindled to anger—it leads but to evil :
9 For evildoers shall be cut off,
     But the land shall be theirs, that wait on the Lord.

10 Yet but a little, and the wicked vanish :
     Look at his place—he is there no more.
11 But the patient—the land shall be *theirs*,
     And the rapture of peace in abundance.

12 The wicked plotteth against the righteous,
     He gnasheth upon him with his teeth;
13 The Lord laugheth at him,
     For He sees that his day is coming.

14 The wicked have drawn the sword,
     To slay men who walk uprightly;
15 But their sword shall pierce their own heart,
     And their bows shall be broken in pieces.

16 Better is the righteous man's little
     Than the wealth of many wicked.
17 For the arms of the wicked shall be broken,
     But the Lord upholdeth the righteous.

PSALM XXXVII

18 The Lord watcheth over the days of the blameless,
   Their heritage shall continue for ever.
19 They shall not be shamed in the evil time,
   In the days of famine they shall be satisfied.

20 Because the wicked shall perish :
   But the foes of the Lord, like a brand in the oven,
   Shall vanish—like smoke they shall vanish.

21 The wicked must borrow and cannot pay back,
   But the righteous is lavish and giveth.
22 For those whom He blesses inherit the land,
   While those whom He curses shall be cut off.

23 The Lord supporteth the steps
   Of the man with whom He is pleased.
24 Though he fall, he shall not be cast headlong,
   For the Lord holdeth his hand.

25 Never, from youth unto age,
   Have I seen the righteous forsaken,
   Or his children begging bread.
26 He is ever lavishly lending,
   And his children are fountains of blessing.

27 Depart from evil and do good—
   So shalt thou dwell (in the land) for ever.
28 For the Lord loveth justice,
   He does not forsake His friends.

   The unrighteous shall be destroyed[a] for ever,
   And the seed of the wicked shall be cut off.
29 But the land shall belong to the righteous,
   They shall dwell upon it for ever.

PSALM XXXVII

30 The mouth of the righteous murmureth wisdom,
    And words of justice are on his tongue.
31 The law of his God is in his heart,
    His steps are never unsteady.

32 The wicked watcheth the righteous,
    And seeketh to put him to death.
33 But the Lord leaves him not in his hand :
    At his trial he will not be held guilty.

34 Wait on the Lord, and observe His way :
    He will lift thee to honour—the land shall be thine,
    Thou shalt feast thine eyes on the doom of the wicked.

35 I have seen the wicked exultant,
    Lifting himself like a cedar of Lebanon.
36 But the moment I passed, behold! he had vanished;
    I sought for him, but he could not be found.

37 Preserve thine honour and practise uprightness,
    For such a man fares well in the end.
38 But transgressors shall perish together.
    Cut off are the wicked for ever.

39 The righteous are saved by the Lord,
    Who in time of distress is their refuge :
40 The Lord doth help and rescue them,
    From the wicked He rescues and saves them,
    Because they take refuge in Him.

PSALM XXXVIII

PSALM XXXVIII

A Confession of Sin and Prayer for Deliverance

Reprove me not, Lord, in Thine anger,
    And chasten me not in Thy wrath;
2 For Thine arrows have sunk into me,
    And Thy hand lieth heavy upon me.

3 In my flesh is no soundness
    Because of Thine anger,
No health in my bones,
    Because of my sin.
4 For that my guilt
    Is gone over my head:
It weighs like a burden
    Too heavy for me.

5 My wounds stink and fester,
    For my foolishness I am tormented.
6 Bent and bowed am I utterly,
    All the day going in mourning.

7 My loins are filled with burning,
    And in my flesh is no soundness.
8 I am utterly crushed and numb:
    I cry louder than lion roars.

9 Lord, Thou knowest all that I long for,
    My groans are not hidden from Thee.
10 My heart is throbbing,
    My strength has failed me.
The light of mine eyes—
    Even it is gone from me.

PSALM XXXVIII

11 My dear ones and friends keep aloof,
    And my neighbours stand afar off.
12 They that aim at my life lay their snares,
    They that seek my hurt speak of ruin,
    Nursing treachery all the day long.

13 But I turn a deaf ear and hear not;
    Like the dumb I open not my mouth.
14 I am as a man without hearing,
    With no arguments in his mouth.

15 For my hope, O Lord, is in Thee.
    Thou wilt answer, O Lord my God,
16 When I utter the hope that those
    Who made scorn of my tottering feet
    May not rejoice over me.

17 For I am ready to fall,
    My pain forsaketh me never.
18 Yea, I acknowledge my guilt,
    I am anxious because of my sin:

19 My wanton assailants are strong,
    Those who wrongfully hate me are many,
20 Who render me evil for good,
    And oppose me, because I make good my goal.
    They have cast me out into solitude,
    Like to a corpse abhorred.[1]

21 Do not forsake me, O Lord;
    My God, be not far from me.
22 Haste Thee to help me,
    O Lord my Saviour.

PSALM XXXIX

PSALM XXXIX

The Pathos of Life

I VOWED to watch my words,
And sin not with my tongue,
But to put on my mouth a bridle,
While the wicked were in my presence.
2 I was silent and dumb,
Not a rash word spake I:
But my pain was stirred up.
3 My heart was hot in my bosom;
As I mused, the fire was kindled,
Till at last the words came to my tongue.

4 " Teach me, O Lord, mine end,
And the sum of my days—what it is.
Let me know how transient I am.
5 See! my days Thou hast made but a span,
And my life is as nothing before Thee.
It is but as a vapour that every man stands:
6 It is but in mere semblance man walks to and fro,
And all his noise is for nothing.
He heaps up, and knoweth not who shall gather."

7 And now, what wait I for, Lord?
My hope is in Thee.
8 From all my transgressions deliver me;
Make me not the scorn of the fool.
9 I am dumb, never opening my mouth,
For this is Thine own doing.
10 Remove Thy stroke from off me:
By the might of Thy hand I am spent.

PSALM XL

11 When Thou chastenest sinful man with rebuke,
    Thou dost waste, like the moth, his beauty.
    Every man is naught but a vapour.

12 Hear my prayer, O Lord;
    Give ear to my cry for help.
    Hold not Thy peace at my tears.
13 For I am but a guest of Thine,
    And a pilgrim, like all my fathers.
14 Look away from me, let me smile again,
    Ere I go away and be no more.

PSALM XL

Thanksgiving and Petition

For Jehovah I waited and waited,
    Till, inclining to me,
    He heard my cry.
2 From the horrible pit He drew me,
    Up out of the miry clay;
    He set my feet on a rock,
    And my steps He made firm.
3 He put a new song in my mouth,
    Even praise to our God.
    Many see it, and, filled with awe,
    Put their trust in Jehovah.

4 Happy the man that hath put
    In Jehovah his trust,
    Not turning aside to defiant
    And lying apostates.

PSALM XL

5 With us Thou hast wrought in rich measure,
   Jehovah our God,
Thy marvels and purposes for us—
   None may compare with Thee—
Were I to declare or to tell them,
   Past counting are they.

6 In offerings bloody or bloodless
   Thou hast no delight,
But with open ears Thou hast made me.[1]
Burnt-offering and offering for sin
   Are not what Thou askest.
7 Then said I, " Behold I am come,
   As the roll of the book hath enjoined.
8 My delight, O God, is to do Thy will,
   And Thy law is within my heart."
9 Well, O Jehovah, Thou knowest
   That, with lips unrestrained,
The glad news of salvation I told
   In the great congregation,
10 Not hiding it in my heart.
   I have told of Thy steadfast help,
From the great congregation I hid not
   Thy love and Thy faithfulness.
11 So restrain not thou, O Jehovah,
   Thy pity from us.
Thy love and Thy faithfulness—ever
   May they be our shield.

12 For evils that cannot be numbered
   Have compassed me round.
My transgressions have followed me up—
   I can bear it no more.

PSALM XLI

    They are more than the hairs of my head,
        And my heart hath forsaken me.
13 O Jehovah,[2] be pleased to deliver me,
        Haste to my help, O Jehovah.
14 May those that are seeking my life
        Be ashamed and confounded together;
    May those that delight in my hurt
        Be defeated and brought to dishonour.
15 May those who hurrah over me
        Be dumbfounded because of their shame.
16 But may all who seek after Thee
        Rejoice and be glad in Thee.
    May all who love Thy salvation
        Say, " Great is the Lord " evermore.
17 As for me, I am weak and needy,
        Yet the Lord careth for me.
    Thou art my help and deliverer;
        Tarry not, O my God.

PSALM XLI

A Prayer for Healing and Vindication

HAPPY is he that considers the weak;
    In the day of misfortune the Lord will deliver him.
2 He will keep him safe, happy, and long in the land,
      And not give him up to the rage of his foes.
3 The Lord will sustain him on bed of languishing;
      Tending his sickness, as long as he lies.

4 For this cause I say, " O Lord, show me Thy favour;
      Heal me, because I have sinned against Thee."

PSALM XLI

5 Mine enemies speak of me nothing but evil,
   " When will he die, and his name pass away ? "
6 When one comes to see me, his words ring hollow ;
   His heart keeps gathering mischief the while ;
   And when he goes out, he giveth it speech.
7 In secret they whisper together against me,
   All those that hate me plot evil against me.
8 " Some fell disease has fastened upon him ;
   And now that he lies, he will rise up no more."
9 Yea, mine own bosom friend, in whom I trusted,
   Who ate of my bread, is disdainful to me.

10 But do Thou, Lord, graciously raise me up,
   That I may pay them their due reward.
11 Herein shall I know Thou delightest in me,
   If my foes may not shout over me in triumph.
12 As for me, in mine innocence Thou wilt uphold me,
   And set me for ever before Thy face.

Blessed be Jehovah, the God of Israel,
From everlasting to everlasting,
Amen and Amen.

BOOK II

PSALMS XLII and XLIII

Yearning for God

L IKE as the hart which longeth
    After the brooks of water,
Even so longeth my soul
    After Thee, O God.
2 My soul is athirst for God,
    For my living God.
When shall I enter in,
    And see the face of God?
3 My tears have been to me food
    By day and by night;
For they say to me all the day long,
    " Where is thy God ? "

4 I would pour out my soul within me,
    As I call these things to mind—
How I used to pass on with the throng,
    At their head, to the house of God,
With glad shouts and giving of thanks,
    In the throng that kept festival.

5 *O soul of mine, why art thou downcast?*
    And why art thou moaning within me?
Hope thou in God;
    For yet shall I praise Him,
    My Saviour, my God.

PSALMS XLII—XLIII

6 My soul is cast down within me.
  I will therefore call Thee to mind
  From the land of Jordan and Hermon,
  The mountain Mizár.
7 Flood is calling to flood
  At the noise of Thy cataracts ;
  All Thy waves and Thy billows
  Have passed over me.

8 In the day I cry to the Lord
  To summon His kindness ;
  And the song that I sing in the night
  Is a prayer to the living God.
9 I say unto God my rock,
  " Why hast Thou forgotten me ?
  Why must I walk so sadly,
  So hard pressed by the foe ? "
10 It pierces me to the heart
  To hear the enemy's taunts,
  As all the day long they say to me,
  " Where is thy God ? "

11 *O soul of mine, why art thou downcast ?*
  And why art thou moaning within me ?
  Hope thou in God ;
  For yet shall I praise Him,
  My Saviour, my God.

xliii.
1 Right me, defend my cause
    Against a pitiless people.
  From crafty and crooked men,
    O God, deliver me.

PSALM XLIV

2 For Thou art God my protector:
    Why hast Thou cast me off?
  Why must I walk so sadly,
    So hard pressed by the foe?
3 Send forth Thy light and Thy truth,
    Let *them* be my guides:
  To Thy holy hill let them bring me,
    To the place where Thou dwellest.
4 Then will I go to God's altar,
    To God my rejoicing;
  And with joy on the lyre I will praise Thee,
    O Lord my God.

5 *O soul of mine, why art thou downcast?*
    And why art thou moaning within me?
  Hope thou in God;
    For yet shall I praise Him,
    My Saviour, my God.

PSALM XLIV

A Lament in Defeat

O God, we have heard with our ears,
    Our fathers have told us the story
  Of the work that Thou wroughtest in their day,
    Thy wonders in days of old,
2 Uprooting and crushing the nations,
    Then planting and settling *them*.[1]
3 For 'twas not their own sword that won them the land,

PSALM XLIV

It was not their own arm that brought them the
victory.
Thine was the hand and the arm,
Thine was the face that shone on them with favour.
4 It was Thou, my King and my God,
That ordainedst the victories of Jacob.

5 Through Thee we can thrust back our foes,
And by Thy name tread down our assailants:
6 For not in my bow do I trust,
Nor can *my* sword win me the victory.
7 Our victory cometh from Thee,
And confusion to those who hate us.
8 In God we boast all the day long,
And Thy name will we praise for ever.

9 Yet Thou hast spurned and disgraced us,
In not going forth with our hosts,
10 And in making us flee from the foe,
So that those who hated us spoiled us.
11 Thou hast let us be eaten like sheep,
Thou hast scattered us over the world,
12 Selling Thy folk for a pittance,
And getting no gain from their price.
13 Thou hast made us the butt of our neighbours,
The derision and scorn of all round us.
14 O'er the world Thou hast made us a by-word,
The nations at us shake their heads.
15 My disgrace is for ever before me,
My face is covered with shame,
16 At the words of blasphemer and scoffer,
At the sight of the foe and the vengeful.

PSALM XLV

17 All this has come upon us,
   Yet we have not forgotten Thee,
   Nor falsely dealt with Thy covenant.
18 Our heart has not turned back,
   Nor our steps declined from Thy way,
19 That Thou thus shouldst have crushed us down,
   And covered us over with gloom,
   In the place where the jackals roam.
20 Had we forgotten the name of our God,
   Or stretched out our hands to a god that was strange,
21 Would God not have searched this out?
   For He knoweth the heart and its secrets.
22 But in Thy cause it is we are killed all the day,
   And counted as sheep for the slaughter.

23 Bestir Thee, why sleepest Thou, Lord?
   Awake, cast us not off for ever.
24 Why dost Thou hide Thy face,
   Forgetting our stress and our misery?
25 For our soul is bowed to the dust,
   Our body cleaves to the ground.
26 Arise, come to our help:
   Ransom us for Thy kindness' sake.

PSALM XLV

Song for the Marriage of a King

My heart is astir with a goodly matter:
   A song will I sing, concerning the king,
With tongue like the pen of a ready writer.

PSALM XLV

2 Thy beauty is more than mortal,
    Grace is shed over thy lips :
    Therefore God hath blessed thee for ever.

3 Warrior, gird thy sword on thy thigh.
    What glory and splendour !
4 Good fortune attend thee, as forth thou dost ride
    In the cause of good faith, and as champion of justice.
    May thine arm instruct thee in deeds of dread.
5 Sharp are thine arrows ; nations fall under thee :
    Pierced to the heart are the foes of the king.

6 Thy throne shall endure for ever and ever—
    Thy royal sceptre a sceptre of equity.
7 Right thou lovest and wrong thou hatest :
    Therefore Jehovah thy God doth anoint thee
    With oil of gladness above thy fellows.

8 With myrrh, aloes, and cassia thy robes are all fragrant,
    Thou art ravished with music of ivory harps.
9 King's daughters stand ready with jewels for thee,
    At thy right hand the queen in gold of Ophir.

10 Listen, daughter, and see ; and incline thine ear :
    Forget thy folk and thy father's house.
11 And when the king desireth thy beauty,
    Bow unto him—for he is thy lord.
12 So shall the Tyrians come with gifts,
    And the richest of people will do thee homage.

PSALM XLVI

13 The king's daughter is glorious altogether,
    With dress of pearls inwrought with gold.
14 In gay-coloured robes she is led to the king,
    With the virgin companions she brought in her train.
15 The king's palace they enter with joy and rejoicing.

16 May sons of thine take the place of thy fathers,
    Whom thou shalt make princes in all the land.
17 Thy name will I celebrate world without end,
    So that nations shall praise thee for ever and ever.

PSALM XLVI

A Safe Stronghold our God is Still

GOD is to us a refuge and strength,
    A help right trusty in distresses.
2 No fear have we therefore, though earth should change,
    And the hills totter into the heart of the ocean.
3 Let its waters roar and foam,
    Let the mountains shake with the swelling thereof:
On our side is the Lord of hosts,
Our sure defence is the God of Jacob.[1]

4 A river there is, whose streams make glad
    God's city, the home the Most High hath hallowed.
5 God is within her : she cannot be shaken.
    God helpeth her at the turn of the morning.
6 Nations roared, kingdoms tottered :
    He uttered His voice, earth melted away.

PSALM XLVII

7 *On our side is the Lord of hosts,*
    Our sure defence is the God of Jacob.

8 Come and see what the Lord hath done,
    Working appallingly in the earth.
9 He stilleth wars to the ends of the earth—
    Breaking the bow, snapping the spear,
    Burning the chariots in the fire.
10 " Refrain ; and know surely that I am God,
    High over the nations, high over the world."[2]
11 *On our side is the Lord of Hosts,*
    Our sure defence is the God of Jacob.

PSALM XLVII

Jehovah's Universal Sovereignty

C LAP your hands, all ye peoples :
    Shout to God in ringing cries.
2 For the Lord is most high and dread,
    A great King over all the earth.

3 He subdueth the peoples under us,
    The nations under our feet ;
4 He chooseth our heritage for us,
    The glory of Jacob whom He loveth.

5 God is gone up with a shout,
    The Lord with the sound of a trumpet.
6 Sing praise to our God, sing praises :
    Sing praise to our King, sing praises.

PSALM XLVIII

7 For King of all earth is He :
    Praise God in a skilful song.
8 God is King over all the nations,
    God sits on His holy throne.

9 Princes of nations gather
    With the people of Abraham's God :
    For the shields[1] of the earth are God's ;
    Greatly exalted is He.

PSALM XLVIII

The Marvellous Deliverance of Zion

GREAT is Jehovah and worthy all praise
    In the city of our God.
2 His holy mountain, that rises so fair,
    Is the joy of all the world.
    Like the mount of the gods [1] is mount Zion,
    The city of the great King.

3 Once God made Himself known
    As the defence of her palaces.
4 For see ! a concert of kings
    Passed over the frontier together.
5 But one glance, and they were astounded ;
    They hastened away in dismay.
6 Trembling took hold of them there,
    Like the pangs of a woman in travail.
7 They were shattered, as east wind shatters
    The giant ships in pieces.

PSALM XLIX

8 Even as we heard, have we seen
    In the city of Jehovah of hosts,
  The city of our God.
  God will uphold her for ever.

9 We think, O God, of Thy love,
    In the midst of Thy temple.
10 Thy fame, like Thy name, shall extend
    To the ends of the earth.
  Victory fills Thy hand.
11   Let mount Zion be glad ;
  Let the daughters of Judah rejoice
    Because of Thy judgments.
12 Walk about Zion, go round her ;
    Count ye her towers.
13 Set ye your mind on her ramparts,
    Consider her palaces ;
  That ye tell to the next generation
14   That such is Jehovah,
  Our God—He it is that shall guide us
    For ever and ever.

PSALM XLIX

The Problem of the Prosperity of the Wicked

HEAR this, ye peoples all ;
    Give ear, all ye that dwell in the world :
2 Men of low degree and high,
    The rich and the poor together.
3 My mouth shall utter wisdom,
    The thoughts of a seeing heart.

PSALM XLIX

4 I incline mine ear to a proverb,[1]
   On the lyre I will open my riddle.
   Man in honour abides not,
   He is like to the beasts that perish.

5 Why should I be afraid in the days of misfortune,
   When circled by wicked and cunning men
6 Who put their trust in their wealth,
   And boast of their boundless riches?

7 For assuredly no man can ransom himself,
   Or give unto God the price of his life,
8 To keep him alive for ever and ever,
9 So as never to see the pit at all.

10 But see it he shall. Even wise men die,
   The fool and the brutish perish alike,
   And abandon their wealth unto others.
11 The grave is their everlasting home,
   The place they shall dwell in for ever and ever,
   Though after their own names they called whole lands.[2]
12 *Man in honour abides not,*
   He is like to the beasts that perish.

13 This is the fate of the confident fool,
   And the end of those who are pleased with their portion.
14 Like sheep they descend to Sheol
   With Death for their shepherd;
   Down they go straight to the grave,
   And their form wastes away in their home below.[3]

PSALM L

15 But God will assuredly ransom my life
   From the hand of Sheol;
   For He will receive me.
16 So be not afraid when a man grows rich,
   When the pomp of his house increases.
17 Not a shred of it all can he take when he dies,
   His pomp cannot go down after him.
18 Though he counts himself happy, when he is alive,
   And wins praise from men for faring so well,
19 He must join the race of his fathers,
   Who see the light nevermore.
20 *Man in honour, that hath no insight,*
   Is like to the beasts that perish.

PSALM L

True Worship

THE Lord God hath spoken: He summons the earth
   From sunrise to sunset.
2 From Zion, perfection of beauty,
   God's glory shines forth.
3 Our God cometh, He cannot keep silence,
   Devouring fire is before Him,
   And furious tempest around Him.
4 He summons the heavens above
   And the earth to judge His people.
5 Gather to Him His saints
   By covenant-sacrifice bound to Him;
6 That the heavens may declare His justice,
   For a God of justice is He.

PSALM L

7 "Hear, O my people, and I will speak,
    And protest unto thee, O Israel:
    I am Jehovah, thy God.
8 Not for thy sacrifices will I reprove thee—
    Thy burnt-offerings are ever before me—
9 Not a bullock will I take from thy house,
    Nor he-goats out of thy folds;
10 For all beasts of the forest are mine,
    And the kine on a thousand hills.
11 I know all the birds of the air,
    All that moves on the fields is mine.
12 Were I hungry, I would not tell *thee*,
    For the world and its fulness are mine.
13 Am I such as to eat bulls' flesh,
    Or drink the blood of goats?
14 Offer to God a thank-offering,[1]
    Pay the Most High thy vows.
15 Summon me in the day of distress,
    I will rescue thee, so shalt thou honour me."

16 But unto the wicked God saith:
    "What right hast thou to talk of my statutes,
    Or take my covenant into thy mouth—
17 While thou thyself hatest correction,
    And castest my words behind thee?
18 When thou seest a thief, thou dost run with him;
    With adulterers thou keepest company.
19 Thou lettest thy mouth loose for evil,
    Thy tongue contriveth deceit.
20 Thou dost shamefully speak of thy brother,
    And slander the son of thy mother.

PSALM LI

21 And because I kept silence at this,
   Thou didst take me for one like thyself.
   But I will convict thee and show thee plainly.

22 Now ye that forget God, mark this,
   Lest I rend you, past hope of deliverance.
23 He who brings a thank-offering honours me;
   But to him who gives heed to his ways,
   I will show the salvation of God."

PSALM LI

God be Merciful to Me, the Sinner

IN Thy kindness, O God, be gracious to me,
   In Thine own great pity blot out my transgressions.
2 Wash me clean of my guilt,
   Make me pure of my sin.

3 For well I know my transgressions,
   My sin is ever before me.
4 Against Thee, only Thee, have I sinned,
   And done that which is wrong in Thy sight:
   Thou therefore art just when Thou speakest,
   And clear when Thou utterest judgment.
5 See! in guilt was I brought to the birth,
   And in sin did my mother conceive me.
6 'Tis the innermost[1] truth Thou desirest,
   Give me therefore true wisdom of heart.

7 Purge Thou me clean with hyssop,
   Wash me whiter than snow.

PSALM LI

8 Fill me with joy and gladness,
    Let the bones Thou hast broken rejoice.
9 Hide Thy face from my sins,
    And blot out my guilt altogether.

10 Create me a clean heart, O God,
    Put a new steadfast spirit within me.
11 Cast me not forth from Thy presence,
    Withdraw not Thy holy spirit.
12 Give me back the joy of Thy help,
    With a willing spirit sustain me.

13 I will teach Thy ways to transgressors,
    And sinners shall turn unto Thee.
14 Save me from blood, O God,
    And my tongue shall ring out Thy faithfulness.
15 Open my lips, O Lord,
    And my mouth shall declare Thy praise.

16 For in sacrifice Thou hast no pleasure,
    In gifts of burnt-offering no delight.
17 The sacrifice pleasing to God
    Is a spirit that is broken ;
  A heart that is crushed, O God,
    Thou wilt not despise.

18 Do good in Thy pleasure to Zion,
    Build Thou the walls of Jerusalem.
19 Then shalt Thou welcome the due forms of sacrifice,
    Then on Thine altar shall bullocks be offered.

PSALM LII

PSALM LII

The Doom of Arrogance

WHY glory in mischief, thou hero?
  God's kindness is all the day.
2 Engulfing ruin thou plottest,
  Thy tongue like a razor whetted,
  Thou practiser of deceit.
3 Evil, not good, thou lovest,
  And falsehood, not words of truth.
4 But thou lovest all words that devour,
  And a tongue that is given to deceit.

5 But God, on His part, shall destroy thee for ever,
  Grasp thee and pluck thee out of thy tent,
  And root thee out of the land of the living.
6 Smitten with awe at the sight,
  The righteous shall laugh at him.
7 "Look"—(they will say)—"at the hero
  Who made not God his stronghold,
  But trusted in his great wealth
  And in the strength of his substance."

8 As for me, like a fresh olive-tree
  In the house of God am I.
  I trust in the kindness of God
  For ever and evermore.
9 I will render Thee thanks for ever
  For this that Thou hast done.
  I will tell how good Thou art
  In the presence of them that love Thee.

PSALM LIII

PSALM LIII[1]

The Folly of Denying God

Fools say in their heart,
  "There is no God."
Vile, hateful their life is ;
  Not one doeth good.

2 From heaven God looked
    Upon men, to see
  If any was wise,
    And cared for God.

3 But all have swerved,
    The taint is on all ;
  Not one doeth good,
    No, not one.

4 But they learned their lesson,
    Those workers of evil,
  Who ate up my people,
    Eating, devouring,
    And feared not God.

5 Sore afraid were they there,
    Where no fear was ;
  For God scattered the bones
    Of the godless people.
  Put to shame were they,
    For God had rejected them.

PSALM LIV

6   O that from Zion
    Came help for Israel!
    When God brings His people
    A change of fortune,
    How glad shall be Jacob,
    And Israel how joyful!

PSALM LIV

A Prayer for Deliverance from Oppression

SAVE me, O God, by Thy name,
    By Thy power secure for me justice.
2 Hearken, O God, to my prayer,
    Give ear to the words of my mouth.
3 For proud men have risen against me
    And terrible men seek my life,
    Men who do not set God before them.

4 But see! God is my helper,
    The Lord is sustaining my soul.
5 Let their evil fall back on my foes:
    Cut them off in Thy faithfulness, Lord.

6 Then will I bring Thee glad sacrifice,
    Praising Thy gracious name;
7 For from all distress Thou hast saved me,
    And feasted mine eyes on my foes.

PSALM LV

PSALM LV

Prayer for Help against a Treacherous Friend

The Confused and Desperate City

GIVE ear, O God, to my prayer,
    Hide Thee not from my supplication.
2 Attend unto me, and answer;
    For bitter is my lament.
3 I am wild with the noise of the foe,
    With the clamour of the ungodly;
For they hurl mischief upon me,
    And persecute me with fury.
4 My heart is awhirl within me,
    And terrors are fallen upon me.
5 Fear and trembling assail me,
    And horror wrappeth me round.
6 O for the wings of a dove:
    I would fly away and rest.
7 I would wander far away,
    And lodge me in the wilderness.
8 I would with all haste escape
    From the raging wind and tempest.

9 Confuse, O Lord, their tongue;
    For I see Wrong and Strife in the city.
10 By day and by night they go round her
    (Like sentries) upon her walls.
While within her are mischief and trouble,
11   Within her is ruin complete.
Evermore is her market-place haunted
    By fraud and by oppression.

PSALM LV

The Treacherous Friend

12   The taunts were not those of a foe—
     That I could have borne;
    The disdain was not that of an enemy—
     I could have shunned him:
13   But 'twas thou, a man, mine equal,
     My dear and familiar friend.
14   Oft took we sweet counsel together,
     And walked in God's house with the throng.
15   May death fall stealthily on them,
     May they go down to Sheol alive,
    Thither hurled, as their infamy merits.

16   As for me, I will call upon God—
     He it is that will help me.
17   Evening and morning and noon
     I lament and make moan.
    He will hear my voice; and, in peace,
18   He will ransom my soul
    From the battle before me, where many
     Are measured against me.
19   He that sits on His ancient throne
     Will hear and will humble them—
    Strangers to law as they are [1]
     And to reverence for God.

20   He has let his hand loose on his friends,
     Thus profaning his covenant.
21   His mouth was smoother than butter,
     But war filled his heart.
    His words were softer than oil,
     But sharper than swords.

PSALM LVI

22 Cast thou thy care on the Lord,
   And He will sustain thee.
   He will not suffer the righteous
   To totter for ever.
23 But Thou, God, wilt hurl them down
   To the nethermost pit.
   Bloody and treacherous men
       Shall not live out half their days;
       As for me, I will trust in Thee.

PSALM LVI

The Tears of the Saints

O God, be gracious to me,
   For mortal men trample upon me,
   All the day fighting and pressing me.
2 All the day enemies trample me;
   Many there be
   That contend with me bitterly.
3 In the day of my terror
   I trust in Thee.
4 *In God I maintain my cause,*
   In God I fearlessly trust.
   What can flesh do unto me?

5 They torture me all the day,
   They ceaselessly plan to hurt me,
6 Banded together in secret,
   Watching mine every step,
   As those who hope for my death.
7 Pay them out for their sin, O God,
   Hurl down the strong in Thine anger.

PSALM LVII

8 Thou Thyself countest my wanderings.
    Put in Thy bottle my tears—
    Are they not in Thy book? [1]
9 Then shall my foes be turned back
    In the day that I call.
    Of this I am sure,
    Because God is for me.
10 *In God I maintain my cause,*
    In the Lord I maintain my cause.
11 *In God I fearlessly trust,*
    What can man do unto me?

12 Thy vows are upon me, O God,
    I will render thank-offerings to Thee;
13 Because Thou hast saved me from death,
    Yea, my feet from stumbling,
    To the end that I walk before God
    In the light of the living.

PSALM LVII

A Prayer for Protection from Persecution

BE gracious, O God, be gracious to me,
    For in Thee has my soul taken refuge.
In Thy sheltering wings I take refuge,
    Till ruin be overpast.
2 I cry to the Most High God,
    To the God who accomplishes for me.
3 He will send me His succour from heaven,
    He will thrust away those who would trample me. [1]

PSALM LVIII

4 In the midst of lions I lie,
    Who devour the children of men.
  Their teeth are spears and arrows,
    And their tongue is a whetted sword.
5 *Be exalted, O God, o'er the heavens,*
    And Thy glory o'er all the earth.

6 They set a net for my feet,
    But in it was their own foot caught.
  Before me they dug a pit,
    But they fell into it themselves.

7 My² heart is steadfast, O God,
    My heart is steadfast.
  I would sing, yea, I would make music;
8   Awake, Thou art my pride.
  Awake, harp and lyre;
    Fain would I waken the dawn.
9 I would praise Thee among the peoples, O Lord,
    And make music among the nations to Thee;
10 For great unto heaven is Thy love,
    And Thy faithfulness unto the clouds.
11 *Be exalted, O God, o'er the heavens,*
    And Thy glory o'er all the earth.

PSALM LVIII

A Prayer for Vengeance upon Unjust Judges

SPEAK ye indeed what is right, ye gods?
    With equity judge ye the children of men?
2 In the land ye practise iniquity—all of you—
    Violence do ye dispense with your hands.

PSALM LIX

3 The wicked are aliens to God from the womb—
   Liars and wanderers, even from their birth.
4 Venom have they like the venom of snakes,
   They are like the deaf adder that stoppeth her ears,
5 And refuses to listen to the voice of the charmer,
   Or binder of spells, be he never so cunning.

6 O God, break to pieces the teeth in their mouth,
   Tear out the great teeth of the young lions, Lord.
7 May they melt away like running water !
   Like tender grass, cut down may they be !
8 Like the snail that dissolves on its crawling path,
   Like the birth untimely which sees not the sunlight.
9 Before your pots feel (the fire of) the thorns,
   He will come with His tempest and sweep them away.[1]
10 The sight of such vengeance will gladden the righteous ;
   His feet he shall wash in the blood of the wicked.
11 " Yes," men will say, " the just have their reward :
   Yes, on the earth is a God who is Judge."

PSALM LIX

A Prayer for Vengeance upon Insolent Foes

SAVE me, O God, from mine enemies ;
   Secure me from mine assailants.
2 Save me from those that do wrong
   Save me from men of blood.

PSALM LIX

3 For see ! they lay ambush for me,
      Strong men are banded against me—
    Not for sin or transgression of mine,
4   For no guilt of mine, O Lord,
    They run and make ready. Awake !
      Come forth to meet me, and see !
5 Thou, O Jehovah of hosts,
      O God of Israel, awake !
    And punish the proud, every one ;
      Spare none of the traitors vile.

6   *At evening they come,*
      And, howling like dogs,
      Make their round in the city.
7 Look at their venomous mouths
      And their lips whereon sitteth insult.
8 But Thou, Lord, laughest at them,
      Thou mockest at all the insolent.
9 *O my strength, I will sing unto Thee,*
      For God is my sure retreat.
10 *My God with His love will meet me,*
      And feast mine eyes on my foes.

11   Slay them not, lest my people forget,
      Let Thy hosts keep them roaming and wandering.
12   In their sinful speech snare them, O Lord ;[1]
      And may they be trapped in their pride,
    For the curses and lies that they utter.
13   In Thy wrath make a clean end of them,
      That men, to the ends of the earth,
      May know that God ruleth in Jacob.

PSALM LX

14 *At evening they come,*
And, howling like dogs,
Make their round in the city.
15 They roam about for a feast,
And snarl, if they get not their fill.
16 As for me, I will sing of Thy might;
I will ring out Thy love in the morning.
For to me Thou hast been a sure refuge,
A retreat in the day of my trouble.
17 *O my strength, I will sing praise to Thee,*
For God is my sure retreat.
My God with His love (will meet me,
And feast mine eyes on my foes).

PSALM LX

A Prayer after Defeat in Battle

O GOD, Thou hast spurned and broken us,
Routing us in Thy wrath.
2 Thou hast shaken the land and cleft it;
Heal Thou its tottering breaches.
3 Thou hast made Thy people drink hardship,
And given us wine of reeling.

4 Thou hast given those that fear Thee a banner,
A rallying-place from the bow,[1]
5 For the rescue[2] of Thy beloved.
Save by Thy right hand and answer us.

6 God did solemnly swear:
" As victor will I divide Shechem,
And mete out the valley of Succoth.

PSALM LX

7 Mine is Gilead, mine is Manasseh,
    Ephraim is the defence of my head,
    Judah my sceptre of rule,
8 Moab the pot that I wash in,
    Edom—I cast my shoe over it,³
    I shout o'er Philistia in triumph."

9 O to be brought to the fortified city!
    O to be led into Edom!
10 Hast Thou not spurned us, O God?
    Thou marchest not forth with our armies.
11 Grant us help from the foe,
    For vain is the help of man.
12 With God we shall yet do bravely:
    He Himself will tread down our foes.

PSALM LXI

A Prayer for the King

HEAR my cry, O God,
    Be attentive unto my prayer.
2 From the ends of the earth I call
    Unto Thee, when my heart is faint:
Be my guide on the slopes of the rock
    That is too high for me (unaided).
3 For Thou art a refuge to me,
    A strong tower in face of the foe.

4 O to be guest in Thy tent for ever,
    Hiding beneath Thy sheltering wings!
5 For Thou, O God, dost hear my vows,
    And dost grant the desires of those that fear Thee.

PSALM LXII

6 Add many days to the life of the king ;
   May his years endure throughout all generations.
7 In the presence of God be he throned for ever ;
   May kindness and faithfulness watch over him.
8 And I will sing praise to Thy name for ever,
   Paying my vows day after day.

PSALM LXII

Quietness and Confidence

Be still in God only, O soul of mine ;
   From Him cometh my help.
2 *Yes, He is my rock, my help, my retreat,*
   I shall not be shaken too sorely.
3 How long will ye, all of you, batter a man,
   As one might a leaning wall ?
4 Yea, from his height they are planning to thrust him,
   As one might a tottering wall.
   They take pleasure in falsehood ; they bless with their mouth,
   But inwardly they curse.

5 *Be still in God only, O soul of mine,*
   For from Him cometh my hope.
6 *Yes, He is my rock, my help, my retreat,*
   I shall not be shaken too sorely.
7 On God rests mine honour and safety,
   In God is my strong rock, my refuge.
8 Trust in Him, all ye people assembled,
   Pour out your heart in His presence ;
   God is a refuge for us.

PSALM LXIII

9 The lowly are nought but a breath,
    The lofty are but an illusion:
  In the balances up they go,
    They are lighter than breath altogether.
10 Trust not in gain of extortion,
    Set no vain hopes in robbery.
  As for wealth, if it beareth fruit,
    Set not your heart upon it.

11 One thing God hath uttered,
    Two things there are which I heard—
  That power belongs unto God,
12   And to Thee, too, O Lord, belongs kindness;
  For Thou dost requite each man
    According to what he hath done.

PSALM LXIII

Athirst for God

O GOD, my God, Thee, Thee do I seek:
    My soul is athirst for Thee,
My flesh fainteth for Thee
    In a parched and waterless land.

2 As I in the temple have seen Thee,
    Beholding Thy power and Thy glory,
4 Even so, while I live, will I bless Thee,
    And lift up my hands in Thy name.

3 For better than life is Thy kindness:
    My lips shall utter Thy praise.
5 As with marrow and fat am I feasted;
    With joyful lips I will praise Thee.

PSALM LXIV

6 Yea, I call Thee to mind on my bed,
    And muse on Thee in the night watches;
7 For Thou hast been my help,
    'Neath Thy sheltering wings I will sing.
8 My soul clingeth close after Thee,
    Thy right hand holdeth me up.

9 But those that seek after my life
    Shall go down to the depths of the earth,
10 Given o'er to the power of the sword,
    Or as prey for jackals to devour.

11 But the king shall rejoice in God:
    All who own His allegiance will glory.
    For the mouth of the false shall be stopped.

PSALM LXIV

A Prayer for Deliverance from Malicious Foes

HEAR, O my God, the voice of my plaint:
    Guard my life from the foe who affrights me.
2 Hide me from villains who secretly plot,
    From the blustering throng of the workers of evil,
3 Who have whetted their tongue like a sword,
    And aimed bitter words like arrows,
4 Which from ambush they launch at the blameless,
    Shooting swiftly and unafraid.

5 They strengthen their wicked purpose,
    They tell of the snares they have hidden,
    They say to themselves, " Who can see ? "
6 They think out their crimes full cunningly
    In their mischievous bosoms and crafty hearts.[1]

PSALM LXV

7 But God with His arrow will shoot them,
    Swiftly shall they be smitten.
8 For their tongue He will bring them to ruin,
    So that all shake their head at the sight of them.

9 Then every man, touched to awe,
    As he ponders what God has wrought,
    Will tell the tale of His doings.
10 In the Lord shall the righteous rejoice,
    In Him shall they take refuge;
    And all the true-hearted shall glory.

PSALM LXV

Hymn for a Thanksgiving Festival

It is seemly to praise Thee, O God, in Zion,
    And to Thee shall the vow be performed in Jerusalem.
2 O Thou that hearest prayer,
    Unto Thee shall all flesh come.
3 Our sins are too mighty for us,
    Our transgressions—Thou only canst cover them.
4 Happy the man whom Thou choosest
    To dwell beside Thee in Thy courts.
    O may we be filled with the joys
    Of Thy house, even Thy holy temple.

5 In dread deeds Thou dost loyally answer us,
    O God of our salvation,
    Whom all ends of the earth put their trust in,
    And islands far away.

PSALM LXVI

6 By Thy strength Thou dost stablish the hills,
  Being girded with might;
7 Thou stillest the roaring of seas,
  And the tumult of nations,
8 So that those who dwell at (earth's) bounds
  Are awed at Thy signs:
  The lands of the sunrise and sunset
  Thou makest to ring with joy.

9 Thou dost visit and water the earth;
  Thou greatly enrichest her
  With the river of God, which is full of water.
  Thou preparest the corn thereof,
10 Watering her furrows,
  Settling her ridges;
  Thou makest her soft with showers,
  And blessest what grows thereon.

11 Thou crownest the year with Thy goodness,
  Thy chariot-tracks drip with fatness.
12 The wilderness pastures are dripping,
  The hills wear a girdle of joy.
13 The meadows are clothed with flocks,
  The valleys are covered with corn;
  They shout to each other and sing.

PSALM LXVI

Thanksgiving for National Deliverance

2 SHOUT unto God, all the earth,
  Sing praise to His glorious name,
  Sing ye His glorious praise.

PSALM LXVI

3   Say unto God, " How dread are Thy works,
        So great is Thy might that Thine enemies cringe
            to Thee.
4   All the earth doeth homage to Thee,
        Singing praises to Thee,
        Singing praise to Thy name."

5   Come and see what God hath done,
        Awe-inspiring is He in His works among men.
6   He turneth the sea into dry land,
        And men cross the river on foot.
    ' Let us therefore rejoice in Him,
7   The mighty Ruler eternal,
    Whose eyes keep watch on the nations,
        That no rebel lift up his head.

8   O bless our God, ye peoples ;
        Sound aloud His praise,
9   Who hath set our soul in life,
        And not suffered our foot to totter.
10 For Thou, O God, hast proved us,
        Hast tried us, as silver is tried.
11 Thou didst bring us into prison,
        And put chains upon our loins,
12 Thou didst let men ride over our head.
        We went through fire and through water,
        But Thou leddest us out to a spacious place.

13 I will enter Thy house with burnt-offerings,
        I will pay unto Thee my vows,
14 Which mine open lips have uttered,
        And my mouth hath declared in my straits.

PSALM LXVII

15 I will offer Thee offerings of fatlings,
   With the odour of burning rams,
   I will sacrifice bullocks with goats.

16 Come and hear my story—
   All ye that reverence God—
   Of what He has done for me.
17 For my mouth had no sooner invoked Him
   Than His praise was under my tongue.
18 Had I cherished sin in my heart,
   The Lord would never have listened.
19 But assuredly God *has* listened,
   And attended to my loud prayer.

20 Blessed be God, who turned not aside
   My prayer, nor withdrew His kindness from me.

PSALM LXVII

A Harvest Thanksgiving

BLESS us, O God, with Thy favour,
   Let the light of Thy face fall upon us;
2 That the world may know Thy way,
   And all nations Thy power to save.

3 *Let the peoples praise Thee, O God;*
   Let the peoples—all of them—praise Thee.
4 Let the nations ring out their joy;
   For Thou governest the peoples with equity,
   And guidest the nations on earth.
5 *Let the peoples praise Thee, O God;*
   Let the peoples—all of them—praise Thee.

PSALM LXVIII

6 The earth hath yielded her increase
　　By the blessing of God, our God.
　May this blessing of ours win men to Him
　　Unto all the ends of the earth.

PSALM LXVIII
Victory

God arises, His enemies scatter :
　　They that hate Him flee before Him.
2 As smoke before wind is driven,
　　As wax doth melt before fire,
　　So before God vanish the wicked.
3 But the righteous rejoice in God's presence,
　　They exult with exceeding joy.

4 Sing unto God, make music to His name,
　　By His name Jah praise Him who rides on the clouds,
　　And exult in His presence.
5 Father of orphans, Defender of widows,
　　Is God in His holy abode.
6 God bringeth home the lonely,
　　He leads forth the prisoner to comfort,
　　So that none but the rebel dwells cheerless.[1]

7 O God, when Thou wentest in front of Thy folk
　　In Thy march through the desert,
8 Earth shook, the heavens dropped (rain)
　　At the presence of God—
　At the presence of God, even Israel's God.
9 Rain in abundance, O God, Thou didst sprinkle,
　　Restoring the languishing land of Thy heritage.

PSALM LXVIII

10 A dwelling therein Thy people found:
   In Thy goodness, O God, Thou didst care for the poor.

11 The Lord spake the glad tidings[2] (of victory)
   And great was the army of those that proclaimed it:
12 "Kings of armies—they flee, they flee,
   And the housewife divideth the spoil:—
13 Dove's wings covered with silver
   And pinions with shimmer of gold,
14   Set with stones, like snow upon Zalmon."[3]

15 A mountain of God is the mountain of Bashan,
   A mountain of peaks is the mountain of Bashan.
16 Ye high-peaked mountains, why look ye askance
   At the mountain which God hath desired for His home—
   Yea, whereon Jehovah will dwell for ever?
17 The chariots of God are twice ten thousand:
   The Lord came from Sinai, His holy place.
18 Thou didst mount the height[4] with trains of Thy captives,
   And gifts that Thou hadst received among men.
   Yea, the rebels shall dwell with Jehovah God.

19 Blest be the Lord who sustaineth us daily,
   The God who is also our Saviour.
20   Yea, our God is a God who is Saviour.
   The ways of escape from death
   Are known to Jehovah the Lord.
21 Yes, God will shatter the head of His foes—
   The rough scalp of him who struts on in his sins.

PSALM LXVIII

22 The Lord said: "I will bring thee home from Bashan,
  Home from the depths of the sea,
23 That thy feet thou mayest bathe in blood,
  And thy dogs lick their share of the foe."

24 In the temple appear God's triumphal processions,
  Processions in praise of my King and my God,
25 With singers in front, and minstrels behind,
  And maidens with timbrels between them (singing),
26 "Ye of the well-spring of Israel,
  Bless the Lord God in the dance."
27 There, in front, is Benjamin the little,
  The princes of Judah beside them,[5]
  The princes of Zebulon, princes of Naphtali.

28 Summon Thy might, O God—
  Thy godlike might, wherewith
  In the past Thou hast wrought for us—
29 From Thy temple that crowneth Jerusalem.
  Kings shall bring tribute to Thee.
30 Rebuke Thou the beast of the reed,[6]
  The herd of bulls, with the calves of the peoples.[7]
  Trample Thou down the lovers of lies.[8]
  Scatter the nations whose joy is in war.
31 May they come from Egypt with gifts of oil,[9]
  Ethiopia haste with full hands unto God.

32 Sing unto God, O ye kingdoms of earth,
  Make melody unto the Lord.
33 Praise Him who rides on the ancient heavens.
  See! He utters His voice, His mighty voice.

PSALM LXIX

34 Ascribe ye strength to the God over Israel,
  Whose strength and majesty dwell in the skies.
35 Awe-inspiring is God in His holy place,
  Even Israel's God—He it is
   That gives strength and might to His people.
    Blessed be God.

PSALM LXIX

A Prayer for Deliverance and Vengeance

SAVE me, O God; for the waters
  Are threatening my life.
2 I am sunk in depths of mire,
  Where ground there is none.
 I am come into deep deep waters,
  The flood overwhelms me.
3 I am weary of crying, my throat is parched,
  Mine eyes are wasted with waiting for God.

4 More than the hairs of my head
  Are those that wantonly hate me.
 More than my bones in number
  Are those that are falsely my foes.
 That which I never robbed,
  How am I then to restore?
5 O God, Thou knowest my folly,
  My guilt is not hidden from Thee.
6 Through me let not any be shaméd,
  Who wait for Thee, Lord God of hosts.
 Through me let not those be confounded
  That seek Thee, O God of Israel.

PSALM LXIX

7 'Tis in Thy cause that I have borne taunts,
    And my face has been covered with shame;
8 I became to my brethren a stranger,
    To sons of my mother an alien.

9 It was zeal for Thy house that consumed me,
    And the insults they hurled at Thee fell upon me.
10 When I chastened my soul with fasting,
    They took occasion to taunt me.
11 When I put on a garment of sackcloth,
    They made me the theme of a taunt-song.
12 Those that sit in the gate make sport of me
    In the music of drunken songs.

13 As for me, I pray unto Thee.
    Grant me, O Lord, Thy favour.
    In Thy manifold mercy answer me;
    With Thy loyal help, O save me
14 From sinking down in the mire.
    Lift me out of the deep deep waters,
15 That the rushing flood may not drown me,
    That the deep may not swallow me up,
    Nor the pit close her mouth upon me.
16 Answer me, Lord, in Thy gracious kindness,
    Turn unto me in Thy manifold pity.
17 Hide not Thou Thy face from Thy servant,
    For I am in trouble; O answer me speedily.
18 Draw nigh to my soul and redeem it;
    Because of mine enemies, ransom me.

19 Thou knowest how I am insulted;
    In Thy sight are all my foes.

PSALM LXIX

20 Insult has broken my heart,
    Past cure are my shame and confusion.
    For pity I looked—there was none!—
    And for comforters, but I found none.
21 Poison they gave me for food,
    And to slake my thirst they gave vinegar.

22 May their table, outspread, be a trap to them,
    And their peace-offerings be a snare.
23 May their eyes be darkened and blind,
    Make their loins to shake without ceasing.
24 Pour Thine indignation upon them,
    Let Thy burning wrath overtake them.
25 May their camp be a desolation,
    In their tents be there none to dwell.
26 For him whom Thou smotest they persecute,
    And those whom Thou woundedst, they pain yet more.
27 Charge them with sin upon sin,
    May they not be acquitted by Thee.
28 From the book of life be they blotted,
    May their names not be written with the righteous.

29 Lift me, O God, by Thy help
    Above my pain and misery.
30 Then will I praise God in song
    And magnify Him with thanksgiving,
31 Which shall please the Lord better than ox,
    Or than bullock with horns and hoofs.
32 The oppressed shall rejoice at the sight.
    Ye that seek after God, let your heart revive.

PSALM LXX

33 For the Lord listens to the poor,
    He does not despise His prisoners.

34 Let the heavens and the earth sing His praises,
    The seas, and all creatures that move in them.
35 For God will bring help unto Zion,
    And build up the cities of Judah,
    So that men shall dwell there in possession.
36 The seed of His servants shall have it for heritage,
    And those that love Him shall dwell therein.

PSALM LXXI[1]

A Cry for Help in Persecution

O GOD, be pleased to deliver me,
    Haste Thee to help me, O Lord.
2 As for those that are seeking my life,
    Ashamed and confounded be they.
3 May those that delight in my hurt
    Be defeated and brought to dishonour.
4 But may all who seek after Thee
    Rejoice and be glad in Thee.
    May all who love Thy salvation
    Say, " God is great," evermore.
5 As for me, I am weak and needy :
    Make haste, O God, unto me.
    Thou art my help and deliverer ;
    O Lord, tarry Thou not.

PSALM LXXI

PSALM LXXI

Forsake me not, when I am Old

In Thee, O Lord, I take refuge,
    Let me never be put to shame.
2 In Thy faithfulness save me and rescue me,
    Bend Thine ear unto me and save me.
3 Be to me a rock of defence,
    A fortified house, to save me;
    For my rock and my fortress art Thou.[1]

4 Save me, my God, from the hand of the wicked,
    From the grasp of the unjust and cruel man.
5 For Thou, O Lord, art my hope,
    In whom from my youth I have trusted.
6 On Thee have I leaned from my birth;
    From my mother's womb it was Thou that didst draw me.
    In Thee is my hope evermore.

7 I have been as a wonder to many,
    For Thou art my refuge and strength.
8 All the day long my mouth
    Is filled with Thy praise and Thy glory.
9 Cast me not off in the time of old age;
    When my strength is spent, forsake me not.
10 For my foes lie in ambush for me,
    They that watch me take counsel together;
11 "God has left him," they say: "pursue
    And seize him, for he is helpless."

12 O God, be not far from me,
    Haste, O my God, to my help.

PSALM LXXI

13 Put my foes to shame and dishonour,
  With insult and shame be they covered.
14 As for me, I will hope evermore,
  And more and yet more will I praise Thee.
15 All the day long shall my mouth
  Tell Thy faithfulness and Thy salvation,
  Though I know not how they may be counted.

16 I will show forth the might of the Lord,
  And Thy faithfulness praise—Thine alone.
17 Thou hast taught me, O God, from my youth,
  And till now have I told of Thy wonders.
18 Yea, even to old age and grey hair,
  O God, forsake me not.
  Still would I tell of Thy might
  Unto all generations to come.

19 Thy power and Thy justice, O God,
  Extend as far as the heavens:
  For great are the things Thou hast done.
  Who is like unto Thee, O God?
20 Thou hast caused us to see troubles many,
  But Thou wilt revive us again.
  From the nethermost parts of the earth
  Thou wilt bring us up again.
21 Thou wilt multiply my greatness,
  And comfort me again.

22 As for me, with the harp I will praise Thee,
  And Thy faithfulness, O my God;
  And make music to Thee on the lyre,
  O Thou Holy One of Israel.

PSALM LXXII

23 My lips shall ring out their joy,
   My mouth shall sing praises to Thee;
   My soul, too, which Thou hast redeemed.
24 Yea, all the day long shall my tongue
   Utter Thy righteousness;
   For ashamed and confounded are they
   That were seeking my hurt.

PSALM LXXII

A Prayer for a Just and Glorious Reign

GIVE the king, O God, Thine own spirit of justice—
   Thy spirit of right to the son of the king,
2 That with right He may judge Thy people,
   And Thy downtrodden ones with justice.

3 May the mountains bear weal for the people,
   And the hills yield fruits of justice.
4 The weak may he help to their rights,
   May he save the sons of the needy
   And crush the oppressor in pieces.

5 May he live as long as the sun,
   While the moon shines—for ages and ages.
6 May he come like the rain on the meadow,
   Like showers that besprinkle the earth.

7 In his days may justice flourish,
   And welfare abound, till the moon be no more.
8 May he reign from ocean to ocean,
   From the river to the ends of the earth.

PSALM LXXII

9 May his foes bow down before him,
    His enemies lick the dust.
10 May tribute be rendered by kings
    Of the isles and of Tarshish;
  May gifts be brought by the kings
    Of Sheba and Seba.

11 Yea, may all kings fall prostrate before him,
    And all nations yield him their service.
12 For he saveth the poor when he crieth,
    The helpless and the downtrodden.

13 He pities the weak and the poor,
    He saveth the lives of the poor.
14 He redeems them from wrong and from violence,
    For dear is their blood in his sight.

15 Long may he live;
    And may gold of Sheba be given him;
  Prayer, too, be made for him ceaselessly,
    All the day long may men bless him.

16 May the land have abundance of corn,
    To the tops of the hills may it wave.
  May the fruit thereof flourish like Lebanon,
    May men spring from the city like grass of the earth.

17 May his name be blessed for ever,
    May his fame endure as the sun.
  May all nations envy his blessedness,
    All tribes of the earth call him happy.

PSALM LXXII

18 Blest be Jehovah, Israel's God,
    The God who alone doeth wondrous things.
19 And blest be for ever His glorious name.
    Let all the earth be filled with His glory.
        Amen and Amen.

BOOK III

PSALM LXXIII

Fellowship with God Here and Hereafter

Y ES, God is good to the upright,
    The Lord to the pure in heart.
2 But my feet were almost gone,
    My steps had well nigh slipped,
3 Through envy of godless braggarts,
    When I saw how well they fared.

4 For never a pang have they,
    Their body is sound and sleek.
5 They have no trouble like mortals,
    No share in human pain.
6 So they wear their pride like a necklace,
    They put on the garment of wrong.
7 Their eyes stand out with fatness,
    Their heart swells with riotous fancies.
8 Their speech is mocking and evil,
    Condescending and crooked their speech.
9 They have set their mouth in the heavens,
    While their tongue struts about on the earth.
10 Small wonder that people resort to them,
    And drink deep draughts of their lore.[1]
11 " How does God know ? " they say,
    " And has the Most High any knowledge ? "
12 See ! these are the godless,
    With wealth and ease ever increasing.

13 Yes, in vain have I kept my heart pure,
    And washed my hands in innocence ;

PSALM LXXIII

14 For all the day long was I plagued—
     Not a morning but I was chastised.
15 But resolving to speak like this
     Were treachery unto Thy children.

16 So I sought to understand it,
     But a wearisome task it seemed:
17 Till I entered the holy world² of God
     And considered their latter end.

18 Yes, Thou dost set them on slippery places;
     Down to destruction Thou hurlest them.
19 One moment—and then what a horror of ruin!
     They are finished and ended—in terrors.
20 Like a dream, when one wakes, shall they be,
     Whose phantoms the waker despises.

21 So my bitterness of heart
     And the pain that stabbed my bosom
22 Show how dull I was and stupid—
     Just like a beast before Thee.

23 As for me, I am with Thee alway,
     Thou hast hold of my right hand.
24 By a plan of Thine Thou guidest me
     And wilt afterward take me to glory.

25 Whom have I in the heavens but Thee?
     And on earth there is none I desire beside Thee.
26 Though flesh and heart waste away,
     Yet God is my portion for ever.

PSALM LXXIV

27 For see! those that are far from Thee must perish,
    Thou destroyest all that are false to Thee.
28 As for me, I am happy when close to God;
    The Lord my God I have made my refuge,
    That I may discourse of all Thy works.

PSALM LXXIV

Lament on the Devastation of the Temple

WHY, O God, hast Thou spurned us for ever?
    Why smoketh Thy wrath against the sheep
    of Thy pasture?
2 Remember the folk Thou hast purchased of old
    To become by redemption the tribe of Thy
        heritage—
    Zion, the mountain Thou madest Thy home.
3 Rouse Thee, and visit its ruins complete.
    In the temple the foe hath made havoc of all
        things.

4 Like lions Thine enemies roared through Thy house,
    Replacing our symbols by signs of their own,
5 Hacking, like woodsmen that lift
    Axes on thickets of trees,
6 Smashing with hatchets and hammers
    All of its carved work together.
7 They have set Thy temple on fire,
    To the very ground they have outraged
    The place where dwelleth Thy name.
8 They have said in their heart, " Let us utterly smite
        them."
    They have burned all the houses of God in the
        land.

PSALM LXXIV

9 No symbol of ours do we see any more :
   No prophet is there any more,
   None is with us that knoweth how long.
10 How long, O God, is the foe to insult ?
   Shall the enemy spurn Thy name for ever ?
11 Why, O Lord, dost Thou hold back Thy hand,
   And restrain Thy right hand within Thy bosom ?

12 Yet God is our King from the ancient days,
   In the midst of the earth working deeds of salvation.
13 It was Thou[1] that didst cleave the sea by Thy might,
   And shiver the heads of the ocean monsters.
14 It was Thou that didst crush many-headed Leviathan,
   And give him as food to the beasts of the wilderness.
15 It was Thou that didst cleave the fountains and torrents ;
   It was Thou that didst dry the perennial streams.
16 Thine is the day ; Thine, too, is the night,
   It was Thou that didst stablish the sun and the star.
17 It was Thou that didst fix all the borders of earth :
   Summer and winter—'tis Thou that hast made them.

18 Yet, for all this, the foe hath insulted Thee, Lord,
   And a nation of fools hath reviled Thy name.
19 Give not the soul of Thy dove to the beasts,
   Do not forget Thine afflicted for ever.
20 Look to the sleek ones—how full they are :
   The dark places of earth[2] are the dwellings of violence.

PSALM LXXV

21 O let not the downtrodden turn back ashamed :
    Let the poor and the needy sing praise to Thy name.

22 Arise, O God, and defend Thy cause :
    Remember how fools all the day insult Thee.
23 Forget not Thou the uproar of Thine enemies,
    The din of Thy foes that ascends evermore.

PSALM LXXV

God the Arbiter of Destiny

WE praise Thee, O God, we praise Thee :
    We would call on Thy name and declare Thy wonders.

2 " Though[1] I may tarry long,
    Yet is my government just.
3 Though earth melt and all her inhabitants,
    It is I that keep steady her pillars."
4 I say to the boasters, " Boast not " ;
    To the godless, " Lift not up your horn :
5 Lift not your horn on high,
    Speak not boldly against the Rock."[2]

6 For 'tis not from the east nor the west,
    Nor yet from the desert or mountains ;[3]
7 But God Himself is the Judge,
    Humbling one and exalting another.

PSALM LXXVI

8 In the hand of the Lord is a cup—
  Foaming wine, richly mixed with spices.
  Out of this He poureth a draught,
  And all the wicked of earth
  Must drain it down to the dregs.

9 As for me, I will joy for ever,
  Singing praise to the God of Jacob.
10 I will hew all the horns of the wicked,
  But the horns of the just shall be lifted.

PSALM LXXVI

A Song of Victory

G od hath made Himself known in Judah,
  His name is great in Israel.
2 His covert is in Salem,[1]
  His habitation in Zion.

3 There He shivered the lightning arrows,
  Shield, sword, and equipment of war.
4 Terrible is Thy splendour
  On the everlasting mountains.

5 Spoiled were the stout of heart;
  In the sleep into which they had fallen,
  Not one of the men of valour
  But lost the power of his hands.

6 At Thy rebuke, God of Jacob,
  Sank chariot and horse to sleep.
7 Awful art Thou : who can stand
  Before Thee, when once Thou art angry ?

PSALM LXXVII

8 The judgment Thou spakest from heaven
  Affrighted the earth into silence,
9 When God arose unto judgment
  To save all the meek of the earth.

10 All nations of men shall praise Thee,
   To Thee shall the remnant hold festival.[2]
11 Vow and pay to your God,
   And let all that are round Him bring presents.

12 He lops off the courage of princes,
   And with terror fills kings of the earth.

PSALM LXXVII

A Prayer for Preservation as in the Days of Old

Loudly will I lift my cry unto God,
  Loudly to God, that He hearken to me.
2 In the day of my trouble I seek the Lord;
  In the night is my hand stretched unweariedly forth,
  But my soul doth refuse to be comforted.

3 When I think of God, I moan;
  When I muse, my spirit is faint.
4 When Thou holdest mine eyes awake,
  And I am restless and speechless,
5 I think of the days of old,
  Call to mind the ancient years.
6 I commune with my heart in the night,
  I muse with inquiring spirit.

PSALM LXXVII

7 " Will the Lord cast us off for ever,
    And will He be gracious no more ?
8 Is His love clean vanished for ever ?
    Is His faithfulness utterly gone ?
9 Hath God forgotten to be gracious,
    Or in anger shut up His compassion ? "

10 Then I said, " This it is that grieves me,
    That the hand of the Most High hath changed."
11 I will think of the deeds of Jehovah,
    And remember Thy wonders of old.
12 I will muse on all Thou hast wrought,
    And meditate on Thy doings.
13 Then Thy way, O God, was majestic :
    What God was great as Jehovah ?
14 Thou wast a God who did marvels,
    Thou didst show Thy power to the world
15 By redeeming Thy folk with Thine arm,
    Even the children of Jacob and Joseph.

16 The waters saw Thee, O God.
    The waters saw Thee and shivered ;
    Yea, to their depths they quivered.
17 Clouds poured torrents of water,
    Thunder rolled in the sky,
    Thine arrows sped to and fro.
18 Loud was the roll of Thy thunder,
    Lightnings lit up the world.
    Earth quivered and trembled.
19 In Thy way, O Lord, through the sea,
    In Thy path through the mighty waters,
    Thy footsteps were all unseen.

PSALM LXXVIII

20 Thou didst guide Thy folk like a flock
    By the hand of Moses and Aaron.

PSALM LXXVIII

The Warnings of History

MY people, give ear to my teaching:
    Bend your ears to the words of my mouth,
2 As I open my mouth in a poem
    On the riddling story of the past.

3 What we have heard and known,
    And what our fathers have told us
4 We will not hide from their children.
    We will tell to the next generation
The praises and might of the Lord,
    And the wonders that He hath done.

5 He set up a testimony in Jacob,
    A law He appointed in Israel,
Which He commanded our fathers
    To make known unto their children,
6 That the next generation should know it,
    That the children yet to be born
Should arise and tell their children;
7   That in God they might put their confidence,
And not forget God's works;
    But that they might keep His commandments,
8 And not be like their fathers,
    A generation defiant and stubborn,
A generation with heart unsteady,
    And spirit unfaithful towards God.

PSALM LXXVIII

9 Sons of Ephraim, armed bowmen,
    Turned back in the day of battle.
10 They did not keep God's covenant,
    They refused to walk in His law.
11 They forgot what He had done,
    And the wonders He had shown them.

12 He did wonders before their fathers
    In the country of Zoan in Egypt.
13 Through the sea which He cleft He brought them,
    Making waters stand up like a heap.
14 He led them by day with a cloud,
    All the night with a light of fire.

15 From the rocks which He cleft in the wilderness,
    He gave them to drink as of ocean's abundance.
16 He brought streams out of the rock,
    And made water run down like rivers.

17 Yet they still went on sinning against Him,
    They defied the Most High in the desert.
18 They tempted God in their hearts,
    Demanding the food that they longed for.
19 " Is God able "—such was their challenge—
    " To spread in the desert a table ?
20 From the rock that He smote there gushed water,
    And torrents that overflowed ;
But can He also give bread,
    Or furnish His people with flesh ?"

21 When the Lord heard this, He was furious,
    And fire was kindled on Jacob,
    Yea, anger went up against Israel.

PSALM LXXVIII

22 For they put no trust in God,
    No confidence in His help.
23 So He summoned the clouds above;
    And, opening the doors of heaven,
24 He rained manna upon them for food,
    And grain of heaven He gave them.
25 Men ate the bread of angels;
    He sent them food to the full.

26 He launched the east wind in the heavens,
    And guided the south by His power.
27 He rained flesh upon them like dust,
    Winged fowl like the sand of the sea.
28 In the midst of their camp He dropped it,
    Just round about their dwellings.

29 They ate and were more than filled;
    He had brought them the thing they desired.
30 But the thing they desired became loathsome:
    While their food was still in their mouths,
31 The wrath of God rose against them.
    He slew the stoutest among them,
    And laid low the young men of Israel.

32 Yet for all this they sinned yet more,
    And refused to believe in His wonders.
33 So He ended their days in a breath,
    And their years in sudden dismay.
34 When He slew them, then they sought after Him,
    They turned and sought God with diligence.

35 They remembered that God was their rock,
    And the Most High God their redeemer.

PSALM LXXVIII

36 But they flattered Him with their mouth,
  And lied unto Him with their tongue.
37 Their heart was not steady with Him,
  They were faithless to His covenant.

38 But He is full of pity:
  He pardoneth sin and destroyeth not.
  Oft He turneth His anger away,
  Without stirring His wrath at all.
39 So He remembered that they were but flesh,
  Breath that passes and does not return.

40 But how oft they rebelled in the desert,
  And caused Him grief in the wilderness,
41 Tempting God again and again,
  And wounding the Holy One of Israel.
42 They did not remember His hand,
  Nor the day He redeemed from the foe—
43 How He set His signs in Egypt,
  In the country of Zoan His wonders.

44 He turned their canals into blood,
  And their streams, that they could not drink them.
45 He sent forth flies, which devoured them;
  Frogs, too, which destroyed them.
46 Their produce He gave to the caterpillar,
  And the fruits of their toil to the locust.
47 He slew their vines with hail,
  And their sycomore trees with frost.
48 He delivered their cattle to the hail,
  And their flocks to bolts of fire.

PSALM LXXVIII

49 He let loose His hot anger among them,
　　Fury and wrath and distress,
　　A band of destroying angels.
50 He made a straight path for His anger,
　　He spared not their soul from death,
　　But delivered their life to the pestilence.

51 He smote all the first-born in Egypt,
　　The chief of their strength in the tents of Ham.
52 He led forth His people like sheep,
　　He was guide to His flock in the desert.
53 Securely He led them, and free from fear,
　　While their foes were drowned in the sea.

54 To His holy border He brought them,
　　To the mount which His right hand had purchased.
55 He drove out the nations before them,
　　And allotted their land for possession,
　　And their tents for Israel to dwell in.

56 Yet they tempted and angered the Most High God,
　　They did not observe His testimonies.
57 They drew back and played false like their fathers;
　　They failed like a treacherous bow.
58 Their high places stirred Him to anger,
　　Their images moved Him to jealousy.

59 When God heard of this, He was furious,
　　And He spurned Israel utterly.
60 He abandoned His home in Shiloh,
　　The tent He had pitched among men.

PSALM LXXVIII

61 He gave His strength[1] up to captivity,
   His glory[1] to the hands of the foe.

62 He delivered His folk to the sword,
   He was furious with His inheritance.
63 Fire[2] devoured their young men,
   And their maidens had no marriage-song.
64 Their priests fell by the sword,
   And their widows made no lamentation.

65 Then the Lord awoke as from sleep,
   Like a mighty man shouting from wine;
66 And he smote His foes on the back,
   Putting them to perpetual scorn.
67 He disowned the tent of Joseph,
   He rejected the tribe of Ephraim;
68 But He chose the tribe of Judah,
   Mount Zion, which He loves.
69 And He built like the heights[3] His sanctuary,
   Like the earth which He founded for ever.

70 And He chose David His servant,
   Taking him from the sheep-folds.
71 From the mother-ewes He brought him,
   To be shepherd to Jacob His people,
   And to Israel His inheritance.
72 With upright heart did he shepherd them,
   And with skilful hands did he guide them.

PSALM LXXIX

PSALM LXXIX

A National Prayer from the Depths of a Bitter Need

HEATHEN, O God, have come into Thy heritage,
　　Defiling Thy holy temple,
　And laying Jerusalem in ruins.
2　They have given the bodies of Thy dead servants
　　To the birds of the air to devour,
　　And the flesh of Thy saints to the beasts of the field.
3　Round about Jerusalem
　　They have poured out their blood like water;
　　And there was none to bury them.
4　On every side our neighbours
　　Revile us and mock us and jeer at us.

5　How long wilt Thou be angry, O Lord?
　　Will Thy jealousy burn like fire for ever?
6　Pour out Thy wrath on the heathen who know Thee not,
　　On the kingdoms that call not upon Thy name.
7　For Jacob they have devoured,
　　They have desolated his dwelling.
8　Remember not against us the sins of the fathers;
　　O meet us soon with Thy pity,
　　For utterly weak are we.

9　Help us, O God our Saviour,
　　For the honour of Thy name:
　For Thine own name's sake deliver us
　　And cover over our sins.

PSALM LXXX

10 Why should the heathen say,
   " Where is their God ? "
   Let revenge for the outpoured blood of Thy servants
   Be shown on the heathen before our eyes.
11 May the groans of the prisoner come before Thee;
   Free the children of death by Thy mighty arm.
12 Pay our neighbours back sevenfold into their bosom
   For the scorn they have heaped upon Thee, O Lord.

13 So shall we, Thy people, the flock of Thy pasture,
   Give thanks unto Thee for evermore,
   And tell Thy praise unto all generations.

PSALM LXXX

A Prayer for the Preservation of Israel, Jehovah's Vine

G IVE ear, O Shepherd of Israel,
   Who Joseph dost lead like a flock ;
From Thy throne on the cherubs shine forth
2   Before Ephraim, Manasseh, and Benjamin.
Stir up Thy mighty power,
   Come Thou to our help.
3 *O Jehovah of hosts, restore us :*
   Show us the light of Thy face,
   So shall we be saved.

4 O Jehovah of hosts,
   How long is Thine anger to smoke,
      Notwithstanding the prayer of Thy people ?
5 Thou hast fed them with bread of tears,
      Thou hast made them drink tears by the measure.

PSALM LXXX

6   The scorn of our neighbours Thou makest us,
     The laughing-stock of our foes.
7   *O Jehovah of hosts, restore us :*
     Show us the light of Thy face,
     So shall we be saved.

8   A vine out of Egypt Thou broughtest ;
     Thou didst drive out the nations, and plant her ;
9   In the ground Thou didst clear she struck root,
     And she filled all the land.
10 The shade of her covered the mountains,
     Her branches the cedars of God.
11 She sent forth her shoots to the sea,
     And her branches as far as the River.
12 Why hast Thou torn down her fences, and left her
     To be plucked at by all who pass by,
13 To be gnawed by the boar from the forest,
     And devoured by the beasts of the field ?

14 O Jehovah of hosts, return :
     Look down from heaven and see
     And visit this vine, and restore her—
15   The vine which Thy right hand hath planted.
16 She is burned with fire and cut down—
     Before Thy stern face they are perishing.
17 Protect Thou the folk Thou hast chosen,
     The men Thou hast reared for Thyself ;[1]
18 Then from Thee we will never draw back.
     Preserve us, and so shall we call on Thy name.
19 *O Jehovah of hosts, restore us :*
     Show us the light of Thy face,
     So shall we be saved.

PSALM LXXXI

PSALM LXXXI
For the Feast of Tabernacles. A Warning against Disobedience

CRY aloud unto God our strength,
    Shout for joy to the God of Jacob.
2 Lift the music, sound the timbrel,
    The pleasant lyre with the harp.
3 On the new moon blow the horn,
    At the full moon, the day of our festival.
4 For this is a statute for Israel,
    Ordained of the God of Jacob,—
5 A witness He set up in Joseph,
    When he marched against Egypt's land,
    Where he heard a tongue that he knew not.

6 " I removed from his shoulder the burden,
    And freed his hands from the basket.
7 At thy call of distress I delivered thee,
    In the thundercloud-covert I answered thee.
    At Meribah's waters I proved thee.

8 Listen, my people, to my charge—
    O Israel, if thou wouldst but listen—
9 ' There shall not be a strange god within thee,
    Thou shalt bow to no alien god.
10 I am Jehovah thy God
    Who brought thee up out of Egypt.
    Open thy mouth, that I fill it.'

11 But my people listened not to my voice,
    Israel would none of me.
12 So to their own hard hearts I left them,
    To walk in devices of their own.

PSALM LXXXII

13 O that my people would listen,
    That Israel would walk in my ways.
14 Soon would I humble their enemies,
    And turn my hand on their foes.
15 Those that hate them should cringe before them
    In everlasting terror.
16 But them would I feed with the richest wheat,
    And with honey from the rock to their heart's desire."

PSALM LXXXII

God the Upholder of Justice

JEHOVAH hath taken His stand
    In the divine assembly:
    In the midst of the gods He holds judgment.
2 "How long will ye crookedly judge,
    And continue to favour the wicked?
3 Do right by the weak and the orphan,
    Acquit the innocent poor.
4 Deliver the weak and the needy,
    Rescue them from the hand of the wicked.

5 They have neither knowledge nor insight,
    In darkness they walk to and fro,
    So that all earth's foundations totter.
6 It was I who appointed you gods,
    Sons of the Most High—all of you.
7 Yet like men ye shall surely die,
    Ye shall fall like one of the demons."[1]

8 Arise, O God, judge the earth,
    For all nations are Thine by inheritance.

PSALM LXXXIII

PSALM LXXXIII

A Prayer for the Destruction of the Enemies of Judah

    BE not so silent, O God :
        Hold not Thy peace, be not still, O God.
2 For see ! Thine enemies roar,
    They that hate Thee lift up their head,
3 Laying crafty plans for Thy people,
    And plotting against Thy jewels.[1]
4 " Come, let us blot them out as a nation,
    That Israel's name be remembered no more."

5 For, conspiring with one accord,
    They have made a league against Thee—
6 Tents of Edom, and Ishmaelites,
    Moab, and the Hagrites.
7 Gebal and Ammon and Amalek,
    Philistia, with the people of Tyre ;
8 Syria, too, is confederate,
    They have strengthened the children of Lot.[2]

9 Deal Thou with them as with Sisera,
    And with Jabin at the torrent of Kishon,
10 Who at Endor were destroyed,
    And became as dung for the ground.
11 Make their nobles like Oreb and Zeeb,
    All their princes like Zebah and Zalmunna,[3]
12 Who have said, " Let us take to ourselves
    The dwellings of God in possession."

13 Whirl them, my God, like dust,
    Like stubble before the wind.

PSALM LXXXIV

14 As the fire that kindleth the forest,
    As flame that sets mountains ablaze,
15 So with Thy tempest pursue them,
    And terrify them with Thy hurricane.
16 Fill with dishonour their faces;
    That they seek Thy name, O Lord.
17 Everlasting shame and confusion,
    Disgrace and destruction be theirs.
18 Teach them that Thou alone
    Art most high over all the earth.

PSALM LXXXIV

The Song of the Pilgrims

How dear is the place where Thou dwellest,
    Jehovah of hosts!
2 With longing my soul was spent
    For the courts of Jehovah.
Now heart and flesh cry for joy
    To the living God.

3 Yea, the sparrow hath found her a home
    And the swallow a nest,
Wherein she layeth her young,
    Even Thine own altars,
Jehovah, Thou God of hosts,
    My King and my God.

4 Happy they that dwell in Thy house,
    Praising thee evermore.
5 Happy the men whose strength is in Thee,
    The men with the pilgrim heart.

PSALM LXXXV

6 As they traverse the valley of tears,[1]
  They make it a place of fountains,
  Clothed with the blessings of early rain.
7 From rampart to rampart on they march,
  Till at last God revealeth Himself in Zion.[2]

8 Jehovah of hosts, hear Thou my prayer,
  Give ear, O God of Jacob.
9 Behold, O God, our defender,
  And look upon Thine anointed.
10 For better a single day in Thy courts
  Than a thousand in mine own chambers:
  Better stand at the door of the house of my God
  Than dwell in the tents of ungodliness.
11 For Jehovah is Sun and Shield,
  Jehovah gives grace and glory.
  No good thing He withholds from the life that is
    blameless.
12 Jehovah of hosts,
  Happy the man whose trust is in Thee.

PSALM LXXXV

A Prayer for National Restoration

ONCE, Lord, Thou didst favour Thy land,
  Granting change of fortune to Jacob,
2 Forgiving the guilt of Thy people,
  And covering all their sin,
3 Withdrawing all Thy fury,
  And turning from Thy hot anger.

PSALM LXXXVI

4 Restore us, O God our Saviour,
 Put away Thy displeasure against us.
5 Wilt Thou cherish Thine anger against us for ever,
 Prolonging Thy wrath unto all generations ?
6 Wilt Thou not revive us again,
 That Thy folk may be glad in Thee ?
7 Show us Thy kindness, O Lord,
 And grant us Thy salvation.

8 I would hear what God will speak ;
 For speak He will—of peace
 To His people, to those that love Him,
 And turn their hearts to Him.[1]
9 Yea, soon those that fear Him shall see how He saves,
 And glory shall dwell in our land.

10 Kindness and loyalty meet ;
 Peace and righteousness kiss.
11 Loyalty springs from the earth ;
 Righteousness looks from the sky.
12 Yea, the Lord shall give all that is good,
 Our land yielding her increase,
13 Righteousness marching before Him,
 And peace on the track of His steps.

PSALM LXXXVI

A Prayer for Divine Guidance and Favour

Incline Thine ear, Lord, and answer me,
 For I am afflicted and needy.
2 Keep me, for I am loyal :
 Save Thy servant, who trusteth in Thee.

PSALM LXXXVI

3 Lord, be gracious to me, for Thou art my God ;
    I cry to Thee all the day.
4 Gladden the soul of Thy servant ;
    For to Thee, O Lord, I lift up my soul.
5 For Thou, Lord, art good and forgiving,
    Rich in love towards all who call on Thee.

6 Give ear, O Lord, to my prayer ;
    Attend to my loud supplication.
7 In the day of my trouble I call on Thee,
    With assurance that Thou wilt answer me.
8 None of the gods is like Thee, O Lord,
    Nor are any works like Thine.
9 All nations which Thou hast made
    Shall come and bow down before Thee,
    Giving glory, O Lord, to Thy name.
10 For great art Thou, and a doer of wonders ;
    Thou art God alone.

11 Teach me, O Lord, Thy way,
    That I may walk in Thy truth :
    So my heart shall rejoice in Thy fear.
12 I will give Thee thanks, O Lord,
    With all my heart, O my God ;
    I will honour Thy name for ever.
13 For great is Thy love towards me,
    From the nethermost world Thou hast rescued me.

14 Haughty men have risen up against me, O God,
    A band of the violent seeking my life,
    Who set not Thee before them.

PSALM LXXXVII

15 But Thou art a God of pity and grace,
   Patient and rich in kindness and faithfulness;
   Turn unto me with Thy grace, O Lord.
16 Grant Thy strength to Thy servant,
   And save the son of Thine handmaid.
17 Work for me some token of good,
   Which those who hate me may see with confusion,
   Since Thou, O Lord, art my helper and comforter.

PSALM LXXXVII

Mother Zion

On the sacred mount is Jehovah's foundation,
   5c Yea, and the Most High Himself shall establish it.
2 Jehovah loveth the gates of Zion
   More than all the dwellings of Jacob.
3 Glorious things He is speaking of thee,
   Thou city of God.

4a " Among those that are mine I name Egypt [1] and Babylon,
4b Behold! Philistia, Tyre, Ethiopia.
5a But as for Zion—her name shall be Mother [2]:
5b For each and all were born in her."
6a Jehovah shall count, when enrolling the peoples,
6b, 4c " This man was born there, and that man was born there."

7 Thus shall they sing, as they dance,
   " All my springs [3] are in Thee."

PSALM LXXXVIII

PSALM LXXXVIII

The Prayer of Despair

O Lord my God,
　　I cry for help in the day-time,
　In the night my cry is before Thee;
2　Let my prayer come into Thy presence,
　　Incline Thine ear to my cry.

3　For my soul is sated with sorrow,
　　My life draws nigh to the world below.
4　I am counted with them that go down to the pit;
　　A man without strength am I.

5　My home is among the dead,
　　Like the slain that lie in the grave,
　Whom Thou dost remember no more—
　　Cut off as they are from Thy hand.

6　In the nethermost pit Thou hast laid me,
　　Amid shadows deep and dark.
7　Thy wrath lieth heavy upon me,
　　Thou hast brought all Thy breakers upon me.

8　Thou hast put mine acquaintance far from me,
　　Thou hast made me of them abhorred.
　I am shut in, and cannot come forth,
9　　Mine eyes are wasted with sorrow.
　I call on Thee, Lord, every day,
　　Spreading my hands out to Thee.

10　For the dead canst Thou work wonders?
　　Can the shades rise again to praise Thee?

PSALM LXXXIX

11 Can Thy kindness be told in the grave,
   Or Thy faithfulness in Abaddon ?[1]
12 Can Thy wonders be known in the darkness,
   Or Thy help in the land of forgetfulness ?

13 I cry for help unto Thee,
   In the morning my prayer comes before Thee.
14 Why, O Lord, dost Thou spurn me,
   And hide Thy face from me ?
15 From my youth I am wretched and dying,
   Benumbed by the terrors I bear.

16 The fires of Thy wrath have passed over me,
   Thine alarms have clean undone me,
17 Surging around me for ever,
   Hemming me in altogether.
18 Those who love me Thou puttest far from me;
   The dark is mine only friend.

PSALM LXXXIX

The Promise to David and the Present Distress

I WILL sing evermore of the love of Jehovah,
   Proclaiming to all generations His faithfulness.
2 For Thy love Thou didst promise to build up for ever,
   Thy faithfulness firm as the heavens themselves.

3 " I have made with my chosen a covenant,
   And sworn unto David my servant,
4 To establish his seed for ever,
   And to build up his throne to all ages."

PSALM LXXXIX

5 Then the holy[1] assembly in heaven
     Praised Thy marvellous faithfulness, Lord.
6 For who in the skies may compare with Jehovah ?
     Who is like to Jehovah among the gods ?

7 A God to be feared in the holy assembly,
     Awful and great above all that are round Him.
8 O Lord God of hosts, who is like unto Thee ?
     Strong art Thou, Jah, with Thy compassing faithfulness.

9 Thou[2] art the Lord of the proud-swelling sea :
     When it lifteth its waves, it is Thou that dost still them.
10 It was Thou that didst pierce and crush Rahab[3] in pieces,
     And scatter Thy foes by Thy mighty arm.

11 Thine are the heavens, Thine also the earth,
     The world and its fulness—'tis Thou that didst found them.
12 The north and the south—'tis Thou hast created them ;
     Tabor and Hermon shout praise to Thy name.

13 Thou hast an arm with the might of a hero ;
     Strong is Thy hand, high uplifted Thy right hand.
14 Justice and right are the stays of Thy throne,
     Kindness and faithfulness ever attend Thee.

15 Happy the people that knows the glad shout,[4]
     That walks, O Lord, in the light of Thy face.

PSALM LXXXIX

16 They exult in Thy name all the day,
    And Thy righteousness shall they extol.

17 For Thou art our strength and our pride.
    Thy favour will lift us to honour.[5]
18 For the holy Jehovah of Israel
    Doth keep our defender and king.

19 In a vision of old Thou didst speak
    In this wise to the man whom Thou lovedst,[6]
    " A crown have I set on the hero
    I chose to be over the people—

20 Even David, the servant I found me,
    And anointed with holy oil.
21 My hand shall be with him for ever,
    Mine arm shall endue him with strength.

22 Not a foe shall dare to assail him,
    Nor a son of wrong to oppress him;
23 But his foes I will shatter before him,
    I will strike down those that hate him.

24 My loyal love shall attend him,
    And I will lift him to honour.[7]
25 I will set his hand on the sea,
    And his right hand on the rivers.

26 As for him, he will call me ' My father,
    My God, and my Rock of salvation.'
27 And *I* will make him my first-born,
    Highest of kings on the earth.

PSALM LXXXIX

28 My love will I keep for him ever,
    My covenant with him shall stand fast.
29 His race will I make everlasting,
    And his throne as the days of the heavens.

30 If his sons forsake my law,
    And walk not as I have ordained;
31 If they profane my statutes,
    And do not keep my commandments;

32 I will punish their sin with the rod,
    Their iniquity with scourges.
33 But my love will I not take from him,
    Nor will I belie my faithfulness.

34 I will not profane my covenant
    By changing the word that has passed my lips.
35 Once have I solemnly sworn—
    And I would not lie unto David—

36 That his race should endure for ever,
    And his throne as the sun before me,
37 Firm as the moon which for ever
    And ever is fixed in the sky."

38 But Thou hast cast off in contempt,
    And been furious with Thine anointed.
39 Thou hast spurned the covenant with Thy servant,
    And his sacred crown dashed to the ground.

40 Thou hast broken down all his walls,
    And laid his bulwarks in ruins.

PSALM LXXXIX

41 All who pass on their way despoil him,
  The scorn of his neighbours is he now.

42 Thou hast given his foes the victory,[8]
  And made all his enemies glad.
43 Thou hast turned back his sword from the foe,
  Thou didst not lift him up in the battle.

44 The sceptre Thou tookst from his hand,
  And his throne Thou didst hurl to the ground.
45 Thou hast shortened the days of his youth,
  And covered him with shame.

46 How long, O Lord, wilt Thou hide Thee for ever?
  How long are the fires of Thy wrath to burn?
47 Remember, O Lord, the shortness of life—
  How fleeting Thou madest all sons of men.

48 What man shall live without seeing death?
  Who can rescue his life from the clutch of Sheól?
49 Where, O Lord, is Thy kindness of old,
  Which Thou in Thy faithfulness swarest to David?

50 Remember, O Lord, how Thy servants are mocked,
  How I bear in my bosom the scorn of all nations—
51 The scorn which Thine enemies hurl, O Lord,
  Which they hurl at the footsteps of Thine anointed.

  Blest be Jehovah, for ever and ever,
  Amen and Amen.

BOOK IV

PSALM XC

Hymn of Eternity

L ORD, Thou hast been a home to us
   One generation after another.
2 Before the mountains were born,
   Or the earth and the world were brought forth,
   From everlasting to everlasting
   Art Thou, O God.

3 Thou bringest man back to the dust,
   Thou summonest men to return.
4 For Thou seest a thousand years
   As the passing of yesterday,
   As a watch in the night.

5 Thy floods sweep them away;
   They become like unto a sleep,
   Or like grass which sprouts in the morning,
6 Which blossoms and sprouts in the morning,
   But by evening is cut and withered.

7 For Thine anger it is that consumes us,
   The heat of Thy wrath that confounds us.
8 Our sins Thou hast set before Thee,
   Our secrets in the light of Thy face.
9 For through Thy wrath our days are declining,
   We bring our years to an end as a sigh.

PSALM XCI

10 Our years, at their height, are three score and ten,
    Or, by reason of strength, perchance fourscore ;
    Yet is their breadth but empty toil,
    For swiftly they go, and we fly away.

11 Who layeth to heart the power of Thine anger ?
    Or who stands in reverent awe of Thy wrath ?
12 O teach us so to number our days
    That we may win us a heart of wisdom.

13 Return, O Lord ; why so long ?
    Relent concerning Thy servants.
14 Grant us Thy love to the full in the morning,
    That all our days we may shout for joy.

15 Make us glad for the days Thou hast humbled us,
    For the evil years we have seen.
16 Let Thy servants see Thee in action,
    Show Thy majesty unto their children.
17 Let the grace of the Lord our God be upon us,
    Uphold what our hands are striving to do.

PSALM XCI

In the Shelter of the Most High

He whose home is the shelter of God Most High,
    Whose abode is the shadow of God Almighty,
2 Can say to the Lord, " My refuge, my fortress,
    My God, in whom I trust."

PSALM XCI

3 For He saves thee from fowler's snare,
      From the yawning pit of destruction.
4a He sheltereth thee with His pinions,
4b   And under His wings thou mayest hide.

5 Thou needst not be afraid for the terror of night,
      Nor for the arrow that flieth by day,
6 Nor for the plague that stalketh in darkness,
      Nor yet for the pest or the demon of noon.[1]

7 A thousand may fall at thy side,
      And ten thousand at thy right hand:
    But it shall not draw nigh unto thee,
4c   For His truth is a buckler and shield.

8 Thou shalt only look on with thine eyes,
      And see how the wicked are punished.
9 As for thee, the Lord is thy refuge,
      Thou hast made the Most High thy defence.

10 Thou shalt never be met by misfortune,
      No plague shall come near thy tent:
11 For He putteth His angels in charge of thee,
      To keep thee in all thy ways.

12 They shall bear thee up on their hands,
      Lest thou strike thy foot on a stone.
13 Thou shalt tread upon lions and adders,
      And trample young lions and dragons.

14 " Because of His love for me, I will deliver him,
      I will protect him who careth for me.

PSALM XCII

15 I will answer his cry and be with him in trouble,
    Bringing him forth into safety and honour.
16 With length of days will I satisfy him,
    I will feast his eyes upon my salvation."[2]

PSALM XCII
The Ways of God

IT is good to give thanks to the Lord,
    To sing praise to Thy name, O Most High,
2 To declare Thy love in the morning,
    And Thy faithfulness in the night,
3 On a ten-stringed psaltery and harp,
    With music that throbs on the lyre.
4 For Thou makest me glad by Thy doings,
    At the work of Thy hands I will ring out my joy.

5 How great are Thy works, O Lord;
    Thy purposes passing deep!
6 A brutish man cannot know,
    Nor can a fool understand,
7 That, when wicked men flourish like grass,
    And evil-doers all blossom,
    It is but that they perish for ever.

8 But Thou art exalted for ever.
9 For see! Thine enemies, Lord—
    For see! Thine enemies perish,
    All evil-doers are scattered.
10 But Thou dost lift me to honour,[1]
    And anoint me afresh with oil.
11 Mine eyes shall feast on my foes,
    And mine ears shall hear of the doom of the wicked.

PSALM XCIII

12 The righteous shall sprout like the palm,
   He shall grow like a cedar of Lebanon.
13 In the house of the Lord are they planted,
   In the courts of our God they shall sprout.
14 They shall still bear fruit in old age,
   All sappy and fresh shall they be—
15 Thus proclaiming the Lord to be just,
   My Rock, in whom is no wrong.

PSALM XCIII

Jehovah, King of all the World

JEHOVAH hath taken His seat on the throne,
   Clothed with majesty, girt with might.
Now the world stands firm, to be shaken no more,
2   Firm standeth Thy throne from all eternity.
   Thou art from everlasting.

3 The floods, O Jehovah, have lifted,
   The floods have lifted their voice,
   The floods lift up their roar.
4 But more grand than the great roaring waters,
   More grand than the breakers of ocean,
   Grand on the height stands Jehovah.

5 What Thou hast ordained is most sure;
   Most sure shall Thy house stand inviolate,
   O Jehovah, for ever and ever.

PSALM XCIV

PSALM XCIV

A Prayer for Vengeance upon the Cruel. Unswerving Confidence in the Moral Order

O Lord, Thou God of vengeance,
  Thou God of vengeance, shine forth.
2 Lift Thee up, Thou Judge of the earth,
  And pay their deserts to the proud.

3 How long shall the wicked, O Lord,
  How long shall the wicked exult,
4 With their blustering arrogant words,
  Their braggart and wicked speech,
5 Crushing Thy people, O Lord,
  And afflicting Thy heritage,
6 Murdering widows and sojourners,
  Slaying the fatherless?
7 They think that the Lord doth not see,
  Nor the God of Jacob regard it.

8 Bethink you, ye dullest of people;
  When will you be wise, ye fools?
9 Is He deaf, that planted the ear?
  Is He blind, that fashioned the eye?
10 Can He that trains nations not punish them—
  He that teaches knowledge to men?
11 The Lord knoweth the thoughts of men,
  That only a breath are they.

12 Happy the man whom Thou chastenest,
  And teachest out of Thy law,
13 Keeping him calm in the day of misfortune,
  Till a pit be dug for the wicked.

PSALM XCV

14 For the Lord will not leave His people,
   He will not forsake His inheritance.
15 For the righteous shall come to their rights,
   And all true-hearted men shall follow them.

16 Who will rise up for me against men who do evil?
   Who will stand up for me against workers of wrong?
17 Were it not for the help of the Lord,
   My soul were now lying in silence.
18 When I thought that my foot was slipping,
   Thy kindness, O Lord, held me up.
19 When with cares my heart was crowded,
   Thy comforts gladdened my soul.

20 Can a royal knave be Thine ally,
   Who frameth mischief by statute?
21 They assail the life of the righteous,
   And innocent blood condemn.
22 But the Lord is my sure retreat,
   My God is the rock of my refuge.
23 He will bring back their sin upon them,
   For their wickedness He will destroy them;
   Yea, the Lord our God will destroy them.

PSALM XCV

For a Festival. A Hymn of Praise and a Solemn Warning

O COME, let us ring out our joy to the Lord,
   Let us merrily shout to our Rock of salvation.
2 Before His face let us come with thanks,
   With songs of praise let us shout unto Him.

PSALM XCVI

3 For the Lord is a great God,
   King above all gods.
4 In His hand are the depths of the earth,
   The heights of the mountains are His
5 The sea is His, for He made it :
   The dry land was formed by His hands.

6 O come, let us worship and bow
   On our knees to the Lord our creator.
7 For He is our God ; and we
   Are the folk of His pasture, the sheep of His hand.

   O that to-day ye would hear His voice :
8 " Do not harden your hearts as at Meribah,
   Or at Massah, that day in the desert,
9 When your fathers tempted and tried me,
   Notwithstanding the works they had seen.

10 Forty years long was I filled with loathing
   For that generation, and thus I spake :
   ' A people with wandering hearts are they,
   And ignorant of my ways.'
11 So I solemnly swore unto them in mine anger,
   That never should they enter into my rest."[1]

PSALM XCVI
The World-King and the World-Judgment

SING to the Lord a new song,
   Sing to the Lord, all the earth.
2 Sing to the Lord, bless His name,
   From day to day herald His victory.

PSALM XCVI

3   Tell His glory among the nations,
     His wonders among all peoples.

4   For great is Jehovah and worthy all praise;
     Awful is He, above all gods:
5   For all the gods of the nations are idols,
     But Jehovah created the heavens.
6   Before Him are splendour and majesty,
     Beauty and strength in His holy place.

7   Ascribe[1] to Jehovah, ye tribes of the nations,
     Ascribe to Jehovah glory and strength.
8   Ascribe to Jehovah the glory He manifests:
     Bring ye an offering, enter His courts.
9   Bow to Jehovah in holy array:
     Tremble before Him, all the earth.

10 Say to the nations, " Jehovah is King."
     Yea, the world standeth firm—to be shaken no more.
     He will judge the peoples with equity.
11 Let the heavens be glad and the earth rejoice,
     Let the sea[2] and its fulness thunder.

12 Let the field, and all that is in it, exult;
     Let the trees of the forest ring out their joy
13 Before the Lord—for He cometh,
     He cometh to judge the earth.
     He will judge the world with justice
     And the nations with faithfulness.

PSALM XCVII

PSALM XCVII

The World-King a King of Justice

JEHOVAH is King, let the earth rejoice :
　　Let her many isles be glad.
2　Clouds and darkness are round about Him,
　　Justice and right are the base of His throne.
3　Fire goeth before Him,
　　And blazeth around His steps,
4　His lightnings illumine the world :
　　The earth quakes at the sight.
5　Mountains melt like wax
　　Before the Lord of all the earth.
6　The heavens proclaim His justice,
　　All nations behold His glory.

7　Shamed are all image-worshippers,
　　That make a boast of their idols.
　　All the gods bow before Him.
8　Zion is glad at the tidings,
　　The daughters of Judah rejoice
　　Because of Thy judgments, Jehovah.
9　For Thou art most high over all the earth,
　　Greatly exalted above all gods.

10　Jehovah loves those that hate evil,
　　He keepeth the souls of the faithful :
　　From the hand of the wicked He saves them.
11　Light doth arise for the righteous,
　　And joy for the upright in heart.
12　Rejoice in Jehovah, ye righteous :
　　Give thanks to His holy name.

PSALM XCVIII

PSALM XCVIII

The Homage of Nature and Man to Jehovah, the Mighty Judge of the World

SING a new song to Jehovah,
    For He hath done wonders;
His right hand and holy arm
    Have won Him the victory.
2 Jehovah hath made His victory known,
    And revealed to the eyes of the nations His righteousness.
3 Mindful He was of His kindness to Jacob,
    Faithful He was to the house of Israel.
All the ends of the earth have seen
    The victory of our God.

4 Shout, all the earth, to Jehovah:
    Break into cries and music.
5 Play on the lyre to Jehovah,
    On the lyre and with loud melody.
6 With trumpet and sound of horn,
    Shout ye before the King.

7 Let the sea[1] and its fulness roar,
    The world and the dwellers upon it.
8 Let the streams clap their hands,
    Let the hills shout for gladness together
9 Before the Lord—for He cometh,
    He cometh to judge the earth.
He will judge the world with justice
    And the nations with equity.

PSALM XCIX

PSALM XCIX
Jehovah's Just and Holy Rule

JEHOVAH is King; let the nations tremble :
 He is throned upon cherubs ; let earth quake.
2 Jehovah is great in Zion,
 He is high over all the nations.
3 Let them praise Thy great and terrible name
 Holy is He.

4 Thou art a King who loves justice,
 Equity Thou hast established :
 Justice and right Thou hast wrought for Jacob.
5 Exalt ye Jehovah our God,
 Bow ye down at His footstool.
 Holy is He.

6 Among His priests were Moses and Aaron,
 Samuel among those that called on His name.
 They called to Jehovah, and *He* gave them answer.
7 He spake unto them in the pillar of cloud,
 They kept His commands and the statute He gave them.
8 Jehovah our God, Thou gavest them answer.
 A God of forgiveness wast Thou unto them,
 Who suffered their doings to go unpunished.
9 Exalt ye Jehovah our God ;
 Bow down at His holy mountain.
 For holy is Jehovah our God.

PSALMS C—CI

PSALM C

A Call to Worship

SHOUT, all the earth, to Jehovah.
2 Serve Jehovah with gladness,
   Approach Him with ringing cries.
3 Be ye sure that Jehovah alone is God.
   It is He that hath made us, and His we are—
   His people, the sheep of His pasture.

4 Enter ye into His gates with thanksgiving,
   Into His courts with praise.
   Give ye thanks to Him, bless ye His name.
5 For Jehovah is good, His love is for ever,
   And unto all ages endureth His faithfulness.

PSALM CI

A Model King

OF kindness and justice I sing,
   Making melody unto Thee, Lord.
2 I would look to the way that is blameless,
   And make it mine own.

Within mine own house I would walk
   With an innocent heart.
3 I would never direct mine eyes
   To a thing that is base.

The impulse to stray I abhor—
   It shall not cling to me.
4 Far from me be perverseness of heart,
   Or kinship with evil.

PSALM CII

5 Whoso slanders his neighbour in secret,
   I bring him to silence :
The man of high looks and proud heart
   I will not abide.

6 I will favour the true in the land,
   They shall dwell in my court.
He who walks in a way that is blameless
   Shall be mine attendant.

7 No man shall dwell in my house
   That practises guile.
No man that speaketh a lie
   Shall abide in my presence.

8 Morn by morn I will wholly wipe out
   All the bad in the land,
And cut off from Jehovah's own city
   All workers of evil.

PSALM CII

A Prayer for Pity and for the Restoration of Zion

Hear my prayer, O Lord ;
   Let my cry for help come to Thee.
2 Hide not Thy face from me
   In the day of my distress.
Incline Thine ear unto me :
   When I call, O answer me speedily.

3 For my days pass away like smoke :
   My bones are burned through as with fire.

PSALM CII

4 My heart is scorched, withered like grass;
    I forget to eat my bread.
5 By reason of my loud groaning,
    My flesh clings to my bones.

6 Like a pelican of the wilderness,
    Like an owl among ruins am I.
7 I make my sleepless lament
    Like a bird on the house-top alone.
8 All the day wild foes revile me,
    Using my name for a curse.

9 For ashes have been my bread,
    And tears have been mixed with my cup.
10 Because of Thy passionate anger,
    Thou didst raise me, then hurl me to the ground.
11 My days decline as a shadow,
    As for me, I wither like grass

12 But Thou, O Lord, art enthroned for ever,
    Thy fame endureth to all generations.
13 Thou wilt arise and have pity on Zion;
    'Tis time to be gracious—her hour has come.
14 For even in her stones Thy servants take pleasure,
    Her very dust they look on with love.

15 Then the nations will reverence the name of the Lord,
    And all the kings of the earth His glory,
16 When the Lord shall have built up Zion,
    And revealed Himself in His glory,

PSALM CII

17 In response to the prayer of the destitute,
    Whose prayer He will not despise.
18 Let this be recorded for ages to come,
    That the Lord may be praised by a people yet unborn.
19 For He shall look down from His holy height,
    From the heavens the Lord will gaze on the earth,
20 To hear the groans of the prisoner,
    To free those that are doomed to die;
21 That men may rehearse the Lord's fame in Zion,
    And the praise of Him in Jerusalem,
22 When the nations are gathered together,
    And the kingdoms, to worship the Lord.

23 He hath broken my strength on the way,
    He hath shortened my days.
24 I will say, " My God, take me not hence
    In the midst of my days.

    Thy years endure age after age.
25   Of old Thou hast founded the earth,
    And the heavens are the work of Thy hands.
26 They shall perish ; but Thou dost stand.
    They shall all wax old like a garment,
    And change—as a robe Thou shalt change them.
27 But Thou art the same, Thy years are endless.
    The sons of Thy servants abide,
    Evermore shall their seed be before Thee."

PSALM CIII

PSALM CIII
Bless the Lord, O my Soul

O SOUL of mine, bless the Lord;
    And all that is in me, His holy name.
2 O soul of mine, bless the Lord;
    And forget not one of His benefits.
3 He pardoneth all thy sins,
    He healeth all thy diseases.
4 He ransoms thy life from the pit,
    He crowns thee with kindness and pity.
5 He gives thee thy heart's desire,[1]
    Renewing thy youth like the eagle's.

6 The Lord doth execute justice
    And right for all that are wronged.
7 He revealed His ways unto Moses,
    His acts to the children of Israel.
8 Full of pity and grace is the Lord,
    Patient, and rich in kindness:
9 He will not always chide,
    Nor cherish His anger for ever.
10 Not after our sins hath He dealt with us,
    Nor requited us after our wickedness.

11 For high as the heavens o'er the earth
    Is His love over them that fear Him.
12 Far as is east from the west
    Hath he put our transgressions from us.
13 As a father pities his children,
    So the Lord pities them that fear Him;
14 For well He knoweth our frame,
    He remembers that we are dust.

PSALM CIV

15 As for man, his days are as grass ;
    Like a flower of the meadow he blossoms
16 At the breath of the wind² it is gone,
    And the place thereof knows it no more.
17 But the love of the Lord is eternal,
    And His kindness to children's children,
18 To the godly who keep His covenant
    And mindfully do His behests.

19 The Lord hath set His throne in the heavens;
    The whole world is under His sway.
20 Bless the Lord, ye angels of His,
    Mighty heroes performing His word.
21 Bless the Lord, all ye His hosts,
    Ye servants that do His will.
22 Bless the Lord, all ye His works,
    Far as His sway extends.
    O soul of mine, bless the Lord.

PSALM CIV

The Hymn of Creation

O Lord my God, Thou art very great,
    Clad in awful splendour,
2   Covered with robe of light.
Thou dost stretch out the heavens like the cloth of a tent.
3   He layeth the beams of His chambers on water.
He taketh dark clouds for His chariot,
    And rides on the wings of the wind.
4 He taketh the winds for His messengers,
    The fire and the flame for His servants.

PSALM CIV

5 He founded the earth upon pillars,
　　To sustain it unshaken for ever.
6 With the garment of ocean He covered her,
　　Waters towered over the mountains.
7 But at Thy rebuke they fled,
　　Scared by the roar of Thy thunder.
9 They dared not pass the bounds set for them,
　　Or cover the earth any more.
8 Mountains rose, valleys sank down—
　　To the place appointed for them.

10 He sent brooks into the valleys,
　　They meander between the mountains.
11 The wild beasts all drink thereat,
　　And the wild asses quench their thirst.
12 The birds have their home by the banks,
　　And twitter their song 'twixt the branches.
13 From His chambers above He gives drink to the mountains,
　　And satisfies earth with the vials of heaven.

14 He maketh grass grow for the cattle,
　　And herbs for the servants of man.[1]
　He bringeth bread out of the earth;
15 　Wine, to gladden man's heart;
　Oil, to make his face shine;
　　Bread, to strengthen man's heart.
16 The trees of the Lord drink their fill—
　　The cedars He planted on Lebanon,
17 Where the little birds build their nest,
　　And the stork whose home is the cypress.
18 The high hills are for the wild goats,
　　And the rocks are for conies to hide in.

PSALM CIV

19 He created the moon to mark seasons,
   And told the sun when to set.
20 Thou makest it dark : night cometh,
   When all the wild beasts bestir them—
21 Young lions that roar for their prey,
   Seeking their meat from God.
22 At sunrise they glide away,
   And lay them down in their dens.
23 Then man goes forth to his work,
   And toils till the even-tide.

24 How many, O Lord, are Thy works,
   All of them made in wisdom !
   The earth is filled with Thy creatures.
25 And there is the great broad sea,
   Where are countless things in motion,
   Living creatures, both great and small.
26 There go sea-monsters,[1]
   And the dragon Thou madest to play with.

27 They all look in hope to Thee,
   To give them their food in due season.
28 And Thou givest with open hand ;
   They gather and eat to their heart's desire.
29 When Thou hidest Thy face, they are terrified ;
   When Thou takest their breath away,
   They die and go back to their dust.
30 But a breath from Thy lips creates them,
   And renews the face of the earth.

31 May the glory of the Lord be for ever,
   May the Lord rejoice in His works.

PSALM CV

32 A glance of His makes the earth tremble,
    A touch of His makes the hills smoke.
33 I will sing to the Lord while I live,
    I will play to my God while I am.
34 May my musing be sweet unto Him.
    As for me, I rejoice in the Lord.
35 But may sinners be swept from the earth,
    And godless men vanish for ever.
    O soul of mine, bless the Lord.

          Hallelujah.

PSALM CV

The Inspiration of the Past

GIVE thanks to the Lord, call on His name:
    Make known His doings among the nations.
2 Sing unto Him, make music to Him,
    Discourse ye of all His wondrous works.
3 Make your boast in His holy name,
    Be glad at heart, ye who seek the Lord.
4 Seek after the Lord and His strength,
    Seek His face evermore.
5 Remember the wonders He did,
    His portents, the judgments He uttered,
6 Ye seed of Abraham His servant,
    Ye children of Jacob His chosen.

7 He is Jehovah our God:
    In all the earth are His judgments.
8 He remembers for ever His covenant,
    His promise for a thousand generations—

PSALM CV

9 The covenant He made with Abraham,
    The oath He sware unto Isaac,
10 And confirmed as a statute to Jacob,
    A pact everlasting to Israel—
11 To give them the land of Canaan
    As the lot which they should inherit.

12 And when they were very few,
    Yea, few and but pilgrims therein,
13 Wandering from nation to nation,
    Journeying from people to people,
14 He suffered no man to oppress them,
    Even punishing kings for their sakes.
15 He forbade them to touch His anointed,
    Or do any hurt to His prophets.

16 When He called for a dearth on the land,
    And cut off the bread which sustained them,
17 He sent before them a man,
    Even Joseph, who was sold as a slave.
18 His feet were galled with fetters,
    He was laid in chains of iron,
19 Till the time that His word came to pass,
    The word of the Lord that had tried him.

20 The king sent and freed him,
    The ruler of nations released him.
21 He made him lord of his household,
    And ruler of all his substance,
22 To admonish his princes at will
    And instruct his elders in wisdom.

PSALM CV

23 Thus Israel came into Egypt,
　　Jacob sojourned in the land of Ham.
24 His people He made very fruitful,
　　And mightier than their foes.
25 He inspired them to hate His people,
　　And to deal with His servants craftily.

26 He sent His servant Moses,
　　And Aaron whom He had chosen.
27 Portents He wrought in Egypt,
　　And signs in the land of Ham.
28 Darkness He sent, and it fell:
　　Yet they gave no heed to His word.

29 He turned their waters into blood,
　　Thus causing their fish to die.
30 Their land was alive with frogs,
　　Swarming even in the royal chambers.
31 At His command came flies,
　　And lice in all their borders.
32 He gave them hail for rain
　　And fire that flashed through the land,
33 Smiting their vines and figs,
　　Breaking the trees of their border.

34 At His command came locusts,
　　Young locusts beyond all counting,
35 Which ate every herb in the land,
　　Ate up, too, the fruit of their ground.
36 He smote in their land all the first-born,
　　The firstlings of all their strength—
37 Then forth He led them with silver and gold,
　　And among His tribes not a man was weary.

PSALM CVI

38 Egypt was glad when they left,
    For terror had fallen upon them.
39 He spread out a cloud to screen them,
    And fire to give light in the night.
40 He sent quails at their entreaty,
    And heavenly bread in abundance.
41 He opened the rock ; waters gushed :
    In the desert they ran like a river.
42 For He thought on His holy promise
    To Abraham His servant.

43 So He led out His people with joy,
    His elect with a ringing cry.
44 And He gave them the lands of the nations,
    The fruit of their toil for possession,
45 That so they might keep His statutes,
    And be of His laws observant.

        Hallelujah.

PSALM CVI

The Nation's Sin against the Divine Love

Hallelujah !

GIVE thanks to the Lord for His goodness,
    For His kindness endureth for ever.
2 Who can describe His heroic deeds,
    Or publish all His praise ?
3 Happy they who keep the law,
    And do righteousness evermore.

4 Remember me, Lord, as Thou dost Thy people,
    And visit me with Thy gracious help.

PSALM CVI

5   May I see the good fortune of Thine elect,
    May I share in the joy of Thy nation,
    And in the pride of Thy heritage.

6   We, like our fathers, have sinned,
        We have done perversely and wickedly
7   In the land of Egypt our fathers,
        All heedless of Thy wonders,
    And unmindful of Thy great kindness,
        At the Red Sea defied the Most High.
8   But He saved them for His name's sake,
        In order to show His might.
9   He rebuked the Red Sea, and it dried;
        They marched through the depths as through desert,
10 Saved from the hand of the hostile,
        Redeemed from the hand of the foe.
11 The waters covered their enemies:
        Not a man of them was left.
12 So then they believed in His words,
        And began to sing His praise.

13 But soon they forgot His doings:
        They did not wait for His counsel.
14 Full lusty they grew in the desert;
        They put God to the proof in the wilderness.
15 He gave them the thing they had asked for,
        But sent wasting disease among them.

16 The camp grew jealous of Moses
        And of Aaron the saint of the Lord.
17 The earth opened and swallowed up Dathan,
        And covered Abiram's company.

PSALM CVI

18   Fire broke out on their company,
      Flame kindled upon the ungodly.

19   They made a calf in Horeb,
      And bowed to the molten image.
20   They exchanged their glorious God
      For the image of ox that eats grass.
21   They forgot the God who had saved them
      By mighty deeds in Egypt—
22   Wonders in the land of Ham,
      Terrors by the Red Sea.
23   So He vowed, and would have destroyed them,
      But for Moses His elect,
    Who stepped into the breach before Him,
      To divert His deadly wrath.

24   They spurned the delightsome land,
      They refused to believe in His word.
25   They murmured in their tents,
      Would not listen to the voice of the Lord.
26   So He swore with uplifted hand
      To lay them low in the wilderness ;
27   To disperse their seed among heathen,
      To scatter them over the world.

28   Then they joined them to Baal of Peor,
      And ate what was offered the dead.
29   They provoked Him to wrath by their doings,
      And plague broke out among them.
30   Then Phinehas stood between,
      And so the plague was stayed ;
31   And it was counted to him for righteousness
      Unto all generations for ever.

PSALM CVI

32 They angered Him at the waters of Meribah,
    Through them it went ill with Moses.
33 They rebelled against His spirit,
    And he uttered speech that was rash.

34 They did not destroy the nations,
    As the Lord had commanded them ;
35 But they mingled with the heathen,
    And learned to do as they did.
36 Their idol gods they worshipped,
    And they were ensnared by them.
37 They sacrificed their sons
    And their daughters to the demons.
38 They poured out innocent blood—
    The blood of their sons and daughters—
    Whom they offered to Canaan's idols,
    And the land was polluted with blood.
39 They became unclean by their works,
    And adulterous in their doings.
40 Then the Lord was wroth with His people,
    Filled with horror at His inheritance.
41 He delivered them unto the heathen,
    To the sway of those who hated them.
42 Their enemies oppressed them,
    And subdued them under their hand.
43 Many a time He saved them,
    But they rebelled at His counsel,
    And pined away in their guilt.
44 Yet He looked upon their distress,
    When He heard their piercing cry.
45 He remembered for them His covenant,
    And relented in His great kindness.

PSALM CVI

46 He caused them to be pitied
   Of all that carried them captive.

47 Save us, O Lord our God,
   And gather us out of the nations,
   To give thanks to Thy holy name,
   And to make our boast of Thy praise.

> Blessed be the Lord, the God of Israel,
> From everlasting to everlasting.
> And let all the people say "Amen."
> Praise ye the Lord.

BOOK V

PSALM CVII

The Song of the Redeemed

Give thanks to the Lord for His goodness
   For His kindness endureth for ever.
2 Let this be the song of the ransomed,
    Whom the Lord hath redeemed from distress,
3 Gathering them from all lands,
    East, west, north, and south.

4 In the wastes of the desert some wandered,
    Finding no way to a city inhabited.
5 Full of hunger and thirst,
    Their soul fainted within them.
6 *Then they cried to the Lord in their trouble,*
    And He saved them from their distresses,
7 Guiding them straight on the way,
    Till they reached an inhabited city.
8 *Let them praise the Lord for His kindness,*
    For His wonderful works unto men;
9 For the longing soul He satisfies,
    And the hungry He filleth with good things.

10 Some sat in darkness and gloom—
    Prisoners—in irons and misery,
11 For rebelling against God's word,
    And spurning the Most High's counsel.
12 Their heart was bowed with toil;
    There was no one to help when they stumbled.
13 *Then they cried to the Lord in their trouble,*
    And He saved them from their distresses.

PSALM CVII

14 Out of darkness and gloom He brought them,
   And burst their bands asunder.
15 *Let them praise the Lord for His kindness,*
   For His wonderful works unto men.
16 For He shivered the gates of bronze,
   And hewed bars of iron asunder.

17 Some were sick from their wicked ways,
   And suffering because of their sins.
18 All manner of food they hated;
   They had come to the gates of death.
19 *Then they cried to the Lord in their trouble,*
   And He saved them from their distresses.
20 He sent His word and healed them,
   And delivered their life from the pit.
21 *Let them praise the Lord for His kindness,*
   For His wonderful works unto men.
22 Let them offer to Him thankofferings,
   And with joy tell what things He hath done.

23 Some crossed the sea in ships,
   Doing business in great waters.
24 These have seen what the Lord can do,
   And His wonderful deeds on the deep.
25 At His command rose a tempest,
   Which lifted the waves on high.
26 Up to heaven they went, down to the depths;
   Their soul with distress was melting.
27 They staggered and reeled like a drunkard;
   Their skill was all swallowed up.
28 *Then they cried to the Lord in their trouble,*
   And He saved them from their distresses.

PSALM CVII

29 He stilled the storm to a whisper,
    And the waves of the sea were hushed.
30 They were glad, because it was quiet;
    They were led to the haven they longed for.
31 *Let them praise the Lord for His kindness,*
    For His wonderful works unto men—
32 Where the people assemble, extol Him,
    And praise Him in council of elders.

33 He turneth streams into a wilderness,
    And to thirsty land springs of water,
34 A fruitful land into a salt waste,
    Because of the sin of the people.
35 A desert He makes pools of water,
    And a land of drought springs of water.
36 He settles the hungry therein,
    They establish a city to dwell in.
37 They sow fields and plant vineyards,
    Which furnish a fruitful yield.
38 By His blessing they multiply greatly,
    And He lets not their cattle decrease.

39 Yet when they are bowed and diminished
    By oppression, misfortune, or sorrow,
40 " He poureth contempt upon princes,
    And on trackless wastes leads them astray ";[1]
41 He lifteth the poor out of misery,
    And makes families fruitful as flocks.
42 " At this sight shall the upright be glad,
    And all wicked mouths shall be stopped."[2]
43 Let the man that is wise observe this,
    And consider the love of the Lord

PSALM CVIII

PSALM CVIII
A Prayer for Victory

MY[1] heart is steadfast, O God,
   My heart is steadfast.
I would sing, yea, I would make music;
   Awake, Thou art my pride.
2 Awake, harp and lyre;
   Fain would I waken the dawn.
3 I would praise Thee among the peoples, O Lord;
   Make music among the nations to Thee.
4 For great unto heaven is Thy love,
   And Thy faithfulness unto the clouds.
5 Be exalted, O God, o'er the heavens,
   And Thy glory o'er all the earth.

6 For [2] the rescue of Thy beloved,
   Save by Thy right hand and answer us.
7 God did solemnly swear:
   " As victor will I divide Shechem,
   And mete out the valley of Succoth.
8 Mine is Gilead, mine is Manasseh,
   Ephraim is the defence of my head,
   Judah my sceptre of rule,
9 Moab the pot that I wash in,
   Edom—I cast my shoe over it,
   I shout o'er Philistia in triumph."

10 O to be brought to the fortified city!
   O to be led into Edom!
11 Hast Thou not spurned us, O God?
   Thou marchest not forth with our armies.

PSALM CIX

12 Grant us help from the foe,
    For vain is the help of man.
13 With God we shall yet do bravely,
    He Himself will tread down our foes.

PSALM CIX

An Imprecation

  O God whom I praise, keep not silence;
2   For their wicked mouths they have opened against me,
    They speak unto me with tongues that are false.
3 They beset me with words of hatred,
    And fight without cause against me.
4 My love they requite with hostility,
    While for them I lift up my prayer.
5 Evil for good they reward me,
    And hatred for my love.

6 Set over him one that is godless,
    An opponent at his right hand.
7 From his trial let him come forth guilty,
    May his prayer be counted as sin.
8 Grant that his days may be few,
    That his office be seized by another.
9 Grant that his children be fatherless,
    And that his wife be a widow.
10 Up and down may his children go begging,
    Expelled from their desolate home.
11 May all that he owneth be seized by the creditor,
    May strangers plunder the fruits of his toil.

PSALM CIX

12 May none extend to him kindness,
   Or pity his fatherless children.
13 His descendants be doomed to destruction
   Blotted out be his name in one generation!
14 May his father's guilt be remembered,
   And his mother's sin not blotted out:
15 May the Lord keep them ever before Him
   And his memory root from the earth;
16 For he gave no thought to show kindness,
   But pursued the poor and the needy,
   And the downhearted—even unto death.

17 May the curses he loved light upon him,
   May the blessings he loathed be afar.
18 Like a garment he clothed him with curses;
   May they pierce to his inwards like water,
   And cling to his bones like oil.
19 Let them be like the robe he wraps round him,
   Like the girdle he always is girt with.
20 Be this the reward of mine adversaries,
   Of those that speak evil against me.

21 But Thou, O Lord Jehovah,
   For Thy name's sake deal with me;
   In Thy gracious kindness save me.
22 For I am poor and needy,
   And my heart is wounded within me.
23 I am gone like a lengthening shadow,
   I am shaken off like a locust.
24 My knees totter from fasting,
   My flesh is shrivelled and spare.
25 As for me, they heap insults upon me:
   When they see me, they shake their head.

PSALM CX

26 Help me, O Lord my God,
    And save me in Thy kindness.
27 Teach them that this is Thy hand,
    And Thine own doing, O Lord.
28 Let *them* curse, if only *Thou* bless.
    Put mine assailants to shame,
    And make Thy servant glad.
29 Mine opponents be clothed with dishonour,
    And wrapped in a robe of shame.

30 I give thanks to Thee, Lord, with loud voice,
    I give praise in the midst of the throng;
31 For He stands by the poor, at his right hand,
    To save him from those that condemn him.

PSALM CX

Divine Promise of Victory and Dominion to the Priest-King

Thus spake Jehovah concerning my Lord,
    " Sit thou at my right hand,
Till I set thy foot on the neck of thy foes."

2 On Zion Jehovah is wielding
    Thy sceptre of might, and doth charge thee
    To rule in the midst of thy foes.

3 In the day that thou marchest to battle
    Thy people will follow thee gladly—
   Young warriors in holy array,
    Like dew-drops, born of the morning.

PSALM CXI

4 Jehovah hath sworn and will not repent,—
"As for thee, thou art priest for ever
After Melchizedek's manner."

5 By thy side will the Lord shatter kings
On the day of His wrath.
6 He will execute judgment—
Filling the valleys with dead,
The broad fields with shattered heads.
7 He will drink of the brook by the way,
And march onward with uplifted head.

PSALM CXI [1]

In Praise of the Divine Goodness

Hallelujah.

I WILL thank the Lord with all my heart,
In those intimate hours when the upright gather.
2 Great are the things that the Lord hath done,
Worthy of study by those that love them.
3 Majestic and glorious is His work,
And His salvation abideth for ever.
4 For His marvellous deeds He hath made a memorial;
The Lord is gracious and full of compassion.
5 Food He giveth to those that fear Him,
Evermore He remembers His covenant.
6 His mighty works He hath shown to His people,
In giving to them the nations for heritage.
7 All that He doeth is faithful and right,
All His behests are firm and sure.

PSALM CXII

8 They are established for ever and ever,
    Executed with truth and uprightness.
9 Unto His people He sent redemption,
    He hath appointed His covenant for ever.
    Holy and reverend is His name.
10 The fear of the Lord is the choicest of wisdom :
    Those who keep it are wise indeed.
    His praise abideth for ever and ever.

PSALM CXII[1]

The Blessings of Godliness

Hallelujah.

HAPPY the man that feareth the Lord,
    And greatly delighteth in His commandments.
2 Mighty on earth shall be his seed ;
    A blessing shall rest on the race of the upright.
3 Wealth and riches are in his house,
    And his prosperity standeth for ever.
4 To the upright ariseth light in the darkness ;
    Full of favour and pity and kindness is he.
5 It is well with the man who shows pity and lends,
    Who supporteth all his affairs upon justice.
6 For he will for ever abide unshaken ;
    The just shall be had in remembrance for ever.
7 He will not be afraid of evil tidings,
    With steady heart he trusteth the Lord.
8 His heart is firm and unafraid :
    He knows he will feast his eyes on his enemies.

PSALM CXIII

9 With lavish hands he gives to the poor,
    And his prosperity standeth for ever.
    He is lifted to heights of triumph and honour.
10 The sight of him fills with vexation the godless :
    Gnashing their teeth, they melt away.
    The godless are baulked in their expectation.

PSALM CXIII

The Lord loveth the Lowly

Hallelujah.

PRAISE the Lord, ye His servants,
    Praise the name of the Lord.
2 The name of the Lord be blessed
    From now and for evermore.
3 From sunrise unto sunset
    Is the name of the Lord to be praised.

4 High is the Lord above all nations,
    Above the heavens is His glory.
5 Who is like the Lord our God,
    In the heavens or on the earth ?

6 Throned as He is on high,
    He looketh down into the depths.
7 He raiseth the weak from the dust,
    He lifts from the dunghill the needy,
8 And sets him beside the princes,
    Even the princes of His people.
9 He giveth the barren woman a home,
    And makes her the happy mother of children.

Hallelujah.

PSALM CXIV

The Marvel of the Exodus

WHEN Israel went out of Egypt,
  Jacob's house from a barbarous [1] people,
2 Judah He chose for Himself, [2]
  Israel [3] as the land of His sway.

3 The sea saw it, and fled,
  The Jordan turned him back.
4 Mountains skipped like rams,
  Hills like the young of the flock.

5 What aileth thee, sea, that thou fleest?
  Jordan, that backward thou turnest?
6 Mountains, that ram-like ye skip?
  Hills, like the young of the flock?

7 Earth, tremble before the Lord,
  At the presence of Jacob's God,
8 Who turns rocks into pools of water,
  And flint into fountains of water.

PSALM CXV

Israel's Incomparable God

NOT to us, Lord, not unto us,
  But unto Thy name give glory,
For Thy kindness' and faithfulness' sake.
2 Why should the heathen say,
  " Where is now their God ? "

PSALM CXV

3 Our God—He is in heaven ;
   Whatsoever He willeth, He doeth.
4 Their idols ¹ are silver and gold,
   Made by the hands of men.
5 Mouths have they, but they speak not :
   Eyes have they, but they see not.
6 Ears have they, but they hear not :
   Noses have they, but they smell not.
7 Hands have they, but they feel not ;
   Feet have they, but they walk not :
   There is no sound in their throat.
8 Like them be those that make them,
   And all that trust in them.

9 O Israel, trust in the Lord :
   He is their help and their shield.
10 House of Aaron, trust in the Lord :
   He is their help and their shield.
11 Ye that fear the Lord, trust in the Lord :
   He is their help and their shield.

12 The Lord, mindful of us, will bless us :
   He will bless the house of Israel,
   He will bless the house of Aaron.
13 He will bless them that fear the Lord,
   The small and the great together.

14 May the Lord add unto you—
   Unto you and unto your children.
15 Blessed be ye of the Lord,
   Creator of heaven and earth.

PSALM CXVI

16 The heavens are the heavens of the Lord,
    But the earth hath He given unto men.
17 The dead cannot praise the Lord,
    Nor those that go down into silence.
18 But *we* will bless the Lord
    From now and for evermore.
        Hallelujah.

PSALM CXVI

Song of Thanksgiving for Deliverance

I LOVE the Lord, because He hears
    The voice of my supplication.
2 For He hath inclined His ear unto me:
    I will call upon Him as long as I live.

3 About me were snares of death,
    The anguish of hell [1] was upon me:
    Distress and sorrow were mine.
4 Then I called on the name of the Lord:
    " I beseech Thee, O Lord, deliver me."

5 Gracious and just is the Lord,
    Compassionate is our God.
6 The Lord preserveth the simple;
    When I was drooping, He saved me.
7 Return, O my soul, to thy rest,
    For the Lord hath dealt richly with thee.

8 Thou hast rescued my soul from death,
    Mine eyes from tears,
    My feet from stumbling.

PSALM CXVI

9   Before the Lord I will walk
      In the land of the living.

10 I held fast my faith, though I said,
      " Ah me ! I am sore afflicted " :
11 Though in mine alarm I said,
      " Every man is but a delusion."

12 What shall I render the Lord
      For all His bounty to me ?
13 I will lift up the cup of salvation,
      And call on the name of the Lord.
14 I will pay my vows to the Lord
      In the presence of all His people.

15 Grave in the eyes of the Lord
      Is the death of His loyal and loved ones.[a]
16 Ah, Lord ! I am Thy servant,
      Thy servant, the son of Thine handmaid.
      Thou hast loosened my bonds.

17 I will offer to Thee a thank-offering,
      And call on the name of the Lord.
18 I will pay my vows to the Lord
      In the presence of all His people,
19 In the courts of the house of the Lord,
      In the midst of thee, O Jerusalem.

Hallelujah.

PSALM CXVII

A Call to Praise

PRAISE the Lord, all ye nations :
   Laud Him, all ye peoples.
2 For His mighty love is over us :
   The Lord is faithful for ever.

Hallelujah.

PSALM CXVIII

Thanksgiving for Victory

***G**IVE thanks to the Lord for His goodness,
   His kindness endureth for ever.*
2 Let the house of Israel now say :
   His kindness endureth for ever.
3 Let the house of Aaron now say :
   His kindness endureth for ever.
4 Let those that fear the Lord now say :
   His kindness endureth for ever.

5 Out of straits I called on the Lord,
   The Lord answered and gave me room.
6 The Lord is mine ; I am fearless.
   What can man do unto me ?
7 The Lord is mine, as my help :
   I shall feast mine eyes on my foes.
8 It is better to hide in the Lord
   Than to trust in mortal men.
9 It is better to hide in the Lord
   Than to put any trust in princes.

PSALM CXVIII

10 Everywhere heathen swarmed round me;
    In the name of the Lord I cut them down.
11 They swarmed, yea, swarmed around me;
    In the name of the Lord I cut them down,
12 They swarmed around me like bees,
    They blazed like a fire of thorns:
    In the name of the Lord I cut them down.

13 Sore they pushed me, to make me fall;
    But the Lord gave me His help.
14 The Lord is my strength and my song,
    And He is become my salvation.
15 Hark! in the tents of the righteous
    Glad cries of victory are ringing.
    The hand of the Lord hath wrought bravely,
16 The hand of the Lord is exalted,
    The hand of the Lord hath wrought bravely.

17 I shall not die: nay, I shall live,
    To declare the works of the Lord.
18 Though the Lord hath chastened me sore,
    He hath not given me over to death.

(The Procession arrives at the Temple)

19 " Open to me the gates of victory.
    I would enter therein and give thanks to the Lord."

(The Welcome)

20 " This is the gate of the Lord:
    The righteous may enter therein."

21 I thank Thee because Thou hast heard me,
    And art become my salvation.

PSALM CXIX

22 The stone which the builders despised
    Is become the head-stone of the corner.
23 This hath been wrought by the Lord;
    It is marvellous in our eyes.

24 This day is the Lord's own creation:
    In it let us joy and be glad.
25 O Lord, save us, we pray,
    O Lord, prosper, we pray.

26 Blessed is he that doth enter
    In the name of the Lord.
    From the house of the Lord we bless you.
27 The Lord is God,
    He hath given us light.
    Wreathe ye the dance with boughs,
    Till they touch the horns of the altar.
28 Thou art my God, I will thank Thee;
    O my God, I will exalt Thee.
29 *Give thanks to the Lord for His goodness:*
    His kindness endureth for ever.

PSALM CXIX [1]

The Power and Comfort of the Word of God

HAPPY they whose life is blameless,
    Who walk by the law of the Lord.
2 Happy they who keep His charges,
    And seek Him with all their hearts;
3 Who also work no unrighteousness,
    But in Thy ways they walk.
4 Thou Thyself hast appointed Thy precepts
    To be kept with diligence.

PSALM CXIX

5 O to be steadily guided
   In the keeping of Thy statutes!
6 Then unashamed shall I be,
   When I look towards all Thy commandments.
7 I will thank Thee with heart unfeigned,
   When I learn Thy righteous judgments.
8 I will observe Thy statutes:
   O forsake me not utterly.

9 How can a young man keep his life pure?
   By giving heed to Thy word.
10 With all my heart have I sought Thee,
   Let me not stray from Thy commandments.
11 In my heart have I treasured Thy word,
   To keep from sinning against Thee.
12 Blessed art Thou, O Lord;
   Teach Thou me Thy statutes.
13 With my lips have I rehearsed
   All the judgments of Thy mouth.
14 I delight in the way of Thy charges,
   More than in riches of all sorts.
15 I will muse upon Thy precepts,
   And look unto Thy paths.
16 In Thy statutes I delight,
   I will not forget Thy word.

17 Grant that Thy servant may live,
   And I will observe Thy word.
18 Open mine eyes, that I see
   Wondrous things out of Thy law.
19 But a guest am I on the earth:
   Hide not Thy commandments from me.

PSALM CXIX

20 My soul is crushed with longing
    For Thine ordinances at all times.
21 Thou dost rebuke the proud, the accursed,
    Who wander from Thy commandments.
22 Roll away from me scorn and contempt,
    For I have observed Thy charges.
23 Though princes sit plotting against me,
    Thy servant will muse on Thy statutes.
24 Thy charges are my delight,
    They are my counsellors.

25 My soul cleaves to the dust;
    Revive me, as Thou hast promised.
26 I told of my ways, Thou madest answer;
    Teach Thou me Thy statutes.
27 Grant me insight into Thy precepts,
    And I will muse on Thy wonders.
28 My soul melteth away for sorrow;
    Raise me up, as Thou hast promised.
29 Put the way of falsehood from me,
    And graciously grant me Thy law.
30 I have chosen the way of fidelity,
    Thine ordinances I long for.
31 I cleave unto Thy charges:
    O put me not, Lord, to shame.
32 I will run in the way of Thy commandments,
    For Thou givest me room of heart.

33 Teach me, O Lord, the way of Thy statutes,
    And I will keep it unto the end.
34 Instruct me to keep Thy law,
    And I will observe it with all my heart.

PSALM CXIX

35 Guide me in the path of Thy commandments,
    For therein do I delight.
36 Incline my heart to Thy charges,
    And not unto greed of gain.
37 Turn away mine eyes from vain sights,
    Revive me by Thy word.
38 Confirm to Thy servant the promise
    Which is given to those that fear Thee.
39 Remove the reproach which I dread,
    Because Thy judgments are good.
40 Behold, I long for Thy precepts.
    Quicken Thou me in Thy righteousness.

41 Visit me, Lord, with Thy love
    And salvation, as Thou hast promised.
42 So shall I answer my slanderers,
    For my trust is in Thy word.
43 Snatch not from my mouth the word of truth,
    For in Thy judgments I hope.
44 I will keep Thy law continually,
    For ever and evermore.
45 So shall I walk in wide spaces,
    For I give my mind to Thy precepts.
46 I will speak of Thy charge before kings,
    And will not be ashamed thereof.
47 Thy commandments are my delight,
    I love them exceedingly.
48 I will lift up my hands[2] to Thy commandments,
    And muse upon Thy statutes.

49 Remember Thy word to Thy servant,
    On which Thou hast made me to hope.

PSALM CXIX

50 This is my comfort in trouble,
 That Thy word giveth life unto me.
51 The arrogant utterly scorn me,
 But I have not declined from Thy law.
52 When I think of Thy judgments of old,
 O Lord, I take to me comfort.
53 I am seized with glowing anger
 At the wicked who forsake Thy law.
54 Thy statutes have been to me songs
 In the house of my pilgrimage.
55 I remember Thy name in the night,
 O Lord, and observe Thy law.
56 My (happy) lot hath been this,
 That I have kept Thy precepts.

57 My portion art Thou, O Lord:
 I have promised to keep Thy words.
58 I entreat Thee with all my heart;
 Grant me Thy promised favour.
59 I have thought upon my ways,
 And turned my feet to Thy charges.
60 I hasted and tarried not
 To give heed unto Thy commandments.
61 Though the godless have wound their cords round me,
 I have not forgotten Thy law.
62 At midnight I rise to praise Thee
 Because of Thy righteous judgments.
63 With all them that fear Thee I company,
 And with those that observe Thy precepts.
64 The earth, Lord, is full of Thy kindness;
 Teach Thou me Thy statutes.

PSALM CXIX

65 Well hast Thou dealt with Thy servant,
   As Thou hast promised, O Lord.
66 Teach me discretion and knowledge,
   For I have believed Thy commandments.
67 Till trouble came I was a wanderer,
   But now I observe Thy word.
68 Thou art good and doest good ;
   Teach Thou me Thy statutes.
69 The proud have forged lies against me,
   But I keep Thy precepts with all my heart.
70 Their heart is gross like fat,
   But I delight in Thy law.
71 It was good for me to be humbled,
   That I should learn Thy statutes.
72 The law of Thy mouth is better to me
   Than thousands of pieces of silver and gold.

73 Thy hands have made me and fashioned me ;
   Make me wise to learn Thy commandments.
74 Those that fear Thee shall see me with joy,
   For in Thy word have I hoped.
75 I know, O Lord, that Thy judgments are right,
   And in faithfulness Thou hast afflicted me.
76 Let Thy love be a comfort to me,
   For so hast Thou promised Thy servant.
77 Visit me with Thy quickening pity,
   For Thy law is my delight.
78 Put the proud to shame, who have wronged me falsely :
   As for me, I will muse on Thy precepts.
79 Let those turn to me who fear Thee,
   That they may learn Thy charges.

PSALM CXIX

80 Let my heart be sound in Thy statutes,
    That I may not be put to shame.

81 My soul pineth for Thy salvation,
    But in Thy word do I hope.
82 Mine eyes pine away for Thy promise:
    Saying, " When wilt Thou comfort me ? "
83 Though shrivelled like wine-skin in smoke,
    Thy statutes I have not forgotten.
84 How few are the days of Thy servant !
    When wilt Thou judge those who harass me ?
85 Proud men have dug for me pits—
    Men who do not conform to Thy law.
86 All Thy commandments are trusty.
    With falsehood they harass me : help me.
87 They had well nigh made an end of me,
    Yet I did not forget Thy precepts.
88 O spare me in Thy kindness,
    And I will observe the charge of Thy mouth.

89 For ever, O Lord, is Thy word
    Fixed firmly in the heavens.
90 Thy truth endures age after age ;
    It is stablished on earth, and it stands.
91 By Thine appointment they stand this day,
    For the universe is Thy servant.
92 Had not Thy law been my joy,
    In my misery then had I perished.
93 I will never forget Thy precepts,
    For through them Thou hast put life in me.
94 I am Thine, O save me,
    For I give my mind to Thy precepts.

PSALM CXIX

95 The wicked lay wait to destroy me,
    But I give heed to Thy charge.
96 I have seen a limit to all things:
    But Thy commandment is spacious exceedingly.

97 O how I love Thy law!
    All the day long I muse on it.
98 Thy commandment makes me wiser than mine enemies:
    For it is mine for ever.
99 I am prudent above all my teachers,
    For Thy charges are my meditation.
100 I have insight more than the aged,
    Because I observe Thy precepts.
101 I refrain my foot from all wicked ways,
    That I may keep Thy word.
102 I turn not aside from Thy judgments,
    For Thou Thyself art my teacher.
103 How sweet are Thy words to my taste,
    Sweeter than honey to my mouth!
104 Insight I win through Thy precepts
    Therefore every false way I hate.

105 Thy word is a lamp to my feet,
    And a light to my path.
106 I have sworn an oath, and will keep it,
    To observe Thy righteous judgments.
107 I am afflicted sorely:
    Revive me, O Lord, as Thou saidst.
108 Accept, Lord, my willing praise,
    And teach Thou me Thy judgments.
109 My life is in ceaseless peril;
    But I do not forget Thy law.

PSALM CXIX

110 The wicked set traps for me,
   Yet I do not stray from Thy precepts.
111 Thy charges are mine everlasting inheritance,
   They are the joy of my heart.
112 I incline my heart to perform Thy statutes
   For ever, even unto the end.

113 I hate men of divided heart,
   But Thy law do I love.
114 Thou art my shelter and shield
   In Thy word do I hope.
115 Begone, ye wicked men,
   I will keep the commands of my God.
116 Uphold me and spare me, as Thou hast promised:
   O disappoint me not.
117 Hold me up, and I shall be saved:
   And Thy statutes shall be mine unceasing delight.
118 All that swerve from Thy statutes Thou spurnest:
   Their cunning is in vain.
119 All the wicked of earth Thou countest as dross,
   Therefore I love Thy charges.
120 My flesh, for fear of Thee, shudders,
   And I stand in awe of Thy judgments.

121 Justice and right have I practised,
   Do not leave me to mine oppressors.
122 Be Thy servant's surety for good:
   Let not the proud oppress me.
123 Mine eyes pine for Thy salvation,
   And for Thy righteous promise.
124 Deal in Thy love with Thy servant,
   And teach Thou me Thy statutes.

PSALM CXIX

125 Thy servant am I ; instruct me,
   That I may know Thy charges.
126 It is time for the Lord to act :
   They have violated Thy law.
127 Therefore I love Thy commandments
   Above gold, yea, above fine gold.
128 So by all Thy precepts I guide me,
   And every false way I hate.

129 Thy testimonies are wonderful,
   Therefore my soul doth keep them.
130 When Thy word is unfolded, light breaks ;
   It imparts to the simple wisdom.
131 With open mouth I pant
   With longing for Thy commandments.
132 Turn unto me with Thy favour,
   As is just unto those that love Thee.
133 Steady my steps by Thy word,
   So that sin have no power over me.
134 Set me free from the men who oppress me,
   And I shall observe Thy precepts.
135 Shine with Thy face on Thy servant,
   And teach Thou me Thy statutes.
136 Mine eyes run down with rills of water,
   Because men observe not Thy law.

137 Righteous art Thou, O Lord,
   And right are Thine ordinances.
138 The laws Thou has ordered are just,
   And trusty exceedingly.
139 My jealousy hath undone me,
   That my foes have forgotten Thy words.

PSALM CXIX

140 Thy word has been tested well;
    And Thy servant loveth it.
141 I am little and held in contempt,
    But Thy precepts I have not forgotten.
142 Just is Thy justice for ever,
    And trusty is Thy law.
143 Stress and strain are upon me,
    But Thy commandments are my delight.
144 Right are Thy charges for ever,
    Instruct me that I may live.

145 With my whole heart I cry; O answer me.
    I would keep Thy statutes, O Lord.
146 I cry unto Thee: O save me,
    And I will observe Thy charges.
147 Ere the dawn I cry for Thy help:
    In Thy word do I hope.
148 Awake I meet the night-watches,
    To muse upon Thy sayings.
149 Hear my voice in Thy kindness:
    O Lord, by Thy judgments revive me.
150 Near me are wicked tormentors,
    Who are far from thoughts of Thy law;
151 But near, too, art Thou, O Lord,
    And all Thy commandments are trusty.
152 Long have I known from Thy charges
    That Thou hast founded them for all time.

153 Look on my misery, and rescue me;
    For I do not forget Thy law.
154 Defend my cause and redeem me:
    Revive me, as Thou hast promised.

PSALM CXIX

155 Salvation is far from the wicked,
    For their mind is not in Thy statutes.
156 Great is Thy pity, O Lord :
    Revive me, as Thou hast ordained.
157 My foes and tormentors are many,
    But I have not declined from Thy charges.
158 I behold the apostates with loathing,
    For they do not observe Thy word.
159 Behold how I love Thy precepts :
    Revive me, O Lord, in Thy kindness.
160 The sum of Thy word is truth,
    All Thy laws are just and eternal.

161 Princes have harassed me wantonly :
    But my heart stands in awe of Thy word.
162 Over Thy word I rejoice
    As one that findeth great spoil.
163 Falsehood I hate and abhor,
    But Thy law do I love.
164 Seven times a day do I praise Thee
    Because of Thy righteous judgments.
165 Right well do they fare that love Thy law :
    They go on their way without stumbling.
166 I hope for Thy salvation ;
    O Lord, I do Thy commandments.
167 My soul hath observed Thy charges :
    I love them exceedingly.
168 I observe Thy precepts and charges :
    Yea, all my ways are before Thee.

169 Let my cry come before Thee, O Lord :
    Give me insight, as Thou hast promised.

PSALM CXX

170 Let my prayer enter into Thy presence:
  Deliver me, as Thou hast said.
171 My lips shall be fountains of praise,
  That Thou teachest me Thy statutes.
172 My tongue shall sing of Thy word,
  For all Thy commandments are right.
173 Let Thine hand be ready to help me,
  For Thy precepts have been my choice.
174 I long, Lord, for Thy salvation,
  And Thy law is my delight.
175 Revive me that I may praise Thee,
  And let Thy precepts help me.
176 I have strayed like a wandering sheep;
  Seek Thou Thy servant, because
  I do not forget Thy commandments.

PSALM CXX

Prayer for Deliverance from Slander and Treachery

In straits I cried to the Lord,
  And to me He made answer.
2 "Deliver my soul, O Lord,
  From the lip that is false
  And the tongue that is crafty."

3 What shall He give unto thee,
  Thou tongue that art crafty?
  What yet shall He give unto thee?
4 Arrows of warrior, sharpened,
  With glowing broom coals together.

PSALM CXXI

5 Woe is me that I sojourn in Meshech,
    That I dwell by the tents of Kedar.
6 Already too long have I dwelt
    Among men who hate peace.
7 As for me, I am peace altogether:
    But the moment I speak,
    They are for war.

PSALM CXXI

The Omnipotent Keeper

I WILL lift up mine eyes to the mountains.
    O whence shall help for me come?
2 From the Lord cometh help unto me—
    The Creator of heaven and earth.

3 Thy foot He will not let totter:
    He who keepeth thee will not sleep.
4 Behold, the Keeper of Israel
    Shall neither slumber nor sleep.

5 The Lord is He that doth keep thee—
    Thy shelter upon thy right hand.
6 The sun by day shall not smite thee,
    Neither the moon by night.

7 From all evil the Lord shall keep thee,
    The Lord shall keep thy soul.
8 He shall keep thy going and coming
    From now and for evermore.

PSALM CXXII

PSALM CXXII

The Joy and the Prayer of the Pilgrims

I WAS glad when they said unto me,
   " We will go to the house of the Lord."
2 (Happy hour, when) our feet were standing,
   Within thy gates, O Jerusalem.

3 O Jerusalem, built once again
   Like a city without breach or gap,
4 Unto thee do the tribes go on pilgrimage,
   Even the tribes of the Lord,

As the law hath ordained for Israel,
   There to give thanks to the Lord.
5 There once stood thrones of justice—
   Even thrones of the household of David.

6 Pray that all may be well with Jerusalem,
   And well with those that love thee,
7 Well within thy ramparts,
   And well within thy palaces.

8 For the sake of my brethren and friends,
   I will wish thee now prosperity:
9 For the sake of the house of the Lord
   Our God, I will seek thy good.

PSALMS CXXIII—CXXIV

PSALM CXXIII
A Prayer for the Divine Pity

I LIFT up mine eyes unto Thee,
    Who art throned in the heavens.
2 Behold, as the eyes of a servant
    Turn to the hand of his master,
Or the eyes of a maid
    To the hand of her mistress,
So do our eyes turn
    To the Lord our God,
Until He be gracious to us.

3 Be gracious, be gracious to us, Lord.
    Scorn enough, and more, have we borne—
4 Yea, more than enough have we borne
    Of derision from men at their ease,
    Of scorn from those that are haughty.

PSALM CXXIV
A Magnificent Deliverance

" HAD it not been the Lord who was for us "
    Let Israel say—
2 " Had it not been the Lord who was for us
    When men rose against us,

3 Then alive they had swallowed us up,
    When their anger was kindled against us.
4 Then the waters had swept us away,
    And the torrent passed over us clean :
5 Then most sure had passed over us clean
    The wild seething waters."

PSALM CXXV

6 Blest be the Lord who hath suffered us not
   To be torn by their teeth.
7 We are like to a bird that is just escaped
   From the snare of the fowler.

8 The snare is broken,
   And we are escaped.
9 Our help is the name of the Lord,
   The Creator of heaven and earth.

PSALM CXXV

A Sure Defence

THEY that trust in Jehovah
   Shall be as mount Zion,
That cannot be moved,
   But abideth for ever.
2 Round Jerusalem are the mountains,
   And Jehovah is round His people
   From now and for evermore.

3 For He will not suffer
   The sceptre of wrong
To rest on the land
   That has fallen to the righteous;[1]
Else the righteous might put forth
   Their own hand to evil.

4 Do good, O Jehovah,
   To those that be good,
   And to the true-hearted.

PSALM CXXVI

5 But those who swerve
   Into crooked ways
  Shall Jehovah lead forth
   With the workers of evil.

      Peace be upon Israel.

PSALM CXXVI

Sowing in Tears

WHEN the Lord turned the fortunes of Zion,
   Like dreamers were we.
2 Then was our mouth filled with laughter,
   Our tongue with glad shouts;
  Then among the heathen men said,
   " The Lord hath dealt greatly with them."
3 Yea, the Lord had dealt greatly with us,
   And we were rejoicing.

4 Turn our fortunes, O Lord,
   As the streams in the south.[1]
5 They that scatter the seed in tears
   Shall reap with glad shouts.
6 Forth they fare, with their burden of seed,
   And they weep as they go.
  But home, home, with glad shouts they shall come
   With their arms full of sheaves.

PSALM CXXVII

PSALM CXXVII, 1—2

The Need of Heavenly Help

EXCEPT the Lord build the house,
   They that build it labour in vain.
Except the Lord watch the city,
   The watchman waketh in vain.

2 It is vain for you to rise early,
      To sit down (to the meal) so late,
   Thus eating the bread of sorrow;
      For He giveth His loved ones in sleep.

PSALM CXXVII, 3—5

The Blessing of Children

SEE! sons are a gift of the Lord,
   The fruit of the womb a reward.
4 Like arrows, by warriors wielded,
      Even so are the sons of youth.

5 Happy the man who has filled
      His quiver full of them.
   He shall not be ashamed when he speaks
      With enemies in the gate.

PSALMS CXXVIII—CXXIX

PSALM CXXVIII
The Blessings of Home

HAPPY all that fear the Lord,
    Even they that walk in His ways.
2 Thou shalt eat what thy hands have toiled for.
    Happy and prosperous thou!

3 Like a fruitful vine shall thy wife be
    In the innermost room of thy house:
Thy children, like slips of olive,
    Round about thy table.

4 See! this is the blessing
    Of the man that feareth the Lord.
5 The Lord shall bless thee from Zion.
    Thou shalt see Jerusalem flourish
All the days of thy life.
6 Thou shalt see thy children's children.
    Peace upon Israel.

PSALM CXXIX
A Prayer for the Discomfiture of the Enemies of Zion

"SORE have they vexed me from youth"—
    Thus let Israel say—
2 "Sore have they vexed me from youth,
    But they have not prevailed against me.

3 The ploughers ploughed on my back,
    They made their furrows long.
4 But the Lord, who is righteous, hath cut
    The cords of the wicked in sunder."

PSALM CXXX

5 Let all who are haters of Zion
    Be put to shame and defeated.
6 May they be as the grass on the house-top,
    Which withers before it shoots up ;

7 Which fills not the arms of the reaper,
    Nor the bosom of him that binds sheaves :
8 Whereof no one says as he passes,
    " The blessing of God be upon you."

    In the name of Jehovah we bless you.

PSALM CXXX

Out of the Depths

Out of the depths
    I call to Thee, Lord.
2 Lord, list to my voice :
    Give heed with Thine ears
    To my loud supplication.

3 If Thou shouldst mark sin, Jah,
    O Lord, who could stand ?
4 But with Thee is forgiveness,
    That Thou mayest be feared.

5 I wait for the Lord,
    My soul waits for His word,
6 My soul looks for the Lord
    More than watchman for morning,
    Than watchman for morning.

PSALMS CXXXI—CXXXII

7 Israel, hope in the Lord :
    With the Lord there is love—
    With Him plenteous redemption.
8 And *He* redeems Israel
    From all his iniquities.

PSALM CXXXI
As a Little Child

O LORD, my heart is not haughty,
    Mine eyes are not lofty,
I walk not among great things,
    Things too wonderful for me.

2 Yes, I have soothed and stilled my soul,
    Like a weaned child on his mother's bosom ;
    Like a weaned child is my soul.

3 O Israel, hope in the Lord
    From now and for evermore.

PSALM CXXXII
The Ancient Promise to David and Zion

REMEMBER, O Lord, unto David
    His sufferings all—
2 The oath that he sware to the Lord,
    And his vow to the Strong One of Jacob,
3 Never to enter his tent,
    Never to lie on his bed,
4 Never to give his eyes sleep
    Or his eyelids slumber,
5 Till a place he had found for the Lord,
    For the Strong One of Jacob to dwell in.

PSALM CXXXII

6 Behold, in Ephráthah we heard of it,
    In the field of the forest[1] we found it.
7 We went to the place where He dwelt,
    We bowed ourselves low at His footstool.
8 " Arise, Lord, and enter Thy resting-place,
    Thou and Thy mighty ark.
9 Let Thy priests wear a garment of righteousness,
    And Thy saints shout aloud for joy.
10 For the sake of David Thy servant,
    Do not reject Thine Anointed."

11 The Lord sware an oath unto David—
    An oath that He will not break;
" A scion of thine
    Will I set on thy throne.
12 If thy sons keep my covenant
    And the statutes I teach them,
Then their sons, too, for ever,
    Shall sit on thy throne."
13 For the choice of the Lord is Zion;
    She is the home of His heart.

14 " This is for ever my resting-place,
    This is the home of my heart.
15 I will royally bless her provision,
    And give bread to her poor in abundance.
16 Her priests I will clothe with salvation;
    Her saints shall shout for joy.
17 There will I raise up for David
    A dynasty puissant.[2]
I have set mine Anointed a lamp
    That shall never go out.[3]

18 Robes of shame I will put on his foes,
   But on *his* head a glittering crown."

PSALM CXXXIII

Brothers together

B<small>EHOLD</small> ! how good and how pleasant
   Is the dwelling of brethren together !
2 Like precious oil on the head
   That ran down on the beard,
   The beard of Aaron, that flowed
   O'er the head of his robe :
3 Like the dew upon Hermon which falls
   On the mountains of Zion.
   For there hath the Lord ordained blessing—
   Even life that is endless.

PSALM CXXXIV

An Evening Invocation

T<small>HE</small> W<small>ORSHIPPERS'</small> G<small>REETING</small>

A<small>TTEND</small>! Bless the Lord,
   All ye the Lord's servants,
Who stand by night
   In the house of the Lord.
2 Lift your hands to the holy place,
   Bless ye the Lord.

T<small>HE</small> P<small>RIESTS'</small> R<small>ESPONSE</small>

3 The Lord bless thee from Zion,
   Who made heaven and earth.

PSALM CXXXV

PSALM CXXXV

The Divine Power as Revealed in Nature and History

Hallelujah.

PRAISE ye the name of the Lord.
　　Praise the Lord, ye His servants,
2　That stand in the house of the Lord,
　　In the courts of the house of our God.
3　Praise the Lord, for the Lord is good :
　　Sing praise to His name—it is pleasant.
4　The Lord for Himself chose Jacob,
　　Israel as His own special treasure.

5　Yea, I know that Jehovah is great,
　　That our Lord is above all gods.
6　All that He willeth He doeth—
　　In the heavens and on the earth,
　　In the seas and in all the abysses.
7　Clouds He brings up from the ends of the earth,
　　Lightnings He makes for the rain,
　　Wind He brings out of His storehouses.

8　The first-born of Egypt He smote,
　　Man and beast together.
9　Signs and wonders He sent
　　Into thy midst, O Egypt,
　　Upon Pharaoh and all his servants.
10　Many nations He smote,
　　Mighty kings He slew—
11　Sihon, king of the Amorites,
　　Og, king of Bashan,
　　And all the kingdoms of Canaan.

PSALM CXXXVI

12 He gave their land for possession,
    Possession to Israel His people.

13 Thy name, O Lord, is for ever ;
    Thy memorial world without end.
14 For the Lord secures right for His people,
    And takes pity upon His servants.

15 The idols of heathen are silver—
    Made by the hands of men.
16 Mouths have they, but they speak not :
    Eyes have they, but they see not.
17 Ears have they, but they hear not :
    Nor is any breath in their mouth.
18 Like them be those that make them,
    And all that trust in them.[1]

19 House of Israel, *bless the Lord :*
    House of Aaron, *bless the Lord.*
20 House of Levi, *bless the Lord :*
    Ye that fear the Lord, *bless the Lord.*
21 Blest be the Lord out of Zion,
    Who dwelleth in Jerusalem.

    Hallelujah.

PSALM CXXXVI

The Divine Love as revealed in Nature and History

G IVE thanks to the Lord for His goodness :
    For His kindness endureth for ever.
2   Give thanks to the glorious God :
    For His kindness endureth for ever.

PSALM CXXXVI

3 Give thanks to the sovereign Lord :
 For His kindness endureth for ever.

4 To Him who alone does great wonders :
 For His kindness endureth for ever.
5 Whose wisdom created the heavens :
 For His kindness endureth for ever.
6 Who spread forth the earth on the waters :
 For His kindness endureth for ever.
7 Who made great lights :
 For His kindness endureth for ever.
8 The sun to rule over the day :
 For His kindness endureth for ever.
9 Moon and stars to rule over the night :
 For His kindness endureth for ever.

10 Who smote the first-born of Egypt :
 For His kindness endureth for ever.
11 And brought Israel out from their midst :
 For His kindness endureth for ever.
12 With strong hand and outstretched arm :
 For His kindness endureth for ever.
13 Who cut the Red Sea in pieces :
 For His kindness endureth for ever.
14 And brought Israel right through the midst :
 For His kindness endureth for ever.
15 And shook Pharaoh with all his host into the sea :
 For His kindness endureth for ever.

16 Who led His folk through the desert :
 For His kindness endureth for ever.
17 Who smote great kings :
 For His kindness endureth for ever.

PSALM CXXXVII

18 And slew noble kings :
   For His kindness endureth for ever.
19 Sihon, king of the Amorites :
   For His kindness endureth for ever.
20 And Og, king of Bashan :
   For His kindness endureth for ever.
21 Who gave their land for possession :
   For His kindness endureth for ever.
22 Possession to Israel His servant :
   For His kindness endureth for ever.

23 Who remembered our low estate :
   For His kindness endureth for ever.
24 And rescued us from our foes :
   For His kindness endureth for ever.
25 Who giveth to all flesh food :
   For His kindness endureth for ever.
26 Give thanks to the God of heaven:
   For His kindness endureth for ever.

Psalm CXXXVII

By the Waters of Babylon

By the waters of Babylon—there we sat,
   And we wept at the thought of Zion.
2 On the willows therein we hung our harps.
3   For there our captors called for a song :
Our despoilers bade us be merry, saying :
   " Sing us one of the songs of Zion."

PSALM CXXXVIII

4 How can we sing the Lord's song
    In the foreigner's land?
5 If I forget thee, O Jerusalem,
    May this hand of mine wither.
6 May my tongue cleave to my palate,
    If I am unmindful of thee,
  Or forget to exalt Jerusalem
    Above my chief joy.

7 Remember against the Edomites, Lord,
    The day of Jerusalem,
  When they said, " Lay her bare, lay her bare,
    Right down to her very foundation."

8 O daughter of Babylon, thou spoiler,
    Happy be he who shall recompense thee
    For all thou hast done unto us.
9 Happy be he who shall seize and dash
    Thy children against the rocks.

PSALM CXXXVIII

The Constancy of the Divine Care

I will thank Thee, O Lord, with all my heart:
    In the sight of the gods I will sing Thy praise.
2 And, prostrate before Thy holy temple,
    Will praise Thy name for Thy constant love.
    For Thy name Thou hast magnified over all.

PSALM CXXXIX

3 In the day that I called, Thou madest me answer ;
   Thou gavest me room, and didst strengthen my soul.
4 All the kings of the earth shall praise Thee, O Lord,
   When they shall have heard the words Thou hast uttered ;
5 And they shall sing of the ways of the Lord,
   And tell of the Lord's transcendent glory.
6 For, high though the Lord is, He looks on the lowly,
   And strikes down the haughty from far away.

7 Though my way be distressful, yet Thou dost preserve me :
   Thou layest Thine hand on mine angry foes,
   And Thy right hand giveth me victory.
8 The Lord will accomplish all that which concerns me.
   Thy kindness, O Lord, endureth for ever.
   O do not abandon the work of Thy hands.

PSALM CXXXIX

The Ever-Present God

O LORD, Thou searchest and knowest me;
2   When I sit, when I rise—Thou knowest it,
   Thou perceivest my thoughts from afar.

3 When I walk, when I lie—Thou siftest it,
   Familiar with all my ways.
4 There is not a word on my tongue,
   But see ! Lord, Thou knowest it all.

PSALM CXXXIX

5 Behind and before Thou besettest me,
    Upon me Thou layest Thine hand.
6 'Tis too wonderful for me to know—
    Too lofty—I cannot attain it.

7 Whither shall I go from Thy spirit?
    Or whither shall I flee from Thy face?
8 If I climb up to heaven, Thou art there:
    Or make Sheol my bed, Thou art there.

9 If I lift up the wings of the morning
    And fly to the end of the sea,
10 There also Thy hand would grasp me,
    And Thy right hand take hold of me.

11 If I say, " Let the darkness cover me,
    And night be the light about me,"
12 The dark were no dark for Thee,
    But night would be light as the day.

13 For Thou didst prepare my reins;[1]
    In my mother's womb Thou didst weave me.
14 I give thee praise for my fashioning—
    So awful, so wonderful.
    Thy works are wonderful.

    Thou knewest me right well;
15   My bones were not hidden from Thee,
    When I was made in secret,
    And woven in the depths of the earth.

PSALM CXL

16 Thine eyes saw all my days :
  They stood on Thy book every one—
  Written down, before they were fashioned,
  While none of them yet was mine.

17 But how far, O God, beyond measure
  Are Thy thoughts ! how mighty their sum !
18 Should I count, they are more than the sand.
  When I wake, I am still with Thee.

19 Wilt Thou slay the wicked, O God !
  And remove from me men of blood,
20 Who maliciously defy Thee
  And take Thy name in vain.

21 Do I not hate those that hate Thee, Lord ?
  Do I not loathe those that resist Thee ?
22 With perfect hatred I hate them,
  I count them mine enemies.

23 Search me, O God, know my heart :
  Try me, and know my thoughts,
24 And see if guile be in me ;
  And lead me in the way everlasting.

PSALM CXL

A Prayer for Preservation

Rescue me, Lord, from the evil man ;
  From the man of violence guard Thou me—
2 From those who plot evil in their heart,
  And stir up war continually :
3 Who make their tongue as sharp as a serpent's,
  And under whose lips is the poison of adders.

PSALM CXL

4 Preserve me, O Lord, from the hands of the wicked,
    From the man of violence guard Thou me—
    From those who are plotting to trip up my feet.
5 The proud have hidden a trap for me,
    Cords they have spread as a net for my feet:
    Snares they have set at the side of my track.

6 I have said to the Lord, " My God art Thou;
    Give ear, O Lord, to my loud supplication.
7 O Jehovah my Lord, my Saviour mighty,
    Thou didst cover my head in the day of battle.
8 Grant not, O Lord, the desires of the wicked;
    And what they have purposed, promote Thou not."

9 Let them not lift up their heads against me.
    May the mischief they prate bring themselves to destruction,
10 May He rain upon them coals of fire,
    May He smite them down swiftly, to rise no more.
11 No place in the land may there be for the slanderer:
    May the violent be hunted from sorrow to sorrow.

12 I know that the Lord will do right by the weak,
    And will execute justice for those that are needy.
13 Surely the righteous shall praise Thy name,
    And they that are upright shall dwell in Thy presence.

PSALM CXLI

PSALM CXLI

A Prayer for Protection from Persecutors

O Lord, I call to Thee : hasten to me,
   Give ear to my voice, when I call unto Thee.
2 Let my prayer be presented as incense before Thee,
   And mine uplifted hands as the evening meal-offering.

3 Set, O Lord, a watch on my mouth,
   Put Thou a guard on the door of my lips.
4 Incline not my heart to an evil matter,
   To busy myself in deeds of wickedness.
   I hate such men as are workers of evil :
   Never may I partake of their dainties.

5 A wound [1] or reproof from a good man in kindness
   Is oil which my head shall never refuse.
   In their misfortune my prayer is still with them.

6 Abandoned they are to the hands of their judges :
   They shall learn that the word of the Lord is true.

7 Like stones on a country road cleft and broken
   So lie our bones scattered for Death [2] to devour.
8 But mine eyes are turned towards Thee, O Lord.
   Do not pour out my life, for in Thee I take refuge.
9 Keep Thou me safe from the trap they have laid for me,
   Yea, from the snares of the workers of trouble.
10 Into their own nets let wicked men fall ;
   While, as for me, I shall pass by rejoicing.

PSALM CXLII

PSALM CXLII

A Prayer for Deliverance from Persecutors

L OUDLY I cry to the Lord :
To the Lord I make loud supplication,
2 Pouring my plaint before Him,
Telling my trouble before Him.

3 When my spirit is faint within me,
My path is known unto Thee.
In the way I am wont to walk in,
They have hidden a trap for me.

4 I look to the right and the left ;
But not a friend have I.
No place of refuge is left me,
Not a man to care for me.

5 So I cry unto Thee, O Lord :
I say, " My refuge art Thou,
In the land of the living my portion."

6 Attend to my piercing cry,
For very weak am I.
Save me from those who pursue me,
For they are too strong for me.

7 Bring Thou me out of the dungeon,
That I may give thanks to Thy name,
For the righteous are patiently waiting
Till Thou showest Thy bounty to me.

PSALM CXLIII

PSALM CXLIII

A Prayer for Deliverance and Guidance

Hearken, O Lord, to my prayer;
    Give ear to my supplication.
In Thy faithfulness give me answer,
    And in Thy righteousness.
2 With Thy servant O enter Thou not into judgment,
    For in Thy sight can no man alive be justified.

3 For the enemy persecutes me,
    Crushing my life to the ground,
Making me dwell in the darkness,
    As those that have long been dead.
4 My spirit is faint within me,
    My heart is bewildered within me.

5 I remember the days of old,
    And brood over all Thou hast done,
Musing on all that Thy hands have wrought.
6   I spread out my hands unto Thee:
My soul thirsteth for Thee,
    Even as a weary land.

7 Answer me speedily, Lord,
    Because my spirit is spent.
Hide not Thy face from me,
    Else become I like them that go down to the pit.
8 Make me hear Thy love in the morning,
    For my confidence is in Thee.
Teach me the way I should go:
    For to Thee I lift up my soul.

PSALM CXLIV

9 Save me, O Lord, from my foes :
      For to Thee I have fled for refuge.
10 Teach me to do Thy will,
      For Thou Thyself art my God.
   Guide me by Thy good spirit,
      O Lord, on a way that is smooth.

11 Spare me for Thy name's sake,
      Bring me out of distress in Thy faithfulness.
12 In Thy kindness extinguish mine enemies,
      And all those that vex me destroy ;
      For I am Thy servant.

PSALM CXLIV, 1—11

The Warrior's Stay

BLEST be the Lord my Rock,
      Who teacheth my hands to war
   And my fingers to fight.
2 My Rock and my Fortress,
      My Tower, my Deliverer,
   My Shield, behind whom I take refuge,
      Who lays nations low at my feet.

3 O Lord, what is man that Thou carest for him,
      Or the son of man, that Thou thinkest of him ?
4 Man is like unto a breath,
      His days as a shadow that passeth.

5 O Lord, bow Thy heavens and come down :
      Touch Thou the hills, that they smoke.
6 Flash forth lightning and scatter them,
      Thine arrows send forth and confound them.

PSALM CXLIV

7 Stretch out Thy hand from on high;
    Pluck me out of the mighty waters,
    Out of the hand of the aliens,
8 *Who speak with the mouth of falsehood,*
    And lift their right hand to swear lies.

9 O God, a new song I would sing Thee,
    On a ten-stringëd harp make Thee music.
10 For to kings Thou givest the victory,
    And David Thy servant Thou savest.
11 From the cruel sword O snatch me,
    Rescue me from the hand of the aliens,
    Who speak with the mouth of falsehood,
    And lift their right hand to swear lies.

PSALM CXLIV, 12—15

The Prosperity of Jehovah's People

MAY our sons in their youth
    Be as plants well trained:
Our daughters like cornices
    Carved as in palaces.

13 May our garners be bursting
    With produce of all kinds.
In the fields may our sheep bear
    By thousands and ten thousands.

14 May no misfortune
    Or loss betide:
Be no cry of distress
    In our broad open spaces.[1]

PSALM CXLV

15 Happy the people
   That fares thus well:
16 And thus fares the people
   Whose God is Jehovah.

PSALM CXLV [1]

The Gracious Kingdom Everlasting

I WILL exalt thee, my God, O King:
   I will bless Thy name for ever and ever.
2 I will bless Thee every day:
   I will praise Thy name for ever and ever.

3 Great is the Lord and worthy all praise,
   His greatness is unsearchable.
4 One age to another shall praise Thy deeds,
   Declaring the mighty things Thou hast done.

5 Of Thy glorious majesty they shall tell,
   And I will muse of Thy manifold wonders.
6 Of the might of Thy terrible acts they shall speak,
   And the tale of Thy great deeds I will tell.

7 The fame of Thine abundant goodness
   And righteousness they shall pour forth in song.
8 The Lord is full of grace and pity,
   Patient and rich in loving-kindness.

9 The Lord is good to all the world,
   And His pity is over all things that He made.
10 All Thy works give Thee thanks, O Lord,
   And Thou art blessed of those that love Thee.

PSALM CXLV

11 They shall speak of Thy glorious kingdom,
   And of Thy might shall they discourse,
12 Making known unto men His mighty acts,
   And the glorious majesty of His kingdom.

13 Thine is a kingdom that lives through all ages :
   Through all generations extends Thy dominion.
   The Lord is faithful in all that He promises,
   Gracious is He in all that He does.²

14 The Lord upholdeth all that fall ;
   He lifteth up all that are bowĕd down.
15 The eyes of all look in hope unto Thee,
   And Thou dost give them their food in due season.

16 Thou Thyself dost open Thine hand,
   And fill with Thy favour all things that live.
17 The Lord is righteous in all His ways,
   Gracious is He in all that He does.

18 The Lord is nigh unto all that call Him,
   To all that call upon Him in truth.
19 He will do the pleasure of those that fear Him ;
   Their cry for help He will hear and save them.

20 The Lord is the keeper of all that love Him,
   But all the wicked will He destroy.
21 My mouth shall utter the praise of the Lord,
   And all flesh shall bless His holy name
      World without end.

PSALM CXLVI

Psalm CXLVI
The Great Protector

O SOUL of mine, praise the Lord.
 I will praise the Lord, while I live;
I will sing to my God, while I am.

3 Put not your trust in princes—
 Mortal men, in whom is no help.
4 When their breath goes out,
 They go back to the dust:
On that very day
 Their purposes perish.
5 Happy he whose help
 Is the God of Jacob:
Whose hope is set
 On the Lord his God,
6 The Creator of heaven and earth,
 The sea, and all that is in them.

He remaineth eternally loyal.
7 For the wronged He executes justice;
He giveth bread to the hungry;
 The Lord releaseth the prisoners.
8 The Lord giveth sight to the blind:
 The Lord raiseth them that are bowed.
The Lord loveth the righteous.
9 The Lord preserveth the stranger,
Upholdeth the widow and orphan,
 But the wicked He leads to disaster.

10 The Lord shall reign for ever,
 Thy God, O Zion, to all generations.

Hallelujah.

PSALM CXLVII

PSALM CXLVII

The Divine Love and Power as Revealed in Nature

Hallelujah.

It is good to sing praise to our God,
 For praise is sweet and seemly.
2 The Lord doth build up Jerusalem,
 The outcasts of Israel He gathers.
3 He healeth the broken in heart,
 And bindeth up their wounds.
4 He counteth the numberless stars,
 He giveth names to them all.
5 Great is our Lord, rich in power,
 And measureless is His wisdom.
6 The Lord lifteth up the down-trodden,
 The wicked He brings to the ground.

7 Sing songs of thanks to the Lord,
 And play on the lyre to our God.
8 For He covers the sky with clouds,
 He prepareth rain for the earth,
 Maketh grass to grow on the mountains,
 And herbs for the servants of man.[1]
9 He giveth the cattle their food—
 The young ravens when they cry.
10 His pleasure is not in the strength of the (war-) horse,
 His joy is not in the (swift) feet of men;
11 But the Lord hath His pleasure in them that fear Him,
 In them that wait for His kindness.

PSALM CXLVIII

12 Praise the Lord, then, O Jerusalem:
   Sing praise to thy God, O Zion.
13 For He strengthens the bars of thy gates,
   And blesseth thy children within thee.
14 He bringeth peace to thy borders,
   And choicest of wheat in abundance.
15 He sends His command to the earth:
   His word runneth very swiftly.
16 Snow He giveth like wool,
   Frost He scatters like ashes.
17 He casts forth His ice like morsels:
   Who can stand before His cold?
18 He sends forth His word, and melts them:
   His wind blows—the waters flow.

19 He declareth His word unto Jacob,
   His statutes and judgments to Israel.
20 With no other folk hath He dealt so,
   Or brought to their knowledge His judgments.

Hallelujah.

PSALM CXLVIII

The Universal Chorus of Praise

PRAISE the Lord from the heavens,
   Praise Him in the heights.
2 Praise Him, all His angels;
   Praise him, all His hosts.

PSALM CXLVIII

3 Praise Him, sun and moon ;
    Praise Him, all stars of light.
4 Praise Him, ye highest heavens,
    And ye waters above the heavens.

5 Let them praise the name of the Lord,
    For at His command they were made.
6 And He fixed them for ever and ever
    By a law which they dare not transgress.

7 Praise the Lord from the earth :
    Ye depths, with your monsters, all.
8 Fire, hail, snow and ice,
    And stormy wind doing His word.

9 All ye mountains and hills,
    All ye fruit trees and cedars,
10 All ye wild beasts and tame,
    Creeping things, birds on the wing.

11 All ye kings and nations of earth ;
    All ye princes and judges of earth :
12 Young men and maidens together,
    Old men and striplings together.

13 Let them praise the name of the Lord,
    For His name alone is exalted.
  Over heaven and earth is His glory.
14 He hath lifted His people to honour.
  Wherefore this chorus of praise from His saints,
    From Israel, the people who stand in His fellowship.

Hallelujah.

PSALM CXLIX

Song of Victory

Hallelujah.

SING to the Lord a new song,
    Sound His praise where the faithful are gathered.
2 Let Israel rejoice in his Maker,
    Sons of Zion exult in their King.
3 Let them praise His name in the dance,
    Making music with lyre and with timbrel.

4 For the Lord doth delight in His people,
    Adorning the humble with victory.
5 Let the faithful exult and extol Him
    With glad ringing cries at the temple [1]—
6 High praises of God in their mouth,
    And a two-edgëd sword in their hand:

7 On the heathen to execute vengeance,
    And chastisement sore on the nations—
8 Binding their kings with chains,
    And their nobles with fetters of iron:
9 To execute on them the doom that is written.
    For all His saints that is glory indeed.

Hallelujah.

PSALM CL

Hallelujah

Hallelujah.

Praise ye God in His holy place.
  Praise ye Him in His firmament mighty.
2 Praise ye Him for His deeds of power;
  Praise ye Him for His manifold greatness.

3 Praise Him with blast of horn;
  Praise Him with harp and lyre.
4 Praise Him with timbrel and dance;
  Praise Him with strings and with pipe.
5 Praise Him with sounding cymbals,
  Praise Him with clashing cymbals.
6 Let all that hath breath praise the Lord.

Hallelujah.

NOTES

NOTES

LXX. stands for the Septuagint, or Greek version of the Old Testament.

I. 4   So LXX.
II. 2   *I.e.*, king.
   11   This translation rests on a probable rearrangement of the consonants.
IV. 6   Echo of the priestly blessing in Num. vi. 24—26.
VII. 14   *I.e.*, the wicked.
VIII. 1   Or possibly (by a skilful emendation of **Duhm's**) "*I would sing of* Thy majesty, etc., with the lisping . . ."
IX.   An alphabetical arrangement, which, though considerably disturbed, runs through Pss. IX. and X., appears to show that originally, as in LXX., these two psalms constituted one. The text is in many places uncertain and the meaning, esp. in Ps. X., often obscure.
XI. 4   So original text of LXX.
   6   Lit. " the portion *of their cup* "—a figure, in frequent use, drawn from a meal or banquet.
XIV.   This ps. is repeated (with modifications) in Ps. LIII.
   5   On some occasion which we have now no means of discovering.
XVI. 5   Lit. " the share of my portion and my cup "—two figures drawn from the allotment of land and the distribution of drink at a meal (*cf.* XI. 6).
   10   Lit. " Sheol," *i.e.*, the underworld. The word occurs several times in the Psalter (*cf.* XLIX. 14, etc.).
XVII. 4*f.*   The translation of these verses rests on an emended text.
   14   This verse is very difficult and obscure.
XVIII.   This ps. recurs in 2 Sam. XXII.
   2   This and the next word are lit. " the horn of my salvation "—the horn being a symbol of strength.

NOTES

XVIII. 2 Last line added from 2 Sam. XXII. 3.
    35 A.V. and R.V. render "Thy gentleness hath made me great." But text and meaning are uncertain.

XIX. 7 Practically=the Pentateuch. The other terms, which appear again in the cognate Ps. CXIX., are synonyms for the Law, in some of its aspects. The charge—lit. " testimony "—is the Law as *attesting* God's will and man's duty (*v.* 7). The behests or " precepts " (*v.* 8) are its detailed injunctions : the " judgments " (*v.* 9) are its decisions, ordinances.

XXI. Or perhaps upon a Coronation Anniversary.
    9 " In His wrath He shall swallow them up,
        And the fire shall devour them."
These lines appear to have been added to the original psalm.

XXII. 20 Lit. "mine only one," *i.e.*, my unique, priceless possession=my life (soul).
    21 The text reads : "Thou hast answered me," and this may be the transition to the glad mood of the second part of the psalm. But it is very doubtful whether this is the original text.

XXIV. 8 The question asked by the warders at the gate is answered by the approaching procession.

XXV. An alphabetic psalm—the verses beginning with successive letters of the Hebrew alphabet. In such psalms, as a rule, there is no rigorous sequence of thought.

XXVII. 6 So LXX.

XXIX. 1 Lit. "Sons of the gods," *i.e.*, divine beings, angels, conceived as dwelling in the sky and watching the storm.
    6 *I.e.*, Hermon.

XXXI. 1*f.* Repeated in LXXI. 1—3.

XXXIV. An alphabetic psalm, of the same type as Ps. XXV.
    10 This translation, which involves only a difference in vowels, offers a more relevant contrast than the ordinary translation with its "young lions." Besides, the Old Testament attitude to the animals is, as a rule, more kindly : *cf.* Pss. CIV. 21, CXLVII. 9.
    16 The context (*cf. v.* 17) shows that *vv.* 15 and 16 ought to be transposed. The alphabetic order which this involves is also found elsewhere.

NOTES

XXXV. 10 Lit. " bones," *i.e.*, body, contrasted with soul in *v.* 9.
12 The meaning is quite uncertain.
17 *Cf.* XXII. 20.
XXXVI. 2 The meaning is extremely obscure.
6 Lit. " the mountains of God."
12 Apparently in vision.
XXXVII. An alphabetic psalm (*cf.* XXV.)—every second verse beginning with successive letters of the Hebrew alphabet.
28 This reading, presupposed by LXX., is demanded by the alphabetic order.
XXXVIII. 20 The last couplet is added from LXX.
XL. 6 Lit. "ears hast Thou dug (*i.e.*, bored) for me "—ears without which the word to be obeyed could not be heard.
13 *Vv.* 13—17=Ps. LXX. with slight differences.
XLIV. 2 *I.e.*, the fathers.
XLVI. 3 The artistic structure of this psalm renders it highly probable that the refrain (*cf. vv.* 7 and 11) should be here inserted.
10 In this verse Jehovah speaks.
XLVII. 9 Apparently the princes.
XLVIII. 2 Lit. " (on) the sides of the north "—an apparent allusion to the mythical home of the gods on some sacred northern mountain (*cf.* Greek Olympus).
XLIX. 4 The proverb is apparently the refrain (*cf. vv.* 12 and 20) which should perhaps be added here.
11 *Cf.* Alexandria, after Alexander, etc.
14 The text of this verse is in great confusion, and the detailed meaning is exceedingly obscure, though the general sense is clear enough.
L. 14 Or " thanksgiving." Possibly the gratitude is itself the offering, though the material offering appears to be considered as not in itself objectionable (*cf. v.* 8).
LI. 6 The word is rare and the meaning not quite certain.
LIII.=XIV. (with modifications).
LV. 19 A difficult line: but "changes" (A.V., R.V.) is unsatisfactory and improbable.
LVI. 8 This line is perhaps a later explanatory addition.
LVII. 3 The line " He will send forth His kindness and faithfulness " may have been added to explain the first line of the verse.

NOTES

LVII. 7 *Vv.* 7—11 reappear (with slight differences) in CVIII. 1—5.
LVIII. 9 The text and detail of this verse are unusually difficult and obscure.
LIX. 12 By emendation: lit. "abandon them, O Lord, to the (consequences of the) sin of their mouth."
LX. 4 *I.e.,* of the enemy.
  5 *Vv.* 5—12 reappear in CVIII. 6—13.
  8 These are expressions of contempt.
LXIV. 6 Emended text.
LXVIII. 6 Lit. " in a parched land."
  11 Described here implicitly as an oracle.
  14 A very obscure passage. Possibly the precious stones are here conceived as glistening on the feathers like snow on the trees of Zalmon (a mountain near Shechem—Judges ix. 48).
  18 Probably Mount Zion.
  27 The meaning of the word rendered " their council " in A.V. and R.V. is very uncertain.
  30 Apparently Egypt.
  30 The greater and the smaller nations.
  30 The meaning of this clause is hopelessly obscure
  31 Meaning uncertain.
LXX. =Ps. XL. 13—17 (with slight differences).
LXXI. 1—3=Ps. XXXI. 1*f.* (with slight differences).
LXXIII. 10 The meaning of this verse is very obscure.
  17 Lit. " sanctuaries." Some take this as=the great sanctuary, *i.e.,* the temple ; others explain it as " holy mysteries." Probably the reference is primarily to the temple, but it doubtless carries also with it the idea of divine things, which a visit to the temple would suggest to the mind of a profound and devout worshipper. It would thus have a mystic flavour, and may be not unfairly rendered as in the translation.
LXXIV. 13 *Vv.* 13—17: *cf.* LXXXIX. 9—12.
  20 *I.e.,* heathen lands ; or it may be " dark places of *the land* "— caves where the persecuted sought shelter.
LXXV. 2*f.* God speaks.
  5 *I.e.,* God—so LXX. (instead of " neck " of the Hebrew text).

NOTES

LXXV. 6 Apparently for *south* and *north*. "Mountains" translates the words rendered in A.V. by "promotion" and in R.V. by "lifting up."

LXXVI. 2 *I.e.*, Jerusalem.
    10 The first line rests on a probable emendation, the second on LXX.

LXXVIII. 61 *I.e.*, the glorious and mighty ark.
    63 The fire of war.
    69 *I.e.*, the heavenly heights.

LXXX. 17 Lit. "Let Thy hand be upon the man of Thy right hand, upon the son of man whom Thou madest strong for Thyself." The context shows that the meaning is as given in the translation. The "man" and the "son of man" are Israel.

LXXXII. 7 By a very simple emendation. The Hebrew text means "like a (mortal) prince."

LXXXIII. 3 Lit.="Thy treasured ones."
    8 *I.e.*, The Moabites and Ammonites (Gen. xix. 37*f.*).
    11 *Cf.* Judges viii. 3, 5.

LXXXIV. 6 Lit. the valley of *Baca*, the balsam-tree, which grew chiefly on arid soil. But the word closely resembles the word for "weeping" and was so taken by many ancient translators. There is possibly here, as often in Hebrew, a word-play.
    7 So LXX.

LXXXV. 8 So LXX.

LXXXVII. 4 Lit. Rahab (*cf.* LXXXIX. 10; Ezek. XXIX. 3).
    5*a* So LXX.
    7 *I.e.*, of salvation.

LXXXVIII. 11 The place of destruction or ruin: synonymous with or part of, Sheol (the underworld).

LXXXIX. 5 The "holy ones" are the angels.
    9—12 *Cf.* LXXIV. 13—17. Rahab (*v.* 10), mythical sea-monster.
    15 The festal shout.
    17 "Thou wilt lift up *our horn*." The horn is a common figure in the Psalter for strength and triumph.
    19 Probably Nathan (*cf.* 2 Sam. vii.); possibly David.
    24 *Cf. v.* 17.

NOTES

LXXXIX. 42 Lit. " Thou hast exalted the right hand of his adversaries."
XCI. 6 So LXX.
  14—16 In these verses Jehovah speaks.
XCII. 10 Lit. " Thou dost lift up my horn like that of a wild ox." *Cf.* LXXXIX. 17.
XCV. 11 Or " resting-place," *i.e.*, Canaan.
XCVI. 7—9 *Cf.* Ps. XXIX. 1*f.*
  11—13 *Cf.* Ps. XCVIII. 7—9.
XCVIII. 7—9. *Cf.* Ps. XCVI. 11—13.
CIII. 5 The precise meaning is uncertain.
  16 *I.e.*, the hot wind, which withers it.
CIV. 14 *I.e.*, the beasts (= "cattle" of first line).
  26 By a simple and probable change for "ships," which does not well suit the context : nor would *v.* 27 be appropriate to ships.
CVII. 40 A quotation from Job xii. 21a and 24b.
  42 From Job xxii. 19a and v. 16b.
CVIII. 1—5=LVII. 7—11.
  6—13=LX. 5—12.
CXI. and CXII. are both alphabetic psalms, in which each new line, *i.e.*, half verse, begins with a succeeding letter of the alphabet.
CXIV. 1 In the Greek sense of "speaking a strange language."
  2 Lit. " Judah became a holy thing to Him," *i.e.*, a thing set apart.
  2 Israel is here practically synonymous with Judah as often in post-exilic literature.
CXV. 4—8 Reappears in CXXXV. 15—18.
CXVI. 3 Hardly too strong for the original " Sheol."
  15 The single Hebrew word here used conveys both meanings.
CXIX. This is an alphabetic psalm in which each of the eight verses constituting a stanza begins with the same letter. Throughout the psalm changes are rung on the words commandments, precepts, judgments or ordinances, testimonies or charges, statutes, saying, and word or words, which are all practically synonymous with the Law, *i.e.*, the Pentateuch. See note on Ps. XIX. 7.
  48 Almost as if in worship.
CXXV. 3 Israel's land.

NOTES

CXXVI. 4 The region south of Judah, mostly arid and barren except in the rainy season.

CXXXII. 6 *I.e.*, Kirjath-jearim (city of thickets). Ephrathah appears to be the district in which this town lay. For the incident alluded to here, *cf.* 1 Sam. vii. 1*f*; 2 Sam. vi. 2—4.

17 Lit "a horn"—a familiar figure: *cf.* XVIII. 2; LXXXIX. 17.

17 Added to explain the figure of the lamp, as symbolizing the perpetuity of the dynasty.

CXXXV. 15—18. Reappears in CXV. 4—8.

CXXXIX. 13 Representative of the inner organs of the body.

CXLI. 5 The text in *vv.* 5 and 6, esp. 6, is desperate, and the meaning and connection altogether obscure.

7 Lit. "Sheol," *i.e.*, the underworld.

CXLIV. 14 The detail of this verse is very obscure.

CXLV. An alphabetic psalm of the type of Ps. XXV.

13 The last two lines are added from LXX. and demanded by the alphabetic scheme.

CXLVII. 8 This line appears in LXX. This line and the previous one come from Ps. CIV. 14.

CXLIX. 5 The text which reads "on their beds" seems to stand in need of some such emendation. (So Briggs.)

THE PSALMS ARRANGED TOPICALLY

No topical arrangement of the Psalms can be very satisfactory. Most of them are expressions of emotion, and naturally there are frequent transitions from one mood to another. Thanksgiving and petition, reflection and imprecation, are so subtly interwoven into the texture of many a psalm, that not a few of them could find an appropriate place within several groups. But the following classification, which I have drawn in the main from my *Messages of the Psalmists* (James Clarke & Co., London; Charles Scribner's Sons, New York), may be found useful.

PSALMS OF ADORATION

Adoration of God as revealed in Nature: VIII., XIX. 1—6, XXIX., CIV.
Adoration of Jehovah for His love to His people: XXXIII., CIII., CXI., CXIII., CXV., CXVII., CXLVII.
Adoration of Jehovah's glorious Kingdom: CXLV., CXLVI.
Nature's Call to Universal Praise: CXLVIII., CL.

PSALMS CONCERNING JEHOVAH'S UNIVERSAL REIGN

XLVII., LXXXVII., XCIII., XCV., XCVI., XCVII., XCVIII., XCIX., C.

PSALMS CONCERNING THE KING

His marriage: XLV.
Prayers for his welfare and success: XX., XXI., LXI., LXIII.
His character: LXXII, CI.
His dominion: II., XVIII., CX.
Yearning for the Messianic King: LXXXIX., CXXXII.

PSALMS OF REFLECTION

On the Moral order of the World: IX., X., XI., XIV., XXXVI., XXXVII., XXXIX., XLIX., LII., LIII., LXII., LXXIII., LXXV., LXXXII., XC., XCII., XCIV.

THE PSALMS ARRANGED TOPICALLY

On Divine Providence: XVI., XXIII., XXXIV., XCI., CXII., CXXI., CXXV., CXXVII., CXXVIII., CXXXIII., CXXXIX., CXLIV., 12—15.
On the value of Scripture: I., XIX. 7—14, CXIX.
On the Nature of the Ideal Man: XV., XXIV. 1—6, L.

PSALMS OF THANKSGIVING

A general thanksgiving: CVII.
For victory or deliverance from national distress: XXX., XL., XLVI., XLVIII., LXV., LXVI., LXVII., LXVIII., LXXVI., CXVI., CXVIII., CXXIV., CXXVI., CXXIX., CXXXVIII., CXLIV. 1—11, CXLIX.

PSALMS IN CELEBRATION OF WORSHIP

V., XXIV. 7—10, XXVI., XXVII., XLII., XLIII., LXXXIV., CXXII., CXXXIV.

HISTORICAL PSALMS

Emphasizing the unfaithfulness of the people: LXXVIII., LXXXI., CVI.
Emphasizing the love or power of God: CV., CXIV., CXXXV., CXXXVI.

IMPRECATORY PSALMS

LVIII., LIX., LXIX., LXXXIII., CIX., CXXXVII.

PENITENTIAL PSALMS

VI., XXXII., XXXVIII., LI., CII., CXXX., CXLIII.

PSALMS OF PETITION

For deliverance, preservation, or restoration: III., IV., VII., XII., XIII., XVII., XXV., XXXI., XXXV., XLI., XLIV., LIV., LV., LX., LXIV., LXXI., LXXIV., LXXVII., LXXIX., LXXX., LXXXV., LXXXVI., LXXXVIII., CXX., CXXIII., CXXXI., CXL., CXLI., CXLII.
Answered prayers: VI., XXII., XXVIII., XXX., XXXI., LVI., LVII.

ALPHABETIC PSALMS

IX., X., XXV., XXXIV., XXXVII, CXI., CXII., CXIX., CXLV.

BIBLIOGRAPHY

A LIST of books of reference will be found on pp. 320—329 of my *Messages of the Psalmists* (James Clarke & Co., London : Charles Scribner's Sons, New York). This list includes books on Hebrew poetry, commentaries, translations, introductions, books dealing with special problems of the Psalter, the theology of the Psalter, and the use of the Psalms in the Christian Church.

In addition to these fall to be mentioned the two-volume commentary in the *Century Bible;* Gunkel, *Ausgewählte Psalmen;* Kittel, *Die Psalmen,* in *Kommentar zum Alten Testament;* Driver, *Studies in the Psalms; The Psalms of Israel* (Lectures delivered in St. Patrick's Cathedral, 1903, Brown, Langham & Co.); Oesterley, *Life, Death and Immortality* (Studies in the Psalms); John Ker, *The Psalms in History and Biography;* Prothero, *The Psalms in Human Life;* W. G. Jordan, *Religion in Song* (James Clarke & Co., 1916 : in their *Humanism of the Bible* series).

Besides the translations of the Psalter to be found in the Commentaries of Ewald, Delitzsch, Perowne, King, Cheyne and Wellhausen, special mention should be made of Cheyne's translation (Kegan Paul, Trench, 1884), Driver's *Parallel Psalter* (Oxford), and C. F. Kent in vol. v. of his *Student's Old Testament.* Professor A. R. Gordon offers skilful and happy translations of particular psalms in his *Poets of the Old Testament* (Hodder and Stoughton), and a useful edition of the *Vulgate Psalter* has been prepared by A. B. Macaulay and James Brebner (Dent).

A CATALOGUE OF THEOLOGICAL, ILLUSTRATED AND GENERAL BOOKS PUBLISHED BY JAMES CLARKE & CO., 13 & 14, FLEET STREET, LONDON, E.C.

CLASSIFIED ACCORDING TO PRICES,
WITH INDEX OF TITLES AND AUTHORS AT THE END.

New Books and New Editions Marked with an Asterisk.

THE "WORSHIP-SONG" SERIES.

Edited by W. GARRETT HORDER

Including

WORSHIP SONG (803 Hymns).
PSALMS AND CANTICLES (150).
ANTHEMS, ANCIENT AND MODERN (130).

For full particulars as to prices, etc., see separate Catalogue, which will be sent post free on application.

JAMES CLARKE AND CO.'S CATALOGUE 3

12/6 net

The Marprelate Tracts. By WILLIAM PIERCE, Author of "An Historical Introduction to the Marprelate Tracts." Demy 8vo, cloth, 12s. 6d. net.

The "Tracts" reprinted in this volume are among the most famous in history. They were read eagerly everywhere in England, from the Court to the country farmhouse, when they appeared at the end of the sixteenth century. They are racy in style, and the unknown author, "Martin Marprelate," brings great resources of wit, humour and argument to bear in his tremendous onslaught upon the Bishops. Mr. Pierce gives a very scholarly edition of the tracts, enriched by many valuable and illuminating notes.

Dr. JAMES MOFFATT, in *The British Weekly*, says :—" Will rank as a standard edition. It is not possible to convey any idea of the historical scholarship and research which have gone to the making of this book, but Mr. Pierce will have his reward in the consciousness of serving the cause of religious liberty; and in the gratification of those who have to study the religious situation of England during the sixteenth century. . . . Their historical importance is considerable."

" One of the most valuable contributions to our history ever made."
Principal W. B. SELBIE.

10/6 net

THE POLYCHROME BIBLE

A New English Translation of the Books of the Bible. Printed in various colours, showing at a glance the composite nature and the different sources of the Books. With many Notes and Illustrations from Ancient Monuments, &c. Each volume is the work of an eminent Biblical scholar of Europe or America, and the whole work is under the general editorship of PAUL HAUPT, of Johns Hopkins University, Baltimore, assisted by HORACE HOWARD FURNESS.

The Book of Ezekiel. Translated by the Rev. C. H. TOY, D.D., LL.D., Professor of Hebrew and other Oriental Languages, and Lecturer on Biblical Literature in Harvard University. 208 pp. (89 pp. translation and 119 pp. notes). With nine full-page Illustrations (including a Map of Western Asia) and 102 Illustrations in the Notes. Cloth, gilt top, 10s. 6d. net.

For other Volumes in this Series see page 4.

JAMES CLARKE AND CO.'S

7/6 net

A Chronicle of the Archbishops of Canterbury. By A. E. McKilliam, M.A. Demy 8vo. Photogravure Portrait and 16 illustrations. Cloth boards, gilt top, 7s. 6d. net.

Christ's Vision of the Kingdom of Heaven. By James Stirling. Author of "The Stewardship of Life," "Finders of the Way," etc. Demy 8vo. Cloth boards, gilt top, 7s. 6d. net.

Hampstead: Its Historic Houses; Its Literary and Artistic Associations. By Anna Maxwell. Large foolscap 4to. Cloth boards, gilt top. Four illustrations in colour and 32 full-page illustrations. 7s. 6d. net.

7/6

A History of the United States. By John Fiske, Litt.D., LL.D. For Schools. With Topical Analysis, Suggestive Questions and Directions for Teachers, by Frank Alpine Hill, Litt.D., formerly Headmaster of the English High School in Cambridge, and later of the Mechanic Arts High School in Boston. With 180 Illustrations and 39 Maps. Crown 8vo, half leather, gilt top, 7s. 6d.

6/- net

THE POLYCHROME BIBLE

The Book of Joshua. Translated by the Rev. W. H. Bennett, M.A., Litt.D., Principal of Lancashire Independent College, Manchester, formerly Fellow of St. John's College, Cambridge. 94 pp., printed in nine colours (43 pp. translation and 51 pp. notes, including an illustrated Excursus on the Tel-el-Amarna Tablets and a List of Geographical Names). Eleven full-page Illustrations (one in colours) and 25 Illustrations in the Notes. Cloth, gilt top, 6s. net.

The Book of Judges. Translated with Notes, by G. F. Moore, D.D., Professor of Hebrew in Andover Theological Seminary. 98 pp., printed in seven colours (42 pp. translation, 56 pp. notes). Seven full-page Illustrations (including a Map in colours and 20 Illustrations in the Notes). Cloth, gilt top, price 6s. net.

For other Volumes in this Series see page 3.

6/- net (continued)

*The Meaning and Value of Mysticism. By E. HERMANN, Author of "Eucken and Bergson." Demy 8vo, cloth boards, gilt top, 6s. net.

The Person of Christ in Modern Thought. By E. DIGGES LA TOUCHE, M.A., Litt.D. Donnellan Lecturer 1911-1912, Author of "Christian Certitude," etc. Demy 8vo, cloth boards, gilt top, 6s. net.

"A full and exhaustive treatment. . . Dr. Digges La Touche has produced a valuable introduction to the study of Christological speculation of the Modern Period, as well as an apologia for the less fashionable confessional Christology of the sixteenth century."—*The Commonwealth.*

"A book of considerable immediate service. . . There is no side of the subject unvisited."—*Expository Times.*

6/-

Kit Kennedy: Country Boy. By S. R. CROCKETT. With Six Illustrations. Crown 8vo, cloth, gilt top, 6s.

"Mr. Crockett has never given better evidence of originality and dramatic power. . . . "—*Manchester Guardian.*

The House of the Secret. By KATHARINE TYNAN, Author of "For Maisie," "Her Ladyship," &c. Large crown 8vo. Illustrated. Cloth boards, 6s.

"Miss Katharine Tynan can always be depended upon for a good story told in a quiet and charming manner. As ever, it has a well-developed and well-constructed plot. We have thoroughly enjoyed this excellent story, and can recommend it very strongly."—*Bookman.*

The Story of Clarice. By KATHARINE TYNAN. Large crown 8vo, cloth boards, 6s.

"A story which is on a level with the best Miss Tynan has yet written. It is quiet and simple. We like 'The Story of Clarice,' and its reasonableness and soundness mark it out for popularity."—*Morning Post.*

Helga Lloyd. A Romance of Grasmere. By EDMUND LEE. Large crown 8vo, cloth boards, 6s.

Friend Olivia. By AMELIA E. BARR. Crown 8vo, cloth boards, 6s.

Through Science to Faith. By DR. NEWMAN SMYTH, Author of "The Place of Death in Evolution," "Old Faiths in New Lights," "The Reality of Faith," &c. Large crown 8vo, cloth, gilt top, 6s.

"We commend Dr. Smyth's work to the attention of all thoughtful readers."—*Liverpool Mercury.*

America in the East. By WILLIAM ELLIOT GRIFFIS, formerly of the Imperial University of Japan, Author of "The Mikado's Empire," "Corea, the Hermit Nation," &c. Crown 8vo, cloth, gilt top, with 19 Illustrations, 6s.

"We need hardly say that there is much that is interesting in the book." *Spectator.*

Rev. T. T. Lynch: A Memoir. Edited by WILLIAM WHITE. With Portrait. Crown 8vo, cloth, 6s.

5/- net

The Romance of Preaching. Yale Lectures for 1914. By CHARLES SILVESTER HORNE, M.A., Author of "A Popular History of the Free Churches," &c. Large Crown 8vo, cloth boards, gilt top, 5s. net.

Getting Together. Essays by Friends in Council on the Regulative Ideas of Religious Thought. Edited by JAMES MORRIS WHITON, Ph.D. (Yale). Large crown 8vo, cloth boards, gilt top, 5s. net.

Charles Darwin and other English Thinkers. With reference to their Religious and Ethical value. By S. PARKES CADMAN, D.D. Large crown 8vo, cloth boards, gilt top, 5s. net.

Evolution, Life and Religion. By EDWARD BRUCE KIRK, R.F.A.S. (Membre de la Société Astronomique de France, David Elder Lecturer on Astronomy, Glasgow and West of Scotland Technical College). Cloth, 5s. net.

John Smith the Se-Baptist, Thomas Helwys, and the First Baptist Church in England. By WALTER H. BURGESS, B.A. Large crown 8vo, cloth, 5s. net.

5/-

Faith and Verification. With Other Studies in Christian Thought and Life. By PRINCIPAL E. GRIFFITH-JONES, D.D. Large crown 8vo. with Photogravure Portrait, cloth boards, gilt top, 5s.

The Private Relationships of Christ. By T. VINCENT TYMMS, D.D. Author of "The Mystery of God," "The Christian Idea of Atonement," &c. Large crown 8vo, cloth boards, gilt top, 5s.

Theology and Truth. By NEWTON H. MARSHALL, M.A., Ph.D. Large crown 8vo, cloth boards, gilt top, 5s.

"The book is masterly both in constructive power and in exposition. . . . It is a book which ought to be widely read."—*Aberdeen Free Press.*

The Growing Revelation. By AMORY H. BRADFORD, D.D. Crown 8vo, cloth, 5s.

4/6 net

Dante For the People. Selected Passages from the Divine Comedy in English Verse. By GAUNTLETT CHAPLIN. Large Crown 8vo. Cloth boards, gilt top, 4s. 6d. net.

J. B. Paton, M.A., D.D., Educational and Social Pioneer. By JAMES MARCHANT. Large crown 8vo, Photogravure Portrait, and Illustrations on Art Paper, cloth boards, gilt top, 4s. 6d. net.

4/6

The Christian World Pulpit. Half-Yearly Volumes, cloth boards, 4s. 6d.

"A notable collection of the utterances of Protestant preachers on a wide variety of subjects which many people will rejoice to ponder at leisure."—*The Glasgow Herald.*

4/-

The Rosebud Annual for 1916. The Ideal Book for the Nursery. Four coloured plates and printed in colour throughout. Handsome cloth boards, 4s. Coloured paper boards, varnished, 3s.

"A veritable treasury of the best of good things."—*Liverpool Mercury.*

Social Salvation. By WASHINGTON GLADDEN. Crown 8vo, cloth, 4s.

3/6 net

*****Pessimism and Love in Ecclesiastes and the Song of Songs**, with Translations from the same. By DAVID RUSSELL SCOTT, M.A., late Pusey and Ellerton Scholar in the University of Oxford. Large Crown 8vo, cloth boards, gilt top, 3s. 6d. net.

*****Reconstruction : A Help to Doubters.** By ROBERT F. HORTON, M.A., D.D., Author of "My Belief," "Oliver Cromwell," etc. Large Crown 8vo, cloth boards, gilt top, 3s. 6d. net.

***"J.B."** J. Brierley, his Life and Work. By H. JEFFS, Author of "The Art of Exposition," "Portrait Preaching," "Concerning Conscience," etc. Large Crown 8vo, Photogravure and other Portraits, cloth boards, gilt top, 3s. 6d. net.

*****The Great Unfolding.** Notes on the Revelation. By Colonel G. J. VAN SOMEREN, Indian Army (retired), Author of "Babylon : Past, Present and Future." Large Crown 8vo, cloth boards, gilt top, 3s. 6d. net.

Selections from Brierley. ("J.B." of "The Christian World"), Large crown 8vo, cloth boards, gilt top, 3s. 6d. net.

Portrait Preaching. Studies in Bible Characters. By H. JEFFS, Author of "The Art of Exposition," "The Art of Sermon Illustration," etc. Large crown 8vo, cloth boards, gilt top, 3s. 6d. net.

JAMES CLARKE AND CO.'S

3/6 net (continued)

My Daily Meditation for the Circling Year. By J. H. JOWETT, M.A., D.D., Author of "Things that Matter Most." "The Passion for Souls," &c. Handsomely bound in cloth boards, gilt edges, with headband and marker, 3s 6d. net. Leather, 5s. net.

Advent Sermons. Discourses on the First and Second Coming of Christ. By W. E. ORCHARD, D.D., Author of "Sermons on God, Christ and Man." Large Crown 8vo, cloth boards, gilt top, 3s. 6d. net.

Saint Paul's Fight for Galatia. By C. H. WATKINS, M.A., D.Th. Large crown 8vo, cloth boards, gilt top. 3s. 6d. net.

Effectual Words. Sermons that led to Christ. Compiled by JOHN REID, M.A., Author of "The First Things of Jesus," "The Uplifting of Life," etc. Large crown 8vo, cloth boards, gilt top. 3s. 6d. net.

A Modern Man's Theology. By DR. WASHINGTON GLADDEN. Large crown 8vo, cloth boards, gilt top. 3s. 6d. net.

Things that Matter Most. Short Devotional Readings. By J. H. JOWETT, M.A., D.D. Author of "The Transfigured Church," "Sharing His Sufferings," "The Passion for Souls," etc. Handsomely bound in cloth, gilt edges, with headband and marker, 3s. 6d. net. Leather, 5s. net.

Sermons on God, Christ and Man. By W. E. ORCHARD, D.D. Author of "Modern Theories of Sin," "The Evolution of Old Testament Religion." Large crown 8vo, cloth boards, gilt top, 3s. 6d. net.

Constructive Natural Theology. By Dr. NEWMAN SMYTH. Author of "Through Science to Faith," "The Reality of Faith," etc. Cloth boards, 3s. 6d. net.

Saint Paul and His Cities. By R. W. POUNDER, Author of "Historical Notes on the Book of Revelation." Large crown 8vo, cloth boards, gilt top, 3s. 6d. net.

The Song of the Well, and other Sermons. By DAVID BURNS. Author of "Sayings in Symbol." Large crown 8vo, cloth boards, 3s. 6d. net.

Until the Day Dawn. The New Testament Basis for a Doctrine of Inspiration. By REV. J. PULESTON JONES, M.A. Large crown 8vo, cloth boards, gilt top, 3s. 6d. net.

Illustrations from Art for Pulpit and Platform. By REV. JAMES BURNS, M.A. Author of "Sermons in Art." Large crown 8vo, cloth boards, gilt top, 3s. 6d. net.

3/6 net (continued)

The Unfettered Word. A Series of Readings for the quiet hour. By J. D. JONES, M.A., D.D. Author of "The Gospel of Grace," etc. Large crown 8vo, cloth boards, gilt top, 3s. 6d. net.

Heaven and the Sea. By FRANK ELIAS. Large crown 8vo, cloth boards, gilt top, 16 Illustrations from classical paintings, 3s. 6d. net.

Concerning Conscience. Studies in Practical Ethics. By H. JEFFS. Author of "The Art of Sermon Illustration," "Practical Lay Preaching and Speaking to Men," etc. Large crown 8vo, cloth boards, gilt top, 3s. 6d. net.

Voices of To-Day: Studies of Representative Modern Preachers. By HUGH SINCLAIR. Large crown 8vo, cloth boards, gilt top, 3s. 6d. net.

Spoken Words of Prayer and Praise. A Book of Prayers. By S. A. TIPPLE. Author of "Days of Old," "Sunday Mornings at Norwood," etc. Cloth boards, 3s. 6d. net.

Fighters and Martyrs for the Freedom of Faith. By LUKE S. WALMSLEY. 512 pp. Frontispiece in colour and 16 Illustrations on art paper. Large crown 8vo, 3s. 6d. net.

What is the Bible? A MODERN SURVEY. By J. WARSCHAUER, M.A., D.Phil., Author of "Jesus: Seven Questions," "Problems of Immanence," &c. Large crown 8vo, cloth boards, 3s. 6d. net.

The Wisdom of God and the Word of God. By W. HARVEY-JELLIE, M.A., B.D. Large crown 8vo, cloth boards, 3s. 6d. net.

Days of Old, and other Sermons. By S. A. TIPPLE, Author of "Sunday Mornings at Norwood." Large crown 8vo, cloth boards, 3s. 6d. net.

Christ or Chaos? By E. S. WATSON ("Deas Cromarty"). Large crown 8vo, cloth boards, 3s. 6d. net.

The Transfigured Church. By J. H. JOWETT, M.A., D.D., Author of "The Passion for Souls," &c. Large crown 8vo, cloth boards, gilt top, 3s. 6d. net.

The Art of Exposition. By H. JEFFS, Author of "The Art of Sermon Illustration," "Practical Lay Preaching," &c. Large crown 8vo, cloth boards, gilt top, 3s. 6d. net.

Heavenly Visions. Studies in the Book of Revelation. By Rev. CHARLES BROWN, Author of "Letters of Christ," &c. Large crown 8vo, cloth boards, gilt top, 3s. 6d. net.

3/6 net (*continued*)

Westminster Sermons. Dean H. HENSLEY HENSON, formerly of S. Margaret's, Westminster. Large crown 8vo, cloth boards, gilt top, 3s. 6d. net.

Religion and Miracle. By GEORGE A. GORDON, D.D., Author of "Through Man to God," "The Christ of To-day," &c. Crown 8vo, cloth boards, gilt top, 3s. 6d. net.

A Working Woman's Life. The Autobiography of MARIANNE FARNINGHAM. Large crown 8vo, cloth boards, 3s. 6d. net.

The Gospel of Grace. By J. D. JONES, M.A., D.D., Author of "Christ's Pathway to the Cross," &c. Large crown 8vo, cloth boards, gilt top, 3s. 6d. net.

The Winning of Immortality. By FREDERIC PALMER, Author of "Studies in Theologic Definition." Cloth boards, gilt top, 3s. 6d. net.

Christian Certitude: Its Intellectual Basis. By E. DIGGES LA TOUCHE, Litt.D. Large crown 8vo, cloth boards, gilt top, 3s. 6d. net.

Life in His Name. By DAVID M. M'INTYRE, Author of "The Hidden Life of Prayer," &c. Handsomely bound in cloth boards, gilt edges, with headband and marker, 3s. 6d. net.

Interludes in a Time of Change: Ethical, Social, Theological. By JAMES MORRIS WHITON, Ph.D. (Yale), Author of "Divine Satisfaction," "Gloria Patri," &c. Cloth boards, gilt top, 3s. 6d. net.

Modern Theories of Sin. By W. E. ORCHARD, D.D. Thesis approved for the Degree of Doctor of Divinity in the University of London. Demy 8vo, cloth boards, gilt top, 3s. 6d. net.

Evangelical Heterodoxy. By J. MORGAN GIBBON, Author of "The Epistle to the Galatians." Large crown 8vo, cloth boards, gilt top, 3s. 6d. net.

The Christian of To-day. A Brief Descripton of His Thought and Life. By ROBERT VEITCH, M.A., Author of "The First Christians," &c. Large crown 8vo, cloth boards, gilt top, 3s. 6d. net.

The Right Hon. H. H. Asquith, M.P. A Biography and Appreciation. By FRANK ELIAS. Large crown 8vo, cloth boards, gilt top, 3s. 6d. net

The Art of Sermon Illustration. By H. JEFFS, Editor of *The Christian World Pulpit*. Large crown 8vo, cloth boards, gilt top, 3s. 6d. net.

CATALOGUE OF BOOKS 11

3/6 net (*continued*)

The First Things of Jesus. By JOHN REID, M.A., of Inverness, Author of "Jesus and Nicodemus: a Study in Spiritual Life." Large crown 8vo, cloth boards, gilt top, 3s. 6d. net.

Jesus: Seven Questions. By J. WARSCHAUER, M.A., D.Phil., Author of "The New Evangel," &c. Large crown 8vo, cloth boards, gilt top, 3s. 6d. net.

The Evolution of Old Testament Religion. By W. E. ORCHARD, D.D. Large crown 8vo, cloth boards, gilt top, 3s. 6d. net.

The Church and Modern Life. By WASHINGTON GLADDEN, D.D., Author of "Who Wrote the Bible?" &c. Cloth boards, gilt top, 3s. 6d. net.

My Belief. Answers to Certain Religious Difficulties. By R. F. HORTON, M.A., D.D., Author of "Cartoons of St. Mark," &c. Large crown 8vo, cloth boards, 3s. 6d. net.

The Story of Congregationalism in Surrey. By E. E. CLEAL. Demy 8vo, 464 pages, 46 Illustrations on art paper and Map, cloth bevelled boards, 3s. 6d. net.

Jesus and His Teaching. By ERICH VON SCHRENCK, Mag. Theol. Translated by J. WARSCHAUER, M.A., D.Phil. Crown 8vo, cloth boards, 3s. 6d. net.

The Atonement in Modern Thought. A Theological Symposium. By Professor AUGUSTE SABATIER, Professor HARNACK, Professor GODET, Dean FARRAR, Dr. P. T. FORSYTH, Dr. MARCUS DODS, Dr. LYMAN ABBOTT, Dr. JOHN HUNTER, Dr. WASHINGTON GLADDEN, Dean FREMANTLE, Dr. CAVE, Dr. R. F. HORTON, Rev. R. J. CAMPBELL, Principal ADENEY, Rev. C. SILVESTER HORNE, Rev. BERNARD J. SNELL, and Dr. T. T. MUNGER. Cheap Edition. Large crown 8vo, cloth boards, 3s. 6d. net.
   "This interesting work. . . . Among the writers are men of great distinction. . . . Deserves careful attention."—*The Spectator*.

A Voice from China. By GRIFFITH JOHN, D.D.Edin., Hankow. Large crown 8vo, cloth boards, 3s. 6d. net.

The Story of the English Baptists. By J. C. CARLILE. Large crown 8vo, 320 pages, 8 Illustrations on art paper, 3s. 6d. net.

The First Christians; or, Christian Life in New Testament Times. By ROBERT VEITCH, M.A. Crown 8vo, cloth boards, gilt top, 3s. 6d. net.

JAMES CLARKE AND CO.'S

3/6 net (*continued*)
By J. BRIERLEY ("J. B.")

Faith's Certainties. By J. BRIERLEY ("J.B."), Author of "Religion and To-day," "Ourselves and the Universe," etc. Large crown 8vo, cloth boards, gilt top, 3s. 6d. net.

Religion and To-day. Large crown 8vo, cloth boards, gilt top, 3s. 6d. net.

The Life of the Soul. Large crown 8vo, cloth boards, gilt top, 3s. 6d. net.

"Vigorous in thought, rich in literary allusions, and incisive in style. . . Mr. Brierley is always convincing as well as ingenious."—*Methodist Recorder.*

The Secret of Living. Large crown 8vo, cloth boards, gilt top, 3s. 6d. net.

"This author has given several thoughtful volumes, but not one in which the ideal and the practical are so well blended and so skilfully contrasted as in the present."—*Liverpool Courier.*

Life and the Ideal. Large crown 8vo, cloth boards, gilt top, 3s. 6d. net.

"This book is a book to read, and each section is food for constant reference and continued thought."—*Manchester Courier.*

Aspects of the Spiritual. Large crown 8vo, cloth boards, gilt top, 3s. 6d. net.

"These essays are equal to the best he has yet produced. They cover an immense variety of subjects."—*Daily News.*

Sidelights on Religion. Large crown 8vo, cloth boards, gilt top, 3s. 6d. net.

"Delightfully optimistic, a description which sums up as a whole this very interesting and helpful volume. It deserves to be widespread."
Pall Mall Gazette.

3/6
By J. BRIERLEY, (J. B.")

Religion and Experience. Crown 8vo, cloth boards, 3s. 6d.
"This book is quite worthy to be placed alongside of Mr. Brierley's best work."—*Daily News.*

The Eternal Religion. Second Edition. Crown 8vo, cloth boards, 3s. 6d.
"Well written and helpful."—*The Times.*

The Common Life. Second Edition. Crown 8vo, cloth boards, 3s. 6d.
"A book which every minister ought to possess."—*British Weekly.*

Problems of Living. Third Edition. Crown 8vo, cloth boards, 3s. 6d
"These beautiful and charming essays."—*Hibbert Journal.*

Ourselves and the Universe: Studies in Life and Religion. Sixth Edition. Crown 8vo, cloth, 3s. 6d.
"We have not for a long time read a brighter, cheerier, or wiser book." *Daily News.*

Studies of the Soul. Eighth Edition. Crown 8vo, cloth, 3s. 6d.
DR. HORTON says:—"I prefer this book to the best-written books I have lighted on for a year past."

Our City of God. Crown 8vo, cloth boards, 3s. 6d.
"We say without hesitation that this is a most inspiring work."
Westminster Gazette.

3/6 (continued)

A Gamble with Life. By SILAS K. HOCKING, Author of "To Pay the Price." Large crown 8vo, bevelled boards, 3s. 6d.
One of the best stories written by this popular author.

Gloria Patri: or, Our Talks About the Trinity. By J. M. WHITON, Ph.D. (Yale). Cloth, 3s. 6d.

The Christ that Is To Be: A Latter-Day Romance. By Sir J. COMPTON-RICKETT, M.P. New Edition. Demy 8vo, cloth, 3s. 6d.

Family Prayers for Morning Use, and Prayers for Special Occasions, Compiled and Edited by J. M. G. Cloth, pott quarto, 3s. 6d.

Preaching to the Times. By Dean H. HENSLEY HENSON. Crown 8vo, cloth extra, 3s. 6d.
"Sound sense and scholarly solidity."—Dundee Courier.

The Dutch in the Medway. By CHARLES MACFARLANE. Author of "The Camp of Refuge," &c. With a Foreword by S. R. CROCKETT. Crown 8vo, cloth, 3s. 6d.

The Quickening of Caliban. A Modern Story of Evolution. By Sir J. COMPTON-RICKETT, M.P., Author of "Christianity in Common Speech," &c. Large crown 8vo, cloth, 3s. 6d.

EMMA JANE WORBOISE'S NOVELS
Crown 8vo, uniformly bound in cloth, 3s. 6d. each.

Violet Vaughan.	Mr. Montmorency's Money.
Overdale.	Chrystabel.

See page 21 for Popular Edition.

AMELIA E. BARR'S NOVELS
Crown 8vo, cloth extra, 3s. 6d. each.

The Beads of Tasmer.	A Border Shepherdess.
She Loved a Sailor.	Paul and Christina.
The Last of the MacAllisters.	The Squire of Sandal Side.
Woven of Love and Glory.	Between Two Loves.

For other books by this Author see pages 5 and 22 (also 31).

3/6 (continued)

THE MESSAGES OF THE BIBLE

Edited by FRANK KNIGHT SANDERS, Ph.D., Woolsey Professor of Biblical Literature in Yale University, and CHARLES FOSTER KENT, Ph.D., Professor of Biblical Literature and History in Brown University. Super royal 16mo, cloth, red top, 3s. 6d. a vol. (To be completed in 12 Volumes.)

I. THE MESSAGES OF THE EARLIER PROPHETS. By Frank Knight Sanders, Ph.D., and Charles Foster Kent, Ph.D.
II. THE MESSAGES OF THE LATER PROPHETS. By Frank Knight Sanders, Ph.D., and Charles Foster Kent, Ph.D.
III. THE MESSAGES OF ISRAEL'S LAW-GIVERS. By Charles Foster Kent, Ph.D.
IV. THE MESSAGES OF THE PROPHETICAL AND PRIESTLY HISTORIANS. By John Edgar McFadyen, M.A.(Glas.), B.A.(Oxon.)
V. THE MESSAGES OF THE PSALMISTS. By John Edgar McFadyen, M.A.(Glas.), B.A.(Oxon).
VII. THE MESSAGES OF THE POETS. By Nathaniel Schmidt, M.A.
VIII. THE MESSAGES OF THE APOCALYPTICAL WRITERS. By Frank Chamberlin Porter, Ph.D., D.D.
IX. THE MESSAGES OF JESUS ACCORDING TO THE SYNOPTISTS. By Thomas Cuming Hall, D.D.
X. THE MESSAGES OF JESUS ACCORDING TO THE GOSPEL OF JOHN. By James Stevenson Riggs, D.D.
XI. THE MESSAGES OF PAUL. By George Barker Stevens, Ph.D., D.D.
XII. THE MESSAGES OF THE APOSTLES. By George Barker Stevens, Ph.D., D.D.

Volume VI. will appear shortly.

"Such a work is of the utmost service to every student of the Scriptures."
The Dundee Advertiser.

3/- net

The Personality of Jesus. By CHARLES H. BARROWS. Large crown 8vo, cloth boards, 3s. net.

Poems. By MADAME GUYON. Translated from the French by the late WILLIAM COWPER, with a Prefatory Essay by D. MACFADYEN, M.A. F'cap 8vo, handsomely bound in leather, 3s. net.

Quiet Hints to Growing Preachers in My Study. By CHARLES EDWARD JEFFERSON, Pastor of Broadway Tabernacle Church, Now York. Small crown 8vo, cloth, 3s. net.

3/-

The Rosebud Annual for 1916. The Ideal Book for the Nursery. Four Coloured Plates and printed in colour throughout. Coloured paper b ards, varnished, 3s. ; cloth boards, 4s.
"A rich fund of enjoyment for the nursery."—*Aberdeen Free Press.*

School Hymns, for Schools and Missions. With Music. Compiled by E. H. MAYO GUNN. Harmonies Revised by ELLIOTT BUTTON. Large Imp. 16mo, 3s.

2/6 net

*****The Appeal of Jesus.** By T. S. CAIRNCROSS, B.D., Author of "The Making of a Minister," etc. Crown 8vo, cloth boards, 2s. 6d. net.

*****The Chosen Twelve.** By JAMES GOLDER BURNS, B.D., of Glasgow. Crown 8vo, cloth boards, 2s. 6d. net.

*****Simon Peter's Ordination Day.** Studies in the Twenty-first Chapter of St. John's Gospel. By the Rev. JOHN A. PATTEN, M.A. Crown 8vo, cloth boards, 2s. 6d. net.

*****Ambrose Shepherd, D.D.** A Memoir and Sermons. Written by ERIC SHEPHERD. Edited by J. F. SHEPHERD, M.A. Crown 8vo, cloth boards, with Portrait, 2s. 6d. net.

The Making of a Minister. By T. S. CAIRNCROSS, B.D., Author of "Steps of the Pulpit." Crown 8vo, cloth boards, 2s. 6d. net.

A Pulpit Manual. Containing Prayers of Adoration, Confession, Petition, Thanksgiving, and Intercession ; Suggestive Summaries ; Orders of Service for Sacraments, Marriage, Admission to Communion, Church Festivals, and other Public Occasions. Compiled by JAMES BURNS, M.A., Author of "Illustrations from Art for Pulpit and Platform." Crown 8vo, cloth boards. 2s. 6d. net.

The Seriousness of Life. Sermons on Practical Subjects, with an Essay on Preaching. By JAMES S. RUTHERFORD, M.A. Crown 8vo, cloth boards. 2s. 6d. net.

Through Eyes of Youth. A Book of Poems. By E. CECIL ROBERTS, Author of "Phyllistrata, and other Poems." Crown 8vo, cloth boards. 2s. 6d. net.

Homes and Careers in Canada. By H. JEFFS, Author of "The Good New Times," etc. 16 Illustrations on art paper. Crown 8vo, cloth boards. 2s. 6d. net.

Christian Union in Social Service. By J. C. CARLILE, Author of "The Story of the English Baptists," etc. Crown 8vo, cloth boards, 2s. 6d. net.

Self-Realisation. By C. H. BETTS, LL.D., Author of "Fragments of Thought," "The Education of a Soul," "Living Pleasures," etc. Crown 8vo, cloth boards, 2s. 6d. net.

JAMES CLARKE AND CO.'S

2/6 net (continued)

Who was Jesus? The Answer of the New Testament. By D. H. MACONACHIE, B.A., B.D. Crown 8vo, cloth boards, 2s. 6d. net.

The Translation of Faith. By H. BULCOCK, B.A., B.D. Crown 8vo, cloth boards, 2s. 6d. net.

Studies in Christian Mysticism. By REV. W. H. DYSON. Crown 8vo, cloth boards, 2s. 6d. net.

Astronomy Simplified. By Rev. ALEX. C. HENDERSON, B.D., F.R.A.S. Crown 8vo, cloth boards, 2s. 6d. net.

Phyllistrata, and other Poems. By E. CECIL ROBERTS. Crown 8vo, cloth boards, 2s. 6d. net.

Spirit and Power. By Rev. D. M. M'INTYRE, Author of "Life in His Name," "The Hidden Life of Prayer," etc. Crown 8vo, cloth boards, 2s. 6d. net.

Led by a Child; and other Sermons. By Rev. ALFRED HOLBORN, M.A. Crown 8vo, cloth boards, 2s. 6d. net.

Our Protestant Faith. By Rev. J. STEPHENS ROOSE, M.A. Crown 8vo, cloth boards, 2s. 6d. net.

The Story of the Twelve: A Dramatic Poem in eight books. By ARTHUR HAY STORROW. Crown 8vo, cloth boards, gilt top, 2s. 6d. net.

The Waiting Life: By the River of Waters. By HUBERT FOSTON, M.A., D.Lit. Crown 8vo, cloth boards, 2s. 6d. net.

The Uplifting of Life. By Rev. JOHN REID, M.A., Author of "The First Things of Jesus," etc. Crown 8vo, cloth boards, 2s. 6d. net.

The Unveiled Glory; or, Sidelights on the Higher Evolution. By Rev. LUTHER WINTHER CAWS, Author of "The Unrecognised Stranger, "The Unfolding Dawn." Crown 8vo, cloth boards, 2s. 6d. net.

Looking Inwards: Words Addressed to the Soul of the Church. By EDWARD SHILLITO, M.A. Crown 8vo, cloth boards, 2s. 6d. net.

Eucken and Bergson. Their Significance for Christian Thought. By E. HERMANN. Crown 8vo, cloth boards, 2s. 6d. net.

Messages of Hope. By GEORGE MATHESON, D.D., LL.D., F.R.S.E. Author of "Thoughts for Life's Journey," &c. Handsomely bound in cloth boards, gilt edges, 2s. 6d. net; leather, 4s. net.

Problems and Perplexities. By W. E. ORCHARD, D.D., Author of "Modern Theories of Sin," "Evolution of Old Testament Religion," etc. 304 pages, printed on India paper, cloth boards, 2s. 6d. net.

The Imperishable Word. By W. CHARTER PIGGOTT. Crown 8vo, cloth boards, 2s. 6d. net.

2/6 net continued)

Constructive Christianity. By WILLIAM SOUPER, M.A. Crown 8vo, cloth boards, 2s. 6d. net.

Peter in the Firelight. By WILLIAM ALLEN KNIGHT, Author of "Our Syrian Guest," "No Room in the Inn," etc. Illustrated in Colours. Fancy Cover. Large crown 8vo, 2s. 6d. net.

A Young Man's Ideal. By WILLIAM WATSON, M.A., Author of "Prayer," &c. Crown 8vo, cloth boards, 2s. 6d. net.

Modern Minor Prophets. Edited, with a Chapter on "Lay Preaching and its By-Products," by H. JEFFS, Author of "The Art of Sermon Illustration," "Practical Lay Preaching and Speaking to Men." Crown 8vo, cloth boards, 2s. 6d. net.

Fifty Years' Reminiscences of a Free Church Musician. By E. MINSHALL. Crown 8vo, Photogravure Portrait, 2s. 6d. net.

Problems of Immanence. Studies Critical and Constructive. By J. WARSCHAUER, M.A., D.Phil., Author of "The New Evangel," "Jesus: Seven Questions," &c. Crown 8vo, cloth boards, 2s. 6d. net.

Sculptors of Life. A Book for Young Men and Young Women. By THOMAS YATES. Crown 8vo, cloth boards, 2s. 6d. net.

An Impregnable Faith. A Modern Pilgrim's Progress from Scepticism through Morality and Religious Optimism to Jesus Christ and the "Good Kingdom." By Rev. DAVID MELVILLE STEWART. Crown 8vo, cloth boards, 2s. 6d. net.

A Lifted Veil. A Novel. By J. G. STEVENSON. Cheap Edition. Crown 8vo, 4 Illustrations, cloth boards, 2s. 6d. net.

Augustinian Revolution in Theology. By Rev. THOMAS ALLIN, D.D., Author of "Race and Religion." Illustrated by Comparison with the Teaching of the Antiochene Divines of the Fourth and Fifth Centuries. Crown 8vo, cloth boards, 2s. 6d. net.

The Beatitudes and the Contrasts. By HUBERT FOSTON, M.A., D. Litt. Crown 8vo, cloth boards, 2s. 6d. net.

King George and Queen Mary. By HENRY WARWICK. Illustrated by latest portraits on art paper. Crown 8vo, cloth boards, 2s. 6d. net.

Letters to a Ministerial Son. By A MAN OF THE WORLD. Crown 8vo, cloth boards, 2s. 6d. net.

Religion: The Quest of the Ideal. By J. M. HODGSON, M.A., D.Sc., D.D. Crown 8vo, cloth boards, 2s. 6d. net.

The Universal Over-Presence. By C. H. BETTS, Author of "Fragments of Thought" and "The Education of a Soul." Crown 8vo, cloth boards, 2s. 6d. net.

Thoughts for Life's Journey. By GEORGE MATHESON, D.D., LL.D., F.R.S.E., Author of "Leaves for Quiet Hours." Cheap Edition. Cloth boards, gilt edges, 2s. 6d. net; leather, 4s. net.

2/6 net (continued)

Life's Beginnings. Wisdom and Counsel for Daily Guidance. Fifth impression. Printed on India paper and handsomely bound in leather, round corners and gilt edges, boxed, 2s. 6d. net (uniform with "The Pilot"). Also in silk grain cloth, 1s. 6d. net. Velvet calf, round corners, gilt edges, 3s. 6d. net.

"One can easily understand how a compendium of the thoughts of master minds such as this may be a real stimulus in these days of stress. The battle of the world will be entered upon with a cheerful heart after a thoughtful perusal of the most noble passages allotted to each day by these discriminating anthologists. Should be in constant demand. One of the prettiest and most acceptable gift-books this busy season has seen."
Dundee Advertiser.

The True Christ, and other Studies in " Whatsoever things are true." By W. L. WALKER, Author of "The Teaching of Christ," &c. Crown 8vo, cloth boards, 2s. 6d. net.

Christ in Everyday Life. By EDWARD INCREASE BOSWORTH, Dean of Oberlin Theological Seminary. F'cap 8vo, India paper, cloth boards, round corners, 2s. 6d. net.

Things Most Surely Believed. By J. D. JONES, M.A., D.D., Author of "The Gospel of Grace," &c. Crown 8vo, cloth boards, 2s. 6d. net.

Lyrics of the Soul. A Book of Poems. By MARIANNE FARNINGHAM, Author of "Harvest Gleanings," &c. Crown 8vo, cloth boards, gilt edges, 2s. 6d. net.

Conquering Prayer : or, The Power of Personality. By L. SWETENHAM, Author of " Religious Genius." Crown 8vo, cloth boards, 2s. 6d. net.

The Immanence of Christ in Modern Life. By FREDERICK R. SWAN. With Introduction by J. BRIERLEY, B.A. Crown 8vo, cloth boards, 2s. 6d. net.

The New Evangel : Studies in the "New Theology." By Rev. J. WARSCHAUER, M.A., D.Phil. Second Edition. Crown 8vo, cloth boards, 2s. 6d. net.
"May be studied with advantage."—*Spectator.*

Health in the Home Life. By HONNOR MORTEN, Author of "A Complete Book of Nursing," "How to Treat Accidents and Illnesses," &c. Crown 8vo, art leather cloth, 2s. 6d. net.

Ungilded Gold ; or, Nuggets from the King's Treasury. Selected Passages from the Bible, arranged for Daily Devotional Reading (uniform with "The Pilot"). 384 pages, leather boxed, 2s. 6d. net ; also silk grain cloth, gilt lettering, red edges, 1s. 6d. net.

CATALOGUE OF BOOKS

2/6 net (*continued*)

The Challenge, and Other Stories for Boys and Girls. By Rev. J. G. STEVENSON, Author of "The Christ of the Children." 4to, cloth boards, 240 pp. Eight Illustrations. 2s. 6d. net.

Leaves for Quiet Hours. By GEORGE MATHESON, F.R.S.E., D.D., LL.D., Author of "Words by the Wayside," &c. New and cheap edition. Handsomely bound in cloth boards, with chaste design in gold, and gilt edges, 2s. 6d. net. Leather, 4s. net.

The Pilot. A Book of Daily Guidance from Master Minds. Contains nearly 2,000 of the choicest extracts systematically arranged for every day of the year. Printed on India paper and handsomely bound in leather, with round corners and gilt edges, 2s. 6d. net ; velvet calf, 3s. 6d. net.

"A book of real daily value."—*Sheffield Telegraph.*

My Neighbour and God. A Reply to Robert Blatchford's "God and My Neighbour." By W. T. LEE. Crown 8vo, cloth boards, 2s. 6d. net.

Liberty and Religion. By P. WHITWELL WILSON, Author of "Why We Believe," &c. Crown 8vo, cloth boards, 2s. 6d. net.

Why We Believe. Papers on Religion and Brotherhood. By P. WHITWELL WILSON. Crown 8vo, cloth boards, 2s. 6d. net.

The New Testament in Modern Speech. With notes. An idiomatic translation into everyday English from the text of "The Resultant Greek Testament." By the late RICHARD FRANCIS WEYMOUTH, M.A., D.Litt., Fellow of University College, London, and formerly Head Master of Mill Hill School, Editor of "The Resultant Greek Testament." Edited and partly revised by ERNEST HAMPDEN-COOK, M.A., formerly Exhibitioner and Prizeman of St. John's College, Cambridge. New and revised Edition. Cloth boards, 2s. 6d. net. Leather 4s. net. Thumb Indexed, cloth, 3s. 6d. net. Leather 5s. net. Also on Oxford India paper, cloth boards, 3s. 6d. net. Leather, 5s. net. Persian morocco, yapp, leather lined and silk sewn, round corners, red under gold, 8s. net. Turkey morocco, limp, 8s. 6d. net. (*See also p.* 22.)

The Resultant Greek Testament. Exhibiting the Text in which the majority of Modern Editors are agreed. By the late RICHARD FRANCIS WEYMOUTH, D.Litt. Cloth boards, 2s. 6d. net.

A Young Man's Religion and his Father's Faith. By N. MCGHEE WATERS. Small crown 8vo, cloth boards, gilt top, 2s. 6d. net.

"It is an earnestly religious and well-written work."—*The Scotsman.*

2/6

The Good New Times. By H. JEFFS, Author of "Practical Lay Preaching and Speaking to Men." Crown 8vo, cloth boards, 2s. 6d.

The Ten Commandments. By G. CAMPBELL MORGAN, D.D. Pott. 8vo, cloth, 2s. 6d.

2/- net

The Church and the Next Generation. By RICHARD ROBERTS, M.A. Crown 8vo, cloth boards, 2s. net.

The Story of Joseph the Dreamer, told by Himself, and Other Poems. By ALFRED CAPES TARBOLTON. Crown 8vo, cloth boards, 2s. net.

The Judges of Jesus: Judas, Annas, Peter, Caiaphas, Herod, Pilate's Wife, Pontius Pilate. By Rev. J. G. STEVENSON, Crown 8vo, cloth boards, 2s. net.

The Value of the Old Testament. By BERNARD J. SNELL, M.A., Author of "The Value of the Apocrypha," "Gain or Loss?" &c. Crown 8vo, cloth boards, 2s. net.

The Purpose of the Cross. By B. G. COLLINS. Crown 8vo, cloth boards, 2s. net.

Atonement and Progress. By NEWTON H. MARSHALL, M.A., Ph.D., Author of "Theology and Truth." Crown 8vo, cloth boards, 2s. net.

Authority and the Light Within. By EDWARD GRUBB, M.A. Crown 8vo, cloth boards, 2s. net.

Ideals for Girls. By the Rev. H. R. HAWEIS, M.A., Author of "Music and Morals." New Edition, crown 8vo, handsomely bound in bevelled boards, gilt edges, 2s. net.

"A book that all parents should place in the hands of their daughters."

The Glorious Company of the Apostles. Being Studies in the Characters of the Twelve. By the Rev. J. D. JONES, M.A., D.D. Cloth boards, gilt top, 2s. net.

"Many think that a readable sermon is a contradiction in terms. Let them read these pages and discover their mistake."—*Examiner.*

The Model Prayer. A Series of Expositions on the Lord's Prayer. By Rev. J. D. JONES, M.A., D.D. New Edition, cloth boards, gilt top, 2s. net.

"Mr. Jones brings a cultured mind, a well-stored memory, and a gift of spiritual insight to the illustration of the Lord's Prayer."
Sunday School Chronicle.

2/-

Simple Cookery. Comprising "Tasty Dishes" and "More Tasty Dishes." Over 500 Tested Receipts. Crown 8vo, cloth boards, 2s.
"A book that should be in every household."

The Children's Paul. A Life of St. Paul specially written for the Young. By Rev. J. G. STEVENSON. 4to, cloth boards, 8 Illustrations on art paper, 2s.

The Christ of the Children. A Life of Jesus for Little People. By Rev. J. G. STEVENSON. Cheap Edition. 4to, cloth boards, 12 Illustrations, 2s.
"It is the very loveliest life of Jesus for children ever written by a long way."—Rev. KINGSCOTE GREENLAND in *The Methodist Recorder*.

Stories of Old. Bible Stories Retold. By C. D. MICHAEL, Author of "Noble Deeds," "Deeds of Daring," &c. Cheap Edition. 4to, 288 pp., cloth boards, 8 illustrations, 2s.

Early Pupils of the Spirit, and What of Samuel? By J. M. WHITON, Ph.D. New Edition, Crown 8vo, cloth, 2s.

The Religion of Jesus. By J. ALLANSON PICTON, M.A, J.P. Crown 8vo, 2s.

CLARKE'S COPYRIGHT LIBRARY
Crown 8vo, tastefully bound in cloth boards, 2s.
The Black Familiars. By L. B. WALFORD.
Kid McGhie. By S. R. CROCKETT.

POPULAR EDITION OF
EMMA JANE WORBOISE'S NOVELS
Crown 8vo, cloth boards, 2s.; bevelled boards, 2s. 6d.

Abbey Mill, The.
Brudenells of Brude, The.
Canonbury Holt.
Chrystabel.
Emilia's Inheritance.
Esther Wynne.
Father Fabian.
Fortune's Favourite.
Fortunes of Cyril Denham, The.
Grey and Gold.
Grey House at Endlestone, The.
Heirs of Errington, The.
His Next of Kin.
House of Bondage.
Husbands and Wives.
Joan Carisbroke.
Lady Clarissa.
Margaret Torrington.
Millicent Kendrick.
Mr. Montmorency's Money.
Nobly Born.
Oliver Westwood.
Overdale.
Robert Wreford's Daughter.
St. Beetha's.
Singlehurst Manor.
Sissie.
Story of Penelope, The.
Thornycroft Hall.
Violet Vaughan.
Warleigh's Trust.
A Woman's Patience.

For other books by this Author see page 13. (*See also p.* 31.)

2/-
NEW SERIES OF COPYRIGHT BOOKS
Crown 8vo, cloth gilt, 2s.

Woven of Love and Glory. By AMELIA E. BARR.
The Last of the MacAllisters. By AMELIA E. BARR.
The Beads of Tasmer. By AMELIA E. BARR.
A Morning Mist. By SARAH TYTLER.
The Debt of the Damerals. By BESSIE MARCHANT.
A Town Romance ; or, On London Stones. By C. C. ANDREWS.
The Pride of the Family. By ETHEL F. HEDDLE.
Unknown to Herself. By LAURIE LANSFELDT.
The Squire of Sandal Side. By AMELIA E. BARR.
The Scourge of God. By J. BLOUNDELLE-BURTON.
The New Mrs. Lascelles. By. L. T. MEADE.
Miss Devereux, Spinster. By AGNES GIBERNE.
Jan Vedder's Wife. By AMELIA E. BARR.

1/9 net

The New Testament in Modern Speech. By the late RICHARD FRANCIS WEYMOUTH, M.A., D.Litt. Pocket Edition (without notes), cloth boards, 1s. 9d. net. Also on Oxford India paper, cloth boards, round corners, gilt edges, 2s. 6d. net. (*See also p.* 19.)

1/6 net
THE "FREEDOM OF FAITH" SERIES

F'cap 8vo, 128 pp., handsomely bound in Green Leather, with chaste design in gold. Price 1s. 6d. net.

The Simple Things of the Christian Life. By G. CAMPBELL MORGAN, D.D.
The Letters of Christ. By CHARLES BROWN.
Christ's Pathway to the Cross. By J. D. JONES, M.A., D.D.
The Crucible of Experience. By F. A. RUSSELL.
The Passion for Souls. By J. H. JOWETT, M.A.
The Value of the Apocrypha. By BERNARD J. SNELL, M.A.
Inspiration in Common Life. By W. L. WATKINSON, M.A.
Prayer. By WILLIAM WATSON, M.A.
A Reasonable View of Life. By J. M. BLAKE, M.A.

"There are precious things in every volume, and the Series deserves success."—*Dundee Advertiser.*

1/6 net (*continued*)

Through Many Windows. Some Modern Parables. By ERNEST A. BIRCH. Crown 8vo, cloth boards, 1s. 6d. net.

The Man on The Road. By CHARLES H. BETTS, LL.D., A.S.P., Author of "Fragments of Thought," "Living Pleasures," etc. Crown 8vo, cloth boards, 1s. 6d. net.

The Well by Bethlehem's Gate. By WILLIAM ALLEN KNIGHT, Author of "The Song of our Syrian Guest," etc. Handsomely bound in cloth boards, gilt, 1s. 6d. net.

The Way and the Work. A Manual for Sunday School Teachers. By J. W. WIMMS, M.A., B.Sc. (Lecturer on the Theory and Practice of Education, University of London), and the REV. FREDERICK HUMPHREY. Crown 8vo, cloth boards. 1s. 6d. net.

A Popular History of the Free Churches. By C. SILVESTER HORNE, M.A. Cheap Edition, with additional Chapter. Cloth boards. 1s. 6d. net.

Christ and War. The Reasonableness of Disarmament on Christian, Humanitarian and Economic Grounds. A Peace Study Text Book. By WILLIAM E. WILSON, B.D. Preface by Dr. RENDEL HARRIS. Crown 8vo. Cloth boards. 1s. 6d. net. Cloth limp. 1s. net.

Life's Little Lessons. Addresses to Children. By VERNON GIBBERD. Crown 8vo, cloth boards, 1s. 6d. net.

For Childhood and Youth. Ideals of the Modern Sunday School. By THISELTON MARK, D.Lit., B.Sc., Author of "The Teacher and the Child," etc. Crown 8vo, cloth boards, 1s. 6d. net.

Facets of Faith. Aspects of Spiritual Life and Thought. By A. W. BLUE. Crown 8vo, cloth boards, 1s. 6d. net.

Life's Beginnings. Wisdom and Counsel for Daily Guidance. Silk grain cloth, 1s. 6d. net. Also printed on India paper and handsomely bound in leather, round corners and gilt edges, boxed, 2s. 6d. net (uniform with "The Pilot"). Velvet calf, round corners, gilt edges, 3s. 6d. net.

> "An admirable compilation. The authors have read widely and their selections from modern religious writers are made with taste and judgment. A very attractive and helpful little book."—*British Weekly.*

The Wayfarer at the Cross Roads. By ARTHUR PRINGLE. Author of "The Faith of a Wayfarer." Crown 8vo, cloth boards, 1s. 6d. net.

Old Testament Stories in Modern Light. A BIBLE GUIDE FOR THE YOUNG. By T. RHONDDA WILLIAMS, Author of "The Christ Within," &c. Crown 8vo, cloth boards, 1s. 6d. net.

J. H. Jowett, M.A., D.D. A CHARACTER STUDY. By FRANK MORISON. Illustrations on art paper. Fancy paper boards, 1s. 6d. net.

1/6 net (*continued*)

The Way of Prayer. By JOHN EDGAR MCFADYEN, D.D., Author of "The Divine Pursuit," "Prayers of the Bible." Fancy boards, gilt top, 1s. 6d. net.

Chats with Women on Everyday Subjects. By EDITH C. KENYON, Author of "A Queen of Nine Days," &c. Crown 8vo, cloth boards, 1s. 6d. net.

Faith and Form. An Attempt at a Plain Re-statement of Christian Belief in the Light of To-day. By HENRY VARLEY, B.A. Crown 8vo, cloth boards, 1s. 6d. net.

The Invisible Companion and Other Stories for Children. By EDWARD W. LEWIS, M.A., B.D., Author of "The Unescapeable Christ," &c. Crown 8vo, cloth boards, 1s. 6d. net.

Sharing His Sufferings. By J. H. JOWETT, M.A., D.D., Author of "The Passion for Souls," &c. Small crown 8vo, cloth boards, 1s. 6d. net; leather 2s. 6d. net.

The Reasonableness of Jesus. By FRANK Y. LEGGATT, M.A. Crown 8vo, cloth boards, 1s. 6d. net.

The Making of Heaven and Hell. By J. M. BLAKE, M.A., Author of "A Reasonable View of Life," &c. Small 8vo, cloth boards, 1s. 6d. net.

Ideals in Sunday School Teaching. By ALFRED H. ANGUS, B.Sc. With Foreword by J. H. Jowett, M.A., D.D. Crown 8vo, cloth boards, 1s. 6d. net.

Notes on the Life and Teaching of Jesus. By EDWARD GRUBB, M.A., Author of "Authority and the Light Within." Crown 8vo, cloth boards, 1s. 6d. net; limp cloth, 1s. net.

The Faith of a Wayfarer. By ARTHUR PRINGLE. Crown 8vo, cloth boards, 1s. 6d. net.

Jesus or Christ? By Rev. J. WARSCHAUER, M.A., D.Phil., Author of "The New Evangel," "Jesus: Seven Questions." Crown 8vo, cloth boards, 1s. 6d. net.

Who Wrote the Bible? By WASHINGTON GLADDEN, D.D., Author of "The Growing Revelation," &c. New and cheap edition, 256 pages, cloth boards, 1s. 6d. net.

Reasons Why for Congregationalists. By Rev. J. D. JONES, M.A., D.D. Crown 8vo, cloth boards, 1s. 6d. net.

Ungilded Gold; or, Nuggets from the King's Treasury. Selected Passages from the Bible, arranged for Daily Devotional Reading (uniform with "The Pilot"). 384 pages, silk grain cloth, gilt lettering, red edges, 1s. 6d. net; leather, boxed, 2s. 6d. net.

Women and their Work. By MARIANNE FARNINGHAM, Author of "Harvest Gleanings," "Women and their Saviour" Crown 8vo, cloth boards, 1s. 6d. net.

1/6 net (continued)

Sunny Memories of Australasia. By Rev. W. CUFF. Crown 8vo, cloth boards. Portraits and Illustrations. 1s. 6d. net.

Britain's Hope Concerning the Pressing Social Problems. By JULIE SUTTER, Author of "Britain's Next Campaign," &c. Cloth boards, 1s. 6d. net.

Burning Questions. By WASHINGTON GLADDEN. Cheap Edition. Crown 8vo, cloth, 1s. 6d. net.

Reform in Sunday School Teaching. By Professor A. S. PEAKE. Crown 8vo, cloth boards, 1s. 6d. net.

1/6

Storehouse for Preachers and Teachers. A Treasury of Outline Texts and Sermons. By J. ELLIS, Author of "The Seed Basket," &c., &c. Cloth boards, 1s. 6d.

Words by the Wayside. By GEORGE MATHESON, D.D., LL.D., F.R.S.E., Author of "Thoughts for Life's Journey," &c. New Edition. Oblong, cloth boards, gilt top, 1s. 6d.

The Children's Pace; and other Addresses to Children. By Rev. J. S. MAVER, M.A., of Paisley. F'cap, 8vo, cloth, 1s. 6d.

SMALL BOOKS ON GREAT SUBJECTS

Pott 8vo, bound in buckram cloth, 1s. 6d. each. (*See also p.* 30).

The Christ Within. By Rev. T. RHONDDA WILLIAMS.
Old Pictures in Modern Frames. By J. G. GREENHOUGH, M.A.
The Conquered World. By R. F. HORTON, M.A., D.D.
Social Worship an Everlasting Necessity. By JOHN CLIFFORD, D.D.
Types of Christian Life. By E. GRIFFITH-JONES, D.D.
How to Become Like Christ. By MARCUS DODS, D.D.
The Way of Life. By H. ARNOLD THOMAS, M.A.
Character Through Inspiration. By T. T. MUNGER, D.D.
Infoldings and Unfoldings of the Divine Genius, in Nature and Man. By JOHN PULSFORD, D.D. New Edition.
The Jealousy of God. By JOHN PULSFORD, D.D.
The Supreme Argument for Christianity. By W. GARRETT HORDER.
Reconsiderations and Reinforcements. By JAMES MORRIS WHITON.

1/- net

* **Sir Galahad.** By JAMES BURNS, M.A., Author of "The Happy Warrior." With Photogravure Frontispiece of Watts's famous picture "Sir Galahad." Bound in khaki cloth, 1s. net.
* **Around the Guns.** Sundays in Camp. By JAMES BLACK, M.A., of Edinburgh. Crown 8vo, khaki cloth boards, with design in colours, 1s. net.
* **Kaiser or Christ?** Sermons by the BISHOP OF LONDON, DR. JOHN CLIFFORD, DR. S. PARKES CADMAN, DR. GRIFFITH-JONES, DR. C. H. WATKINS, REV. THEODORE WOOD. Demy 8vo, paper covers, 1s.
* **Quaint Rhymes for the Battlefield.** By a QUONDAM CRICKETER (C. D. STUDD, Belgian Congo, 1913). Cloth boards, 1s. net.
* **Sweet Peas and Antirrhinums.** How to Grow Them to Perfection. By WILLIAM CUTHBERTSON, Author of "Pansies, Violas and Violets." Crown 8vo, coloured paper boards and frontispiece in colour, 1s. net. Written in a popular form for the amateur gardener by one who is a thorough master of his subject.
* **The Way of Remembrance.** By J. A. HUTTON, M.A. Tastefully bound in blue and white with gilt lettering. 1s. net.
* **God, Humanity and the War.** By G. CAMPBELL MORGAN, D.D., Author of "Simple Things of the Christian Life," &c. 1s. net.
* **Christ and War.** The Reasonableness of Disarmament on Christian, Humanitarian and Economic Grounds. A Peace Study Text Book. By WILLIAM E. WILSON, B.D. Preface by Dr. RENDEL HARRIS. Crown 8vo, cloth limp. 1s. net. Cloth Boards. 1s. 6d. net.
* **The Christian World Album of Sacred and Standard Compostions for the Pianoforte.** Edited by W. H. JUDE. (Uniform with "The Christian World Album of Sacred Songs."). Paper cover, 1s. net. Cloth boards, 2s. net.
* ***The Call of the King.** National Letters to Women. By ANNIS BURDALANE. Demy 8vo, bound in Purple and Gold with Ribbon. 1s. net.
* **The Great Embassy.** Studies in the Growth of Christianity. By CUTHBERT McEVOY, M.A. Foolscap 8vo, cloth boards, 1s. net.
* **Everychild.** By HAROLD BEGBIE, Author of "Broken Earthenware." Crown 8vo, Frontispiece and cover in colours. 1s. net.
* **The Christian World Album of Sacred Songs.** Containing 94 Sacred Songs, in old notation and tonic-sol-fa, selected from the choicest works of the most eminent composers. Edited by W. H. JUDE. 160 pages, paper cover, 1s. net; cloth boards, 2s. net.
* **The Seed of the Kingdom.** Devotional readings from the letters of Isaac Penington. Selected by JENNIE STREET (*Editor of the Sunday School Times*). Fancy Boards, 1s. net.

1/- net (continued)

How to Cook. The Art of Cooking made easy, with a chapter on the use of a gas oven. By J. S. MARSHALL. Crown 8vo, cloth boards, 1s. net.

Our Life Beyond. By J. D. JONES, M.A., D.D., Author of "Christ's Pathway to the Cross," "The Gospel of Grace," etc., etc. cloth boards, gilt lettering, 1s. net; white cloth, padded, in box, 1/9 net.

Flowers from the Master's Garden. By A. E. WINTER. Cloth boards, gilt lettering, 1s. net.

Ecce Vir: Jesus and Modern Manhood. By D. MELVILLE STEWART. Author of "An Impregnable Faith." F'cap 8vo, cloth boards, 1s. net.

The Garrisoned Soul. Meditations on "Peace, Perfect Peace," by C. E. P. ANTRAM. Fancy cloth, 1s. net.
"It is just the sort of book, chaste and beautiful, contents and binding alike, that would make a pretty present on a birthday or a Church festival. Its size and its type make it suitable also to send to an invalid. Indeed, its cheering chapters would to many such, we are sure, act like a tonic, and be an efficient co-worker with the physician."—*Sheffield Telegraph*.

Women and their Saviour. Thoughts of a Minute for a Month. By MARIANNE FARNINGHAM, Author of "Harvest Gleanings," &c. Cloth, 1s. net.
"These 'thoughts of a minute for a month of mornings,' are the outpourings of an entirely unaffected piety."—*Glasgow Herald*.

Reasons Why for Free Churchmen. By Rev. J. D. JONES, M.A., B.D. Small 8vo, cloth boards, 1s. net.

The Price of Priestcraft. By HOWARD EVANS. Crown 8vo, paper covers, 1s. net; cloth, 1s. 6d. net.
"We wish for it a very large circulation. No one has served the cause of religious freedom better than Mr. Howard Evans by his labours in the Press and elsewhere."—*British Weekly*.

Sunday Afternoon Song Book, with Tunes. Compiled by H. A. KENNEDY and R. D. METCALFE. 1s. net. Words only, 12s. 6d. per hundred net.
"The airs have been selected and arranged under the editorship of Mr. R. D. Metcalfe, and add so much to the value of the collection that this edition will easily supersede all others and give the work a new popularity with choral societies and others interested in church music."
The Scotsman.

1/-

Oliver Cromwell. By R. F. HORTON, D.D., Author of "John Howe," "The Teaching of Jesus," &c., &c. Sixth Edition. Nineteenth Thousand. 1s.
"Worthy a place in the library of every Christian student."
Methodist Recorder.

Rome from the Inside; or, The Priests' Revolt. Translated and Compiled by "J. B." of The Christian World. Third Thousand. F'cap. 8vo, 1s.

PICTURE BOOKS FOR THE YOUNG

Pictures by LOUIS WAIN, HARRY B. NEILSON, J. A. SHEPHERD, ELSIE BLOMFIELD, etc.

Printed in colour, varnished boards, 1s.

1/-

*Animal Fancy-Land.

Animal Picture-Land.

Animal Happyland.

Merry Times in Animal Land.

Animals in Fun-Land.

The Merry Animal Picture Book.

Holidays in Animal Land.

Animal Playtime.

Animal Gambols.

Outline Text Lessons for Junior Classes. By GLADYS DAVIDSON, Author of "Kindergarten Bible Stories," &c. F'cap 8vo, cloth boards, 1s.

"The book is simple and practical, and will be found suggestive and helpful by teachers."—*Sunday School Chronicle.*

How to Read the Bible. Hints for Sunday School Teachers and other Bible Students. By W. F. ADENEY, M.A. New and Revised Edition. Cloth boards, 1s.

"A most admirable little work. We know of no book which deals with this subject so clearly and adequately within so small a compass. It speaks of itself modestly as "Hints for Sunday-school Teachers and other Bible Students," but it is one of the very few manuals which are well worth the study of the clergy."—*The Guardian.*

Short Talks to Boys and Girls. By J. C. CARLILE, Author of "Talks to Little Folks." Crown 8vo, cloth boards, 1s.

A Religion that will Wear. A Layman's Confession of Faith. Addressed to Agnostics, by a SCOTTISH PRESBYTERIAN. Crown 8vo, cloth boards, 1s.

The Divine Satisfaction. A Review of what should and what should not be thought about the Atonement. By J. M. WHITON. Crown 8vo, paper, 1s.

CATALOGUE OF BOOKS 29

1/- (continued)

Health and Home Nursing. By Mrs. LESSELS MATHER, Health Lecturer to the Northumberland County Council. F'cap. 8vo, cloth, 1s.

A book that should be in every household. Contains chapters on The Care of the Invalid, Homely Local Applications, Feeding the Invalid, Infection and Disinfection, Care of the Teeth, The Value of Foods, Influenza, its Causes and Prevention, Consumption, its Causes and Prevention, Digestion and Indigestion, Headaches, Home Nursing of Sick Children, What to do till the Doctor Comes, Habit in Relation to Health, The Health of the Town Dweller.

Helps to Health and Beauty. Two Hundred Practical Prescriptions by a Pharmaceutical Chemist. Price 1s.

"This little book contains two hundred practical prescriptions or formulæ, for preparations for the hair, hands, nails, feet, skin, teeth, and bath, in addition to perfumes, insecticides, and medicaments for various ailments. As far as possible technical language is avoided, and the directions are clear and concise."—*Pharmaceutical Journal.*

Morning, Noon and Night. By R. F. HORTON, M.A., D.D. F'cap 8vo, parchment cover with gold lettering, 1s.

"Deeply suggestive, and as earnest as its fancies are pleasing and quaint."
Dundee Advertiser.

Wayside Angels, and Other Sermons. By W. K. BURFORD. Pott 8vo, cloth, 1s.

Tasty Dishes. A Choice Selection of Tested Recipes, showing what we can have for Breakfast, Dinner, Tea and Supper. It is designed for people of moderate means who desire to have pleasant and varied entertainment for themselves and their friends. It is a book of genuine and tested information. New Edition. Thoroughly revised and brought up to date. 130th Thousand. Crown 8vo, 1s.

"No home ought to be without this timely, useful, and practical family friend."—*Brighton Gazette.*

More Tasty Dishes. A Book of Tasty, Economical and Tested Recipes. Including a Section on Invalid Cookery. A Supplement to "Tasty Dishes." New Edition. Price 1s.

"Every recipe is so clearly stated that the most inexperienced cook could follow them and make dainty dishes at a small cost."—*Pearson's Weekly.*
"The recipes given have been carefully tried and not been found wanting."
The Star.

Talks to Little Folks. A Series of Short Addresses. By Rev. J. C. CARLILE. Crown 8vo, art vellum, 1s.

"No one who reads this book can reasonably doubt that Mr. Carlile is master of the difficult art of catching and sustaining the interest of young people. He is wise enough to dispense with the preacher's framework, texts, introductions, &c., and at once he arrests attention by a direct question or a brief story."—*Literary World.*

Christianity in Common Speech: Suggestions for an Every-day Belief. By Sir J. COMPTON-RICKETT, M.P. Demy 8vo, 1s.

1/-
RECITATION BOOKS
By MARY E. MANNERS
Crown 8vo, Linen Covers, 1s. each.

A Tale of a Telephone, and Other Pieces.
"Narrative pieces, suitable for recitation."—*Outlook.*

Aunt Agatha Ann : and other Ballads. Illustrations by ERNOLD A. MASON and LOUIS WAIN.
"Excellent pieces for recitation from a popular pen."—*Lady's Pictorial.*

SMALL BOOKS ON GREAT SUBJECTS
(CHEAP EDITION).
Bound in red cloth, 1s. each. (*See also p. 25.*)

The Taste of Death and the Life of Grace. By P. T. FORSYTH, M.A., D.D.

The Conquered World. By R. F. HORTON, M.A., D.D.

The Christian Life. By W. M. SINCLAIR, D.D.

The Way of Life. By H. ARNOLD THOMAS, M.A.

Faith and Self-Surrender. By JAMES MARTINEAU, D.D., D.C.L.

Martineau's Study of Religion. By RICHARD A. ARMSTRONG.

The Kingdom of the Lord Jesus. By ALEXANDER A. MACKENNAL, D.D.

6d. net

*****They that Wait.** A Message for War Time. By J. H. JOWETT, M.A., D.D. In this daintily produced brochure, Dr. J. H. Jowett presents an inspiriting message of comfort and hope for these times of anxiety and strain. 6d. net.

Recollections of Newton House. By REV. ISAAC HARTILL, F.R.G.S., F.R.Hist.S. 64 pages, with frontispiece. 6d. net.

C. Silvester Horne. In Memoriam. April 15th, 1865—May 2nd, 1914. 64 pages, with portrait, 6d. net.

The Birthday of Hope. By J. D. JONES, M.A., D.D. Illustrated. Printed on art paper, with fancy cover and ribbon, 6d. net. Padded white cloth, lettering in gold, boxed, 1s. 6d. net.

The Ship's Engines. A Parable. By the late T. CAMPBELL FINLAYSON, D.D. In vellum cover, 6d. net.

> Rev. J. H. JOWETT says:—"I am so glad you are issuing the article in the shape of the little booklet. I am sure it will be very helpful to many people, and will bring light and leading to many bewildered souls."

6d.

England's Danger. By R. F. HORTON, M.A., D.D. Price 6d.
Contents: ROMANISM AND NATIONAL DECAY; ST. PETER AND THE ROCK; TRUTH; PROTESTANTISM; HOLY SCRIPTURE; PURGATORY.

"Good fighting discourses. They contend that Roman Catholicism has ruined every country in which it prevails and controvert the leading positions taken by Roman theologians."—*Scotsman*.

CLARKE'S SIXPENNY SERIES
Demy 8vo, Paper Covers.

Studies of the Soul. By J. BRIERLEY, B.A.
Violet Vaughan. By EMMA JANE WORBOISE.
The Bow of Orange Ribbon. By AMELIA E. BARR.
Jan Vedder's Wife. By AMELIA E. BARR.
A Daughter of Fife. By AMELIA E. BARR.
Ourselves and the Universe. By J. BRIERLEY.

4d. net

Holy Christian Empire. By Rev. PRINCIPAL FORSYTH, M.A., D.D., of Hackney College, Hampstead. Crown 8vo, paper cover, 4d. net.

"Rich in noble thought, in high purpose, in faith and in courage. Every sentence tells, and the whole argument moves onward to its great conclusion. Dr. Forsyth has put the argument for missions in a way that will nerve and inspire the Church's workers at home and abroad for fresh sacrifice."
London Quarterly Review.

3d. net

School Hymns, for Schools and Missions. Words only. Compiled by E. H. MAYO GUNN. Cloth limp, 3d.; cloth boards, 6d.; music, 3s.

2d. net

The Sunday Afternoon Song Book. Containing 137 Hymns. For use at "Pleasant Sunday Afternoons," and Other Gatherings. Compiled by H. A. KENNEDY, of the Men's Sunday Union, Stepney Meeting House. Twentieth Thousand, 2d; music, 1s.

"Contains 137 hymns, the catholic character of which, in the best sense of the term, may be gathered from the names of the authors, which include Tennyson, Ebenezer Elliott, Whittier, G. Herbert, C. Wesley, Thomas Hughes, J. H. Newman, Longfellow, Bonar, and others. While the purely dogmatic element is largely absent, the Christian life, in its forms of aspiration, struggle against sin and love for the true and the good, is well illustrated."—*Literary World*.

INDEX OF TITLES

Title	PAGE
Abbey Mill, The	21
Advent Sermons	8
America in the East	5
Animal Fancyland	28
Animal Gambols	28
Animal Happyland	28
Animal Playtime	28
Animal Picture Land	28
Animals in Fun-Land	28
Apocalyptical Writers, The Messages of the	14
Apostles, The Messages of the	14
Appeal of Jesus, The	15
Around the Guns	26
Aspects of the Spiritual	12
Asquith, The Right Hon. H. H., M.P.	10
Astronomy Simplified	16
Atonement and Progress	20
Atonement in Modern Thought, The	11
Augustinian Revolution in Theology	17
Aunt Agatha Ann	30
Authority and the Light Within	20
Beads of Tasmer, The	13, 22
Beatitudes and the Contrasts, The	17
Between Two Loves	13
Birthday of Hope, The	30
Black Familiars, The	21
Border Shepherdess, A	13
Bow of Orange Ribbon, The	31
Britain's Hope	25
Brudenelle of Brude, The	21
Burning Questions	25
Call of the King, The	26
Canonbury Holt	21
Challenge, The	19
Character through Inspiration	25
Chats with Women on Everyday Subjects	24
Children's Pace, The	25
Children's Paul, The	21
Chosen Twelve, The	15
Christ and War	23, 26
Christ in Everyday Life	18
Christ of the Children, The	21
Christ or Chaos ?	9
Christ that is To Be, The	13
Christ, The Private Relationships of	6
Christ Within, The	25
Christ's Pathway to the Cross	22
Christ's Vision of the Kingdom of Heaven	4
Christian Certitude	10
Christian Life, The	30
Christian of To-day, The	10
Christian Union in Social Service	15
Christian World Album of Sacred Songs, The	26
Christian World Album of Sacred and Standard Compositions for the Pianoforte	26
Christian World Pulpit, The	7
Christianity in Common Speech	29
Chronicle of the Archbishops of Canterbury, A	4
Chrystabel	13, 21
Church and Modern Life, The	11
Church and the Kingdom, The	25
Church and the Next Generation, The	20
Common Life, The	12
Concerning Conscience	9
Conquered World, The	25, 30
Conquering Prayer	18
Constructive Christianity	17
Constructive Natural Theology	8
Crucible of Experience, The	22
Dante for the People	7
Darwin, Charles, and other English Thinkers	6
Daughter of Fife, A	31
Days of Old	9
Debt of the Damerals, The	22
Divine Satisfaction, The	28
Dutch in the Medway, The	13
Earlier Prophets, The Messages of the	14
Early Pupils of the Spirit	21
Ecce Vir	27
Effectual Words	8
Emilia's Inheritance	21
England's Danger	31
Esther Wynne	21
Eternal Religion, The	12
Eucken and Bergson	16
Evangelical Heterodoxy	10
Everychild	26
Evolution, Life and Religion	6
Evolution of Old Testament Religion, The	11
Exposition, The Art of	9
Ezekiel, The Book of	3
Facets of Faith	23
Faith and Form	24
Faith and Verification	6
Faith of a Wayfarer, The	24
Faith and Self-Surrender	30
Faith's Certainties	12
Family Prayers for Morning Use	13
Father Fabian	21
Fifty Years' Reminiscences of a Free Church Musician	17
Fighters and Martyrs for the Freedom of Faith	9
First Christians, The	11
First Things of Jesus	11
Flowers from the Master's Garden	26
For Childhood and Youth	23
Fortune's Favourite	21

CATALOGUE OF BOOKS

Title	Page
Fortunes of Cyril Denham, The	21
"Freedom of Faith" Series, The	22
Friend Olivia	5
Gamble with Life, A	13
Garrisoned Soul, The	27
Getting Together	6
Gloria Patri	13
Glorious Company of the Apostles, The	20
God, Humanity and the War	26
Good New Times, The	20
Gospel of Grace, The	10
Great Embassy, The	26
Great Unfolding, The	7
Grey and Gold	21
Grey House at Endlestone, The	21
Growing Revelation, The	7
Hampstead, Its historic houses; its literary and artistic associations	4
Health and Home Nursing	29
Health in the Home Life	18
Heaven and the Sea	9
Heavenly Visions	10
Heirs of Errington, The	21
Helga Lloyd	5
Helps to Health and Beauty	29
His Next of Kin	21
History of the United States, A	4
Holidays in Animal Land	28
Holy Christian Empire	31
Homes and Careers in Canada	15
Horne, C. Silvester	30
House of Bondage, The	21
House of the Secret, The	5
How to Become Like Christ	25
How to Cook	27
How to Read the Bible	28
Husbands and Wives	21
Ideals for Girls	20
Ideals in Sunday School Teaching	24
Illustrations from Art for Pulpit and Platform	8
Immanence of Christ in Modern Life, The	18
Imperishable Word, The	16
Impregnable Faith, An	17
Infoldings and Unfoldings of the Divine Genius	25
Inspiration in Common Life	22
Interludes in a Time of Change	10
Invisible Companion, The	24
Israel's Law Givers, The Messages of	14
Jan Vedder's Wife	22, 31
"J.B." J. Brierley, his Life and Work	7
Jealousy of God, The	25
Jesus and His Teaching	11
Jesus or Christ ?	24
Jesus: Seven Questions	11
Jesus, The Messages of, According to the Gospel of John	14
Jesus, The Messages of, According to the Synoptists	14
Joan Carisbrooke	21
Joshua, The Book of	4
Jowett, J. H., M.A., D.D.	23
Judges of Jesus, The	20
Judges, The Book of	4
Kaiser or Christ	26
Kid McGhie	21
Kingdom of the Lord Jesus, The	30
King George and Queen Mary	17
Kit Kennedy: Country Boy	5, 21
Lady Clarissa	21
Last of the MacAllisters, The	13, 22
Later Prophets, The Messages of the	14
Leaves for Quiet Hours	19
Led by a Child	16
Letters of Christ, The	22
Letters to a Ministerial Son	17
Liberty and Religion	19
Life and Teaching of Jesus, Notes on the	24
Life and the Ideal	12
Life in His Name	10
Life of the Soul	12
Life's Beginnings	18, 23
Life's Little Lessons	23
Lifted Veil, A	17
Looking Inwards	16
Lynch, Rev. T. T.: A Memoir	5
Lyrics of the Soul	18
Making of a Minister, The	15
Making of Heaven and Hell, The	24
Man on The Road, The	23
Margaret Torrington	21
Marprelate Tracts, The	3
Martineau's Study of Religion	30
Meaning and Value of Mysticism	5
Merry Animal Picture Book, The	28
Merry Times in Animal Land	28
Messages of Hope	16
Messages of the Bible, The	14
Millicent Kendrick	21
Miss Devereux, Spinster	22
Model Prayer, The	20
Modern Man's Theology, A	8
Modern Minor Prophets	17
Modern Theories of Sin	10
More Tasty Dishes	29
Morning Mist, A	22
Morning, Noon, and Night	29
Mr. Montmorency's Money	13, 21
My Belief	11
My Daily Meditation for the Circling Year	8
My Neighbour and God	19

JAMES CLARKE AND CO.'S

	PAGE
New Evangel, The	18
New Mrs. Lascelles, The	22
New Testament in Modern Speech, The	19, 22
Nobly Born	21
Old Pictures in Modern Frames	25
Old Testament Stories in Modern Light	23
Oliver Cromwell	27
Oliver Westwood	21
Our City of God	12
Our Life Beyond	27
Our Protestant Faith	16
Ourselves and the Universe,	12, 31
Outline Text Lessons for Junior Classes	28
Overdale	13, 21
Passion for Souls, The	22
Paton, J. B., M.A., D.D.	7
Paul and Christina	13
Paul, The Messages of	14
Person of Christ in Modern Thought, The	5
Personality of Jesus, The	14
Pessimism and Love in Ecclesiastes and Song of Songs	7
Peter in the Firelight	17
Phyllistrata and Other Poems	16
Pilot, The	19
Poems. By Mme. Guyon	14
Poets, The Messages of the	14
Polychrome Bible, The	3, 4
Popular History of the Free Churches, The	23
Portrait Preaching	7
Prayer	22
Preaching to the Times	13
Price of Priestcraft, The	27
Pride of the Family, The	22
Problems and Perplexities	16
Problems of Immanence	17
Problems of Living	12
Prophetical and Priestly Historians, The Messages of	14
Psalmists, The Messages of the	14
Pulpit Manual, A	15
Purpose of the Cross, The	20
Quaint Rhymes for the Battlefield	26
Quickening of Caliban, The	13
Quiet Hints to Growing Preachers in My Study	14
Reasonable View of Life, A	22
Reasonableness of Jesus, The	24
Reasons Why for Congregationalists	24
Reasons Why for Free Churchmen	27
Recollections of Newton House	30
Reconsiderations and Reinforcements	25
Reconstruction, A Help to Doubters	7
Reform in Sunday School Teaching	25

	PAGE
Religion and Experience	12
Religion and Miracle	10
Religion and To-day	12
Religion of Jesus, The	21
Religion: The Quest of the Ideal	17
Religion that will Wear, A	28
Resultant Greek Testament, The	19
Robert Wreford's Daughter	21
Romance of Preaching	6
Rome from the Inside	27
Rosebud Annual, The	7, 15
School Hymns	15, 31
Scourge of God, The	22
Sculptors of Life	17
Secret of Living, The	12
Seed of the Kingdom, The	26
Selections from Brierley	7
Self-Realisation	15
Seriousness of Life, The	15
Sermon Illustration, The Art of	10
Sermons on God, Christ and Man	8
Sharing His Sufferings	24
She Loved a Sailor	13
Shepherd, Ambrose, D.D.	15
Ship's Engines, The	30
Short Talks to Boys and Girls	28
Sidelights on Religion	12
Simon Peter's Ordination Day	15
Simple Cookery	21
Simple Things of the Christian Life, The	22
Singlehurst Manor	21
Sir Galahad	26
Sissie	21
Small Books on Great Subjects	25, 30
Smith, John, the Se-Baptist, Thomas Helwys, and the First Baptist Church in England	6
Social Salvation	7
Social Worship an Everlasting Necessity	25
Song of the Well, The	8
Spirit and Power	16
Spoken Words of Prayer and Praise	9
Squire of Sandal Side, The	13, 22
St. Beetha's	21
St. Paul and His Cities	8
St. Paul's Fight for Galatia	8
Storehouse for Preachers and Teachers	25
Stories of Old	21
Story of Clarice, The	5
Story of Congregationalism in Surrey, The	11
Story of Joseph the Dreamer, The	20
Story of Penelope, The	21
Story of the English Baptists, The	11
Story of the Twelve	16
Studies in Christian Mysticism	16
Studies of the Soul	12, 31
Sunday Afternoon Song Book	27, 31

CATALOGUE OF BOOKS 35

	PAGE
Sunny Memories of Australasia	25
Supreme Argument for Christianity, The	25
Sweet Peas and Antirrhinums	26
Tale of a Telephone, A	30
Talks to Little Folks	29
Taste of Death and the Life of Grace, The	30
Tasty Dishes	29
Ten Commandments, The	20
Theology and Truth	6
They that Wait	30
Things Most Surely Believed	18
Things that Matter Most	8
Thornycroft Hall	21
Thoughts for Life's Journey	17
Through Eyes of Youth	15
Through many Windows	23
Through Science to Faith	5
Town Romance, A	22
Transfigured Church, The	9
Translation of Faith, The	16
True Christ, The	18
Types of Christian Life	25
Unfettered Word, The	9
Ungilded Gold	18, 24
Universal Over-Presence, The	17
Unknown to Herself	22
Until the Day Dawn	8
Unveiled Glory, The; or, Sidelights on the Higher Evolution	16
Uplifting of Life, The	16
Value of the Apocrypha, The	22
Value of the Old Testament	20
Violet Vaughan	13, 21, 31
Voices of To-day: Studies of Representative Modern Preachers	9
Waiting Life, The; By the River of Waters	16
Warleigh's Trust	21
Way and the Work, The	23
Wayfarer at the Cross Roads, The	23
Way of Life, The	25, 30
Way of Prayer, The	24
Way of Remembrance, The	26
Wayside Angels	29
Well by Bethlehem's Gate, The	23
Westminster Sermons	10
What is the Bible?	9
Who was Jesus	16
Who Wrote the Bible?	24
Why We Believe	19
Winning of Immortality, The	10
Wisdom of God and the Word of God, The	9
Woman's Patience, A	21
Women and their Saviour	27
Women and Their Work	24
Words by the Wayside	25
Working Woman's Life, A	10
Woven of Love and Glory	13, 22
Young Man's Ideal, A	17
Young Man's Religion, A	19

INDEX OF AUTHORS

	PAGE
Abbott, Lyman	11
Adeney, W. F.	11, 28
Allin, T.	17
Andrews, C. C.	22
Angus, A. H.	24
Antram, C. E. P.	27
Armstrong, R. A.	30
Barr, Amelia E.	5, 13, 22, 31
Barrows, C. H.	14
Begbie, H.	26
Bennett, Rev. W. H.	4
Betts, C. H.	15, 17, 23
Birch, E. A.	23
Black, J.	26
Blake, J. M.	22, 24
Blomfield, Elsie	28
Bloundelle-Burton, J.	22
Blue, A. W.	23
Bosworth, E. I.	18
Bradford, Amory H.	6
Brierley, J.	7, 12, 31
Brown, C.	9, 22
Bullock, H.	16
Burdalane, Annis	26
Burford, W. K.	29
Burgess, W. H.	6
Burns, David	8
Burns, Rev. J.	8, 15, 26
Cadman, S. P.	6, 26
Cairncross, T. S.	15
Campbell, R. J.	11
Carlile, J. C.	11, 15, 28, 29
Cave, Dr.	11
Caws, Rev. L. W.	16
Chaplin, Gauntlett	6
Cleal, E. E.	11
Clifford, John	25, 26
Collins, B. G.	20
Compton-Rickett, Sir J.	13, 29
Cowper, W.	14
Crockett, S. R.	5, 21
Cuff, W.	25
Cuthbertson, W.	26
Davidson, Gladys	28
Dods, Marcus	11, 25
Dyson, W. H.	16
Elias, F.	9, 10
Ellis, J.	25
Evans, H.	27
Farningham, Marianne	10, 18, 24, 27
Farrar, Dean	11
Finlayson, T. Campbell	30
Fiske, J.	4

JAMES CLARKE AND CO.'S CATALOGUE

	PAGE
Forsyth, P. T.	11, 30, 31
Foston, H.	16, 17
Fremantle, Dean	11
Furness, H. H.	3
Gibberd, Vernon	23
Gibbon, J. Morgan	10
Giberne, Agnes	22
Gladden, Washington	7, 8, 11, 24, 25
Godet, Professor	11
Gordon, George A.	10
Greenhough, J. G.	25
Griffis, W. E.	5
Griffith-Jones, E.	6, 25, 26
Grubb, E.	20, 24
Gunn, E. H. M.	15, 31
Guyon, Madame	14
Hall, T. C.	14
Hampden-Cook, E.	19
Harnack, Professor	11
Harris, Rendel	23, 26
Hartill, I.	30
Harvey-Jellie, W.	9
Haupt, P.	3
Haweis, H. R.	20
Heddle, Ethel F.	22
Henderson, Alex. C.	16
Henson, Dean H.	
Hensley	10, 13
Hermann, E.	5, 16
Hill, F. A.	4
Hocking, S. K.	13
Hodgson, J. M.	17
Holborn, Alfred	16
Horder, W. Garrett	25
Horne, C. Silvester	6, 11, 23
Horton, R. F.	7, 11, 25, 27, 29, 30, 31
Humphrey, F.	23
Hunter, John	11
Hutton, J. A.	26
"J. B." of *The Christian World*	27
J. M. G.	13
Jefferson, C. E.	14
Jeffs, H.	7, 9, 10, 15, 17, 20
John, Griffith	11
Jones, J. D.	9, 10, 18, 20, 22, 24, 27, 30
Jones, J. P.	8
Jowett, J. H.	8, 9, 22, 24, 30
Jude, J. H.	26
Kennedy, H. A.	27, 31
Kent, C. F.	14
Kenyon, Edith C.	24
Kirk, E. B.	6
Knight, W. A.	17, 23
Lansfeldt, L.	22

	PAGE
La Touche, E. D.	5, 10
Lee, E.	5
Lee, W. T.	19
Leggatt, F. Y.	24
Lewis, E. W.	24
London, Bishop of	26
McEvoy, Cuthbert	26
Macfadyen, D.	14
McFadyen, J. E.	14, 24
Macfarlane, Charles	13
M'Intyre, D. M.	10, 16
Mackennal, Alexander	30
McKilliam, A. E.	4
Maconachie, D. H.	16
Manners, Mary E.	30
Man of the World, A	17
Marchant, Bessie	22
Marchant, J.	6
Mark, Thistelton	23
Marshall, J. S.	27
Marshall, N. H.	6, 20
Martineau, Jas.	30
Mason, E. A.	30
Mather, Lessels	29
Matheson, George	16, 17, 19, 25
Maver, J. S.	25
Maxwell, A.	4
Meade, L. T.	22
Metcalfe, R. D.	27
Michael, C. D.	21
Minshall, E.	17
Moore, G. F.	4
Morgan, G. Campbell	20, 22, 26
Morison, F.	23
Morten, Honnor	18
Munger, T. T.	11, 25
Neilson, H. B.	28
Orchard, W. E.	8, 10, 11, 16
Palmer, Frederic	10
Patten, J. A.	15
Peake, A. S.	25
Pharmaceutical Chemist, A.	29
Picton, J. Allanson	21
Pierce, W.	3
Piggott, W. C.	16
Porter, F. C.	14
Pounder, R. W.	8
Pringle, A.	23, 24
Pulsford, John	25
Reid, Rev. J.	8, 11, 16
Riggs, J. S.	14
Roberts, E. Cecil	15, 16
Roberts, R.	20
Roose, Rev. J. S.	16
Russell, F. A.	22
Rutherford, J. S.	15

	PAGE
Sabatier, A.	11
Sanders, F. K.	14
Schimdt, N.	14
Schrenck, E. von	11
Scott, D. R.	7
Scottish Presbyterian, A	28
Sheppherd, E.	15
Shepherd, J. A.	28
Shillito, Edward	16
Sinclair, H.	9
Sinclair, W. M.	30
Smyth, Newman	5, 8
Snell, Bernard J.	11, 20, 22
Someren, J. Van	7
Souper, W.	17
Stevens, G. B.	14
Stevenson, J. G.	17, 19, 20, 21
Stewart, D. M.	17, 26
Stirling, James	4
Storrow, A. H.	16
Street, J.	26
Studd, C. D.	26
Sutter, Julie	25
Swan, F. R.	18
Swetenham, L.	18
Tarbolton, A. C.	20
Thomas, H. Arnold	25, 30
Tipple, S. A.	9
Toy, Rev. C. H.	3
Tymms, T. V.	6
Tynan, Katharine	5
Tytler, S.	22
Varley, H.	24
Veitch, R.	10, 11
Wain, Louis	28, 30
Walford, L. B.	21
Walker, W. L.	18
Walmsley, L. S.	9
Warschauer, J.	9, 11, 17, 18, 24
Warwick, H.	17
Waters, N. McG.	19
Watkins, C. H.	8, 26
Watkinson, W. L.	22
Watson, E. S.	9
Watson, W.	17, 22
Weymouth, R. F.	19, 22
White, W.	5
Whiton, J. M.	6, 10, 13, 21, 25, 28
Wimms, J. W.	23
Williams, T. R.	23, 25
Wilson, P. W.	19
Wilson, W. E.	23, 26
Winter, A. E.	26
Wood, T.	26
Worboise, Emma J.	13, 21, 31
Yates, T.	17

Headley Brothers, Printers, Ashford, Kent; and Bishopsgate, E.C.

www.ingramcontent.com/pod-product-compliance
Lightning Source LLC
Chambersburg PA
CBHW032048230426
43672CB00009B/1511